Time Out

SHORTLIST

Rome
2009
WHAT'S NEW | WHAT'S ON | WHAT'S BEST

timeout.com/rome

Contents

Don't Miss: 2009

Sights & Museums	8
Eating & Drinking	13
Shopping	21
Nightlife	26
Arts & Leisure	30
Calendar	35

Itineraries

Papal Progress	44
Rome on Film	47
Rome in a Rush	50

Rome by Area

Il Centro **54**
  Map: Centro Archaeologico 55
  Map: The Ghetto, Campo de' Fiori,
  Pantheon & Piazza Navona 66
  Map: Roman Forum ... back cover flap

Tridente, Trevi & Borghese **84**
  Map 86

**Esquilino, Celio
& San Lorenzo** **100**
  Map 102

The Aventine & Testaccio **117**
  Map 118

Trastevere & the Gianicolo ... **128**
  Map 130

The Vatican & Prati **139**
  Map 140

Out of Town **151**

Essentials

Hotels **164**
Getting Around **180**
Resources A-Z **184**
Vocabulary **188**
Menu Glossary **189**
Index **190**

Published by Time Out Guides Ltd
Universal House
251 Tottenham Court Road
London W1T 7AB
Tel: + 44 (0)20 7813 3000
Fax: + 44 (0)20 7813 6001
Email: guides@timeout.com
www.timeout.com

Managing Director Peter Fiennes
Financial Director Gareth Garner
Editorial Director Ruth Jarvis
Deputy Series Editor Dominic Earle
Editorial Manager Holly Pick
Assistant Management Accountant Ija Krasnikova

Time Out Guides is a wholly owned subsidiary of Time Out Group Ltd.

© **Time Out Group Ltd**
Chairman Tony Elliott
Financial Director Richard Waterlow
Group General Manager/Director Nichola Coulthard
Time Out Magazine Ltd MD Richard Waterlow
Time Out Communications Ltd MD David Pepper
Time Out International Ltd MD Cathy Runciman
Production Director Mark Lamond
Group IT Director Simon Chappell
Head of Marketing Catherine Demajo

Time Out and the Time Out logo are trademarks of Time Out Group Ltd.

This edition first published in Great Britain in 2008 by Ebury Publishing
A Random House Group Company
Company information can be found on www.randomhouse.co.uk
Random House UK Limited Reg. No. 954009
10 9 8 7 6 5 4 3 2 1

Distributed in the US by Publishers Group West
Distributed in Canada by Publishers Group Canada

For further distribution details, see www.timeout.com

ISBN: 978-1-84670-106-1

A CIP catalogue record for this book is available from the British Library.

Printed and bound by Firmengruppe APPL, aprinta druck, Wemding, Germany.

The Random House Group Limited supports The Forest Stewardship Council (FSC), the leading international forest certification organisation. All our titles that are printed on Greenpeace approved FSC certified paper carry the FSC logo. Our paper procurement policy can be found on www.rbooks.co.uk/environment.

Time Out carbon-offsets all its flights with Trees for Cities (www.treesforcities.org).

Rome Shortlist

The **Time Out Rome Shortlist 2009** is one of a new series of guides that draws on Time Out's background as a magazine publisher to keep you current with what's going on in town. As well as Rome's key sights and the best of its eating, drinking and leisure options, it picks out the most exciting venues to have opened in the last year and gives a full calendar of events from September 2008 to December 2009. It also includes features on the important news, trends and openings, all compiled by locally based editors and writers. Whether you're visiting for the first time in your life or the first time this year, you'll find the *Time Out Rome Shortlist 2009* contains everything you need to know, in a portable and easy to use format.

The guide divides central Rome into six areas, each containing listings for Sights & Museums, Eating & Drinking, Shopping, Nightlife and Arts & Leisure, and maps pinpointing their locations. At the front of the book are chapters rounding up these scenes city-wide, and giving a shortlist of our overall picks. We include itineraries for days out, plus essentials such as transport information and hotels.

Our listings give phone numbers as dialled within Italy. Rome's prefix is 06; you must dial this prefix even if you're calling from within the city. The international code for Italy is 39. When calling from outside Italy do not drop the initial '0' of the Rome prefix. Listed numbers beginning with '3' are mobiles.

We have noted price categories by using one to four euro signs (€-€€€€), representing budget, moderate, expensive and luxury. Major credit cards are accepted unless otherwise stated. We also indicate when a venue is NEW, and give Event highlights.

All our listings are double-checked, but businesses do sometimes close or change their hours or prices, so it's a good idea to call a venue before visiting. While every effort has been made to ensure accuracy, the publishers cannot accept responsibility for any errors that this guide may contain.

Venues are marked on the maps using symbols numbered according to their order within the chapter and colour-coded as follows:

❶ Sights & Museums
❶ Eating & Drinking
❶ Shopping
❶ Nightlife
❶ Arts & Leisure

Map key		
Major sight or landmark		
Railway station		
Park		
Area name		TRIDENTE
Metro line		
Hospital		H
Church		

Time Out Rome Shortlist 2009

EDITORIAL

Editor Anne Hanley
Deputy Editur Tanya Sassoon
Researcher Fulvia Angelini
Proofreader Tamsin Shelton
Indexer Rob Norman

DESIGN

Art Director Scott Moore
Art Editor Pinelope Kourmouzoglou
Senior Designer Henry Elphick
Graphic Designers Gemma Doyle,
    Kei Ishimaru
Digital Imaging Simon Foster
Advertising Designer Jodi Sher
Picture Editor Jael Marschner
Deputy Picture Editor Katie Morris
Picture Researcher Gemma Walters
Picture Desk Assistant Marzena Zoladz

ADVERTISING

Commercial Director Mark Phillips
International Advertising Manager
    Kasimir Berger
International Sales Executive
    Charlie Sokol
Advertising Assistant Kate Staddon
Advertising Sales (Rome)
    Margherita Tedone & Julie Simonsen

MARKETING

Marketing Manager Yvonne Poon
Sales & Marketing Director,
    North America Lisa Levinson
Senior Publishing Brand Manager
    Luthfa Begum
Marketing Designers Anthony Huggins,
    Nicola Wilson

PRODUCTION

Production Manager Brendan McKeown
Production Controller Damian Bennett
Production Co-ordinator Julie Pallot

CONTRIBUTORS

This guide was researched and written by Anne Hanley, with the exception of Papal Progress, Rome on Film, Rome in a Rush, Trevi in our hearts, Secret garden, Chocolate box, Year of Paul, Vatican tours (Julia Crosse) and Pigneto fare (Lee Marshall). The editor would like to thank all the writers of the *Time Out Rome Guide* on which this guide is based.

PHOTOGRAPHY

Photography by Gianluca Moggi, except: page 8, 28, 29, 54, 63, 64, 65, 109, 110, 115, 135, 163, 177, 178, 179 Alessandra Santorelli; page 30 Luigi Fileteci; page 36 Caroline Ablain; page 37 Etsuko Matsuyama; page 71 Soprintendenza speciale per i beni archeologici di Roma; page 134 Olivia Rutherford.

The following images were provided by the featured establishments/ artists: pages 11, 33, 35, 40, 42, 100.

Cover photograph: St. Peter's Basilica. Credit: © Jupiterimages.

MAPS

LS International Cartography, via Decemviri 8, 20138 Milan, Italy (www.geomaker.com).

About Time Out

Founded in 1968, Time Out has expanded from humble London beginnings into the leading resource for those wanting to know what's happening in the world's greatest cities. As well as our influential what's-on weeklies in London, New York and Chicago, we publish more than a dozen other listings magazines in cities as varied as Beijing and Mumbai. The magazines established Time Out's trademark style: sharp writing, informed reviewing and bang up-to-date inside knowledge of every scene.

Time Out made the natural leap into travel guides in the 1980s with the City Guide series, which now extends to over 50 destinations around the world. Written and researched by expert local writers and generously illustrated with original photography, the full-size guides cover a larger area than our Shortlist guides and include many more venue reviews, along with additional background features and a full set of maps.

Throughout this rapid growth, the company has remained proudly independent, still owned by Tony Elliott four decades after he started Time Out London as a single fold-out sheet of A5 paper. This independence extends to the editorial content of all our publications, this Shortlist included. No establishment has been featured because it has advertised, and no payment has influenced any of our reviews. And, for our critics, there's definitely no such thing as a free lunch: all restaurants and bars are visited and reviewed anonymously, and Time Out always picks up the bill.
For more about the company, see www.timeout.com.

Don't Miss
2009

What's best: **Sights & Museums** 8

What's best: **Eating & Drinking** 13

What's best: **Shopping** 21

What's best: **Nightlife** 26

What's best: **Arts & Leisure** 30

What's on: **Calendar** 35

View from the Vittoriano p64

Sights & Museums

History in Rome is not confined to museums and galleries: it tumbles out everywhere. And though the city is reassuringly compact, this doesn't stop the cultural onslaught from being utterly bewildering and exhausting.

It pays to approach the eternal city knowing that you won't see everything. Remember, too, that if you shut yourself up in Rome's extraordinary collections and sites, you'll miss something just as important: the urban landscape and its inimitable inhabitants. To appreciate it, you'll need to walk (bring comfy shoes) and lounge – sitting at a pavement café may crank up the price of your cappuccino, but a front-row seat at the spectacle that is Rome is cheap at any price.

Rome today is looking good: many of its historic buildings have been restored and are gorgeously illuminated at night; the Ara Pacis (p85) has a controversial new enclosure; streets and squares have been repaved with traditional basalt cobbles. Parts of the *centro storico* have been pedestrianised; there are clean green electric buses and the metro is (very gradually) being extended.

Ancient sites

The area with the greatest density of remains lies between the Palatine, Capitoline, Esquiline and Quirinal hills. Located here are the Colosseum (p57), the Roman Forum (p60) and ancient Rome's most desirable residential area, the Palatine (p60). But ancient Rome doesn't stop there: the Museo Nazionale Romano group (Palazzo Massimo alle Terme, p104; Palazzo Altemps, p78; Crypta Balbi, p69;

and the Baths of Diocletian, p101; for all see www.archeorm.arti.beniculturali.it) houses a mind-boggling collection of ancient statuary, of which there's more in the Vatican and Capitoline museums (p145 and p56). And the Pantheon (p76) is a work of art in itself.

Churches

Down the centuries popes, princes and aristocrats all commissioned architects and artists to build and adorn their preferred places of worship, with the result that central Rome is home to more than 400 churches, containing endless artistic treasures.

Churches are places of worship; though only the Vatican imposes its dress code rigidly (both in St Peter's and the Vatican Museums), very short skirts, bare midriffs, over-exposed shoulders and shorts are all frowned upon. Churches ask tourists to refrain from visiting during services. A supply of coins for the meters to light up the most interesting artworks is handy, as is a pair of binoculars.

Museums & galleries

Rome has long boasted some of the world's greatest galleries and museums, but the last few years have seen a rash of new permanent exhibits, and there are new showcases for old ones. The ancient, Renaissance and Baroque dominate, of course; but initiatives such as MACRO and MAXXI (both p98) mean that the city is increasingly catering well for contemporary art.

Opening hours

Though we have given both winter (*orario invernale*) and summer (*orario estivo*) opening hours, the latter may sometimes be extended significantly, with some major museums and sites keeping doors open as late as 11pm in the high

SHORTLIST

Art meets industry
- Classical statuary at the Centrale Montemartini (p122)
- MACRO at the Birreria Peroni (p98)
- MACRO Future at the Mattatoio (p121)

Ancient splendour
- Ara Pacis Museum (p85)
- Colosseum (p57)
- Imperial Fora Museum (p57)
- Pantheon (p76)
- Roman Forum & Palatine (p60)

Ancient collections
- Capitoline Museums (p56)
- Centrale Montemartini (p122)
- Palazzo Altemps (p78)
- Palazzo Massimo alle Terme (p104)
- Vatican Museums (p145)

Breathtaking views
- From the dome of St Peter's (p144)
- From the new lift at the Vittoriano (p64)
- From the Gianicolo hill (p138)
- From the Pincio in Villa Borghese park (p91)

Grand masters
- Capitoline Museums (p56)
- Galleria Borghese (p92)
- Galleria Doria Pamphili (p78)
- Palazzo Barberini (p95)

Impressive *piazze*
- Piazza del Popolo (p84)
- Piazza Farnese (p69)
- Piazza Navona (p76)

Peaceful parks
- Villa Borghese (p91)
- Villa Pamphili (p138)
- Villa Torlonia (p98)

For jewelry
with a difference,
Petochi 1884
have designed
a range of luxury
jewelry using as a
template the Sampietrini,
Rome's world-famous
cobblestones, an essential
feature of the urban landscape
and emblem of the city.
Each of the "cobblestones",
hand-worked in gold,
is unique.

I Sampietrini

PETOCHI
1884

season. Check for current times at information kiosks. Most museums – though not churches – are closed on Mondays.

Note that ticket offices at many museums, galleries and ancient sites stop issuing tickets anything up to 75 minutes before gates shut.

Church opening times should be taken as rough guidelines. And whether doors are open or not often depends on anything from priestly whim to the availability of volunteer staff.

Tickets

Entrance to publicly owned sites and museums is free (*gratuito*) or reduced (*ridotto*) for EU citizens (and citizens of other countries with bilateral agreements) aged under 18 or over 65; you must show photo-ID (for children too) at ticket offices to prove that you are eligible. Under-25s in full-time education may also be eligible for discounts, as may journalists, teachers, motoring association members and others. Carry a range of ID just in case.

Note that many sights now levy an extra charge, generally of €1.50-€3, when special exhibitions are taking place inside; visitors are given no option other than to pay the ticket-plus-exhibition price. In all cases, we have given the basic price in this guide.

Booking

Booking is mandatory for the Domus Aurea (p101) and Galleria Borghese (p92). It is also a good idea for big one-off shows.

Booking is possible – though really not necessary except for large groups for many other sites and museums. Note that agencies charge a booking fee that further bumps up the price of tickets.

The official booking agencies for Rome's major sites are Pierreci (06 0608, www.060608.it or www.pierreci.it) and Ticketeria (06 32 810, www.ticketeria.it). Both accept MasterCard and Visa.

Discounts & passes

The **Roma Pass** is a multi-entrance card that costs €20 and is valid for three days. It gives free access to any two sights, reduced entry to all others, plus free use of the city's public transport system.

MACRO Future p121

For further information, see www.romapass.it.

The **Villa Borghese Card** (€10) lasts for 12 months and allows free access to one of the many museums within this park (p91), as well as giving reduced entrance to the others and discounts at bookshops and bars. For further information, see www.villaborghese.it.

The following tickets can be bought (cash only) at any of the sites involved or at the APT (p187), which charges a €1.50 booking fee.

Appia Card (€6, €3 reductions, valid 7 days) covers the Baths of Caracalla, Tomb of Cecilia Metella and Villa dei Quintili.

Archeologia Card (€20, €10 reductions, valid 7 days) covers the Baths of Caracalla, Baths of Diocletian, Colosseum, Crypta Balbi, Palatine, Palazzo Altemps, Palazzo Massimo alle Terme, Tomb of Cecilia Metella and Villa dei Quintili.

Capitolini Card (€8.50, €6.50 reductions, valid 7 days) covers the Capitoline Museums and Centrale Montemartini.

Museo Nazionale Romano Card (€7, €3.50 reductions, valid for three days) covers the Baths of Diocletian, the Crypta Balbi, the Palazzo Massimo alle Terme and the Palazzo Altemps.

Tours

Trambus's 110 Open bus (06 4695 2252) leaves Termini station every 10mins (8am-8pm). It makes 11 stops on a two-hour circuit. Tours include commentary (in six languages). An all-day stop-and-go ticket costs €16.

The Archeobus passes by the Baths of Caracalla (p117) and along via Appia Antica (Appian Way, p151), leaving Termini station about every 20mins from 9am to 4pm. Stop-and-go tickets cost €13; without stops, the trip takes about two and a half hours.

Tickets for both can be bought at the booth in front of Termini, on board or online (www.trambus open.com). A variety of tickets combining these and other tours, and tours with a trip to or from Ciampino, are also available.

Centrale Montemartini p122

Remo p125

Eating & Drinking

When it comes to the important things in life, Romans value substance over style: the shabby neighbourhood bar, with its excellent coffee and delicious *cornetti,* remains a favourite; and the local trat – where food is hearty and fresh – will always be packed.

But the capital city also offers a host of addresses for sipping and dining in style. And if prices have soared since the introduction of the euro – putting Rome on par with many other European cities – the quality and authenticity of what's on offer here are hard to beat.

Eating

A swathe of designer restaurants opened in Rome around the turn of the millennium, but many have since closed, the survivors being those that offer real culinary excitement, rather than just a few twigs in a vase and the chance of spotting a once-famous TV starlet.

Trattorie and *osterie,* on the other hand, are going great guns, spurred on by a growing demand for value for money. Some are unreconstructed family-run operations; others are recently opened places that take the trattoria formula and give it a twist by upping the creativity quotient in the kitchen.

But it is the focus on the raw materials that is the real innovation. Foodie enthusiasm has upped quality no end; the trickle-down effect of this means that even the most basic trat now generally offers decent extra-virgin olive oil with which to dress your salad.

The other positive note is the increasing variety of the Roman dining scene. Once, the choice was between posh restaurant, humble

ristorante
pizzeria
wine bar
live music
enoteca
emporio libreria
osteria
formaggeria
pesce e ortaggi

the different tastes of Gusto

ristorante pizzeria wine bar piazza augusto imperatore 9 roma tel +39 063226273
osteria formaggeria via della frezza 16 vicolo del corea 2 roma tel +39 0632111482
ristorante cocktail bar pesce & ortaggi piazza augusto imperatore 28 roma tel +39 0668134221
emporio libreria negozio di vini piazza augusto imperatore 7 roma tel +39 063236363

www.gusto.it

trattoria or pizzeria. Today there are wine bars, salad bars, gastropubs and deli-diners. Even the unchanging pizzeria has been shaken up by the arrival of gourmet pizza emporia. And Rome now has more decent Japanese and Indian restaurants than ever before.

It pays to be adventurous when eating in Rome – most of the best places don't have menus in six languages, and may not look like much on the outside. It's also worth getting away from the most heavily touristed parts of the *centro storico* to outlying areas like Testaccio, San Lorenzo or Il Pigneto (see box p125), where you'll find some of the city's best-value creative *trattorie*.

Going the course

The standard Italian running order is: *antipasto* (starter), *primo* (usually pasta, sometimes soup), *secondo* (the meat or fish course) with optional *contorno* (vegetables or salad, served separately) and *dolce* (dessert). You're under no obligation to order four courses – few locals do. It's perfectly normal, for example, to order a pasta course followed by a simple *contorno*.

Top-flight restaurants will occasionally offer a special *menu degustazione* (taster menu), but any establishment with a *menu turistico* should usually be avoided.

Drinks

One of the biggest changes over the last decade has been the way even humble eateries have started to have good wine lists. More and more establishments are now offering a decent selection of wine by the glass (*al bicchiere* or *alla mescita*). In pizzerias, the drink of choice is *birra* (beer) or soft drinks. Mineral water – *acqua minerale* – comes either *gasata* (sparkling) or *naturale* (still) and is usually served by the litre.

SHORTLIST

High-end gourmet
- Antico Arco (p138)
- Il Pagliaccio (p73)
- L'Altro Mastai (p107)

Venues with views
- Caffè Bernini (p81)
- Il Ristoro (p148)
- La Vineria (p75)

Good food, good value
- Cantina Cantarini (p94)
- Bar Necci (p115)
- Satollo (p125)
- Matricianella (p89)
- Tuttifrutti (p125)
- Le Mani in Pasta (p135)

Smart bars for long drinks
- Freni e Frizioni (p133)
- Crudo (p72)
- Etabli (p82)
- Stravinskij Bar (p89)
- Zest bar (roof of Radisson SAS es. Hotel, p176)

Great coffee
- Bar Sant'Eustachio (p81)
- La Caffettiera (p82)
- Dagnino (p107)

Lunch spots
- Casa Bleve (p81)
- Enoteca Corsi (p82)
- Moma (p94)
- Vic's (p91)

Filling snacks
- Forno Campo de' Fiori (p73)
- Lo Zozzone (p82)
- Paninoteca da Guido (p148)

Perfect pizza
- Bir & Fud (p133)
- Da Francesco (p81)
- Dar Poeta (p133)
- Pizza Ciro (p89)
- Remo (p125)

GiNa

eat & drink

restaurant

italian bistrò

wine & cocktail bar

tea room

sweets & ice cream

pic nic basket

music lounge

private party

Via San Sebastianello 7/A
(Next to Spanish Steps)
www.ginaroma.com
tel. 0039.06.678.02.51
Open 7/7 no stop 11 a.m 11 p.m
Gina's kitchen Via Plana 9/11
(piazza Euclide) Roma

GiNa

eat & drink

Prices, tipping and times

Places that add service to the bill are still in the minority; if in doubt, ask, *'il servizio è incluso?'* A good rule of thumb is to leave around five per cent in humbler places, or up to ten per cent in smarter eateries. If service has been slack or rude, you should have no qualms about leaving nothing – or checking the bill in detail, as there is still the occasional restaurateur who gets his sums wrong when dealing with foreigners. Most restaurants accept credit cards, but if there is no sticker on the door, ask, *'accettate le carte di credito?'*

Where we have specified 'Meals served', this is the opening time of the kitchen: the establishment may remain open long after. In the evening, few serious restaurants open before 7.30pm. Pizzerias begin serving earlier, generally by 7pm.

In this guide, we have used the euro (€) symbol to indicate the average price range for a three-course meal without wine for one:

€ – €20 or less
€€ – €21 to €35
€€€ – €36 to €50
€€€€ – over €50

Children, women and (no) smoking

Taking children into restaurants – even the smartest – is never a problem in Rome. Waiters will usually produce a high chair (*un seggiolone*) and are generally happy to serve youngsters *una mezza porzione* – a half-portion.

Women dining alone will rarely encounter problems, though you have to get used to the local habit of staring. Single diners of either sex can have trouble getting a table at busy times: few proprietors want to waste a table that could hold four.

Smoking is now illegal in all restaurants except where there is a designated smoking area that meets stringent regulations.

Booking is recommended for Friday or Saturday evening or Sunday lunch, even in the more humble-looking places.

Pizza

Traditional Roman pizza is thin; Neapolitan pizza is puffier. Either way, make sure it comes from a wood-fired oven (*forno a legna*).

Pizza toppings are strictly orthodox: don't expect pineapple. Note that pizza is an evening thing – very few places serve it for lunch.

Wine bars

Neighbourhood *enoteche* (wine shops) and *vini e olii* (wine and oil) outlets have been around in Rome since time immemorial. Recently, a number of upmarket, international-style wine bars have also sprung up, offering snacks and even full meals to go with their wines.

Snacks

The city's snack culture lurks in unlikely places, such as the humble *alimentari* (grocer's) where they'll fill a crusty white roll (*rosetta*), or a slice of *pizza bianca* (focaccia) with ham, salami or cheese. *Pizza rustica* outlets serve pizza by the take away slab, while most bars have a range of sandwiches and filled rolls.

Vegetarians

Rome has few bona fide vegetarian restaurants; but even in traditional *trattorie*, there's plenty of meatless options to try – from *penne all'arrabbiata* (pasta in a tomato and chilli sauce) through to *tonnarelli cacio e pepe* (thick spaghetti with crumbly sheep's cheese and plenty of black pepper) to *carciofi alla giudia* (deep-fried artichokes). If you are at all unsure about the ingredients of any dish, ask if it has meat in it, *'c'è la carne?'*

Pasticcerie and *gelaterie*

Most *pasticcerie* (cake shops) are bars where freshly baked goodies can be consumed in situ with a drink, or taken away.

Many bars have a freezer cabinet with a sign promising *produzione artigianale* (home-made ice-cream). This is often a con: it may mean industrial ice-cream mix whipped up on the premises. While this doesn't necessarily mean the ice-cream will be bad, you'll need to be selective when seeking a truly unique *gelato* experience. If the colours seem too bright to be real, then they aren't. Banana should be creamy-grey, not electric yellow.

As well as the two main choices of *frutta* or *crema* (fruit- or cream-based ice-cream), there's also *sorbetto* or *granita* (water ices). When you've exhausted these, sample a *grattachecca*, a rougher version of water ice.

Drinking

Cafés and bars

The average Roman starts his or her day with a coffee in a local café or bar (in Italy these amount to the same thing since alcohol and coffee are served all day long in both). They will also have snacks, maybe cigarettes and bus tickets, and fabulous, cheap coffee.

In the touristy *centro storico*, things are different. Standing at the counter like the locals to knock back your tiny cupful is one thing; but occupy a table or, worse, a pavement table, and the bill will double or even treble. Of course, there are moments when nothing is more beguiling than sitting outside with a view of the Pantheon; just be aware that you'll pay for the luxury.

Besides the many variations of *caffè* (the local term for espresso) and *cappuccino*, most bars offer *cornetti* (croissants), *tramezzini*

(sandwiches) and *panini* (filled rolls; one is a *panino*). A small bottle of still or sparkling mineral water (*acqua minerale naturale* or *gassata*) costs around €1.

By law, all bars must have a *bagno* (lavatory), which can be used by anyone, whether or not they purchase anything. Bars must also provide dehydrated passers-by with a glass of tap water, free and with no obligation to buy. Smoking is forbidden inside all bars and cafés.

Pubs and *enoteche*

Many of Rome's *enoteche* and *vini e olii* have recently become charming places to grab a drink and a slice of the *vita romana*. Some of these are chic venues with a *dopocena* (after-dinner) scene and a beautiful, see-and-be-seen crowd.

Rome's pubs are divided between a handful of long-standing British- and Irish-style institutions and a host of newer casual joints.

Casa Bleve p81

sfizi ai fornelli

Via degli Spagnoli, 27
Roma
tel. 06.6872554
06.6864110
www.ilbacaro.com
**OPEN
TO LATE NIGHT**
(closed Sunday)
Reservations advisable

Via Condotti p23

WHAT'S BEST
Shopping

Depending on your attitude towards shopping, you'll find Rome either very refreshing or incredibly frustrating.

There are, for example, no malls in the cramped streets of the *centro*: these recent-ish arrivals are relegated to the drear outer suburbs where visitors rarely venture.

You'll notice, too, a distinct lack of chains – give or take a Benetton or two – or at least of the recognisable ones that in many countries make every high street a carbon copy of all the others.

Instead, there are corner grocery shops, dark and dusty bottle-lined wine shops, one-off boutiques catering to every imaginable taste… and, of course, the opulent outlets of Italy's fashion aristocracy.

Traditionalists can draw comfort from the fact that, for now, the tiny boutique and the family-run store are still managing to retain their presence in Rome's retail sector. Just.

Because in fact, in Rome as elsewhere, the corner shop is being driven out by big-name inner-city mini-markets; and there *are* clothing chains – it's just that they have different names here – and major brands are colonising the Roman high street at a distressing pace.

Where to shop

As a fashion centre, Rome has long been overshadowed by Milan, but the Eternal City remains a more picturesque place to shop. The major Italian names in *alta moda* are huddled around piazza di Spagna and via Condotti, in the Tridente. The main streets here are often packed, so wind your way through the pretty side streets and check out the smaller – though

Franchi p150

often costly – boutiques. Slicing through the Tridente from piazza del Popolo to piazza Venezia is via del Corso, home to mid-range outlets for everything from books and music to clothing and shoes.

Further south along via del Corso, the Galleria Alberto Sordi, a restored early 20th-century arcade, has fast become one of the city's prime shopping and meeting points. As well as the 20 retail outlets, there are a couple of *aperitivo* bars and frequent 'happenings' of a musical and artistic nature, all under one beautifully coloured glass roof.

There are more high street clothing retailers along traffic-clogged via Nazionale; while this street itself is no charmer, the nearby Monti neighbourhood packs unique boutiques and hip originals.

Across the river, beneath the Vatican walls in the Prati area, via Cola di Rienzo is a shorter and slightly less crowded version of via del Corso, with major retail chains, and some great food shopping at divine deli Franchi (p150).

For great independent designers and the city's best vintage gear, on the other hand, head west of piazza Navona to via del Governo Vecchio.

Opening times

Many Rome shop owners now forego the sacred siesta in favour of '*no-stop*' opening hours, from around 10am to 7.30pm, Monday to Saturday. The odd independent store still clings to the 1-4pm shutdown. In the centre, more and more stores also open on Sundays.

Times given in this guide are winter opening hours; in summer (June to September), shops that opt for long lunches tend to reopen later, at say 5.30pm, staying open until around 8pm. Most food stores close on Thursday afternoons in winter, and on Saturday afternoons in summer.

SHORTLIST

Only in Rome
- Ai Monasteri (p83)
- Clerical outfitters along via dei Cestari
- Monks' organic vegetables at Santa Croce in Gerusalemme (p111)
- I Sapori della Legalità (p65)
- Vatican souvenirs in and around Borgo Pio (p143)

Objects of design
- Ilaria Miani (p75)
- Spazio Sette (p76)

Treats to take home
- Buccone (wine; p88)
- Chocolates galore (p134)
- Franchi (deli; p150)
- Volpetti (deli; p126)

Books in English
- Almost Corner Bookshop (p136)
- Anglo-American Book (p91)
- The Lion Bookshop (p91)

Independent designers
- Arsenale (p83)
- Le Gallinelle (p107)
- Le Tartarughe (p83)
- Maga Morgana (p83)

Markets
- Campo de' Fiori (fruit & veg; p64)
- ex-Piazza Vittorio (fruit & veg; p107)
- Piazza San Cosimato (fruit & veg; p136)
- Piazza Testaccio (fruit, veg & shoes; p126)
- Porta Portese (flea market; p136)
- Via Sannio (clothes; p113)

Fine footwear
- Borini (p75)
- Loco (p75)
- Piazza Testaccio (p126)

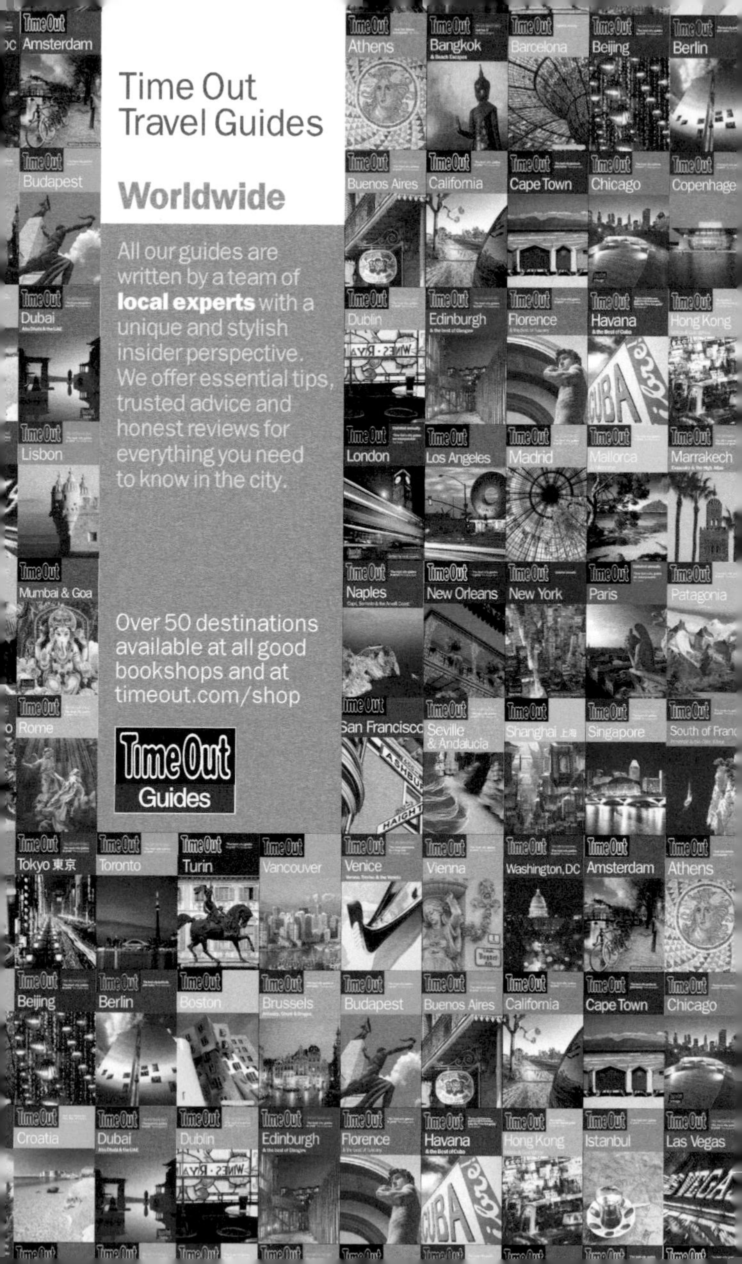

Time Out
Travel Guides

Worldwide

All our guides are
written by a team of
local experts with a
unique and stylish
insider perspective.
We offer essential tips,
trusted advice and
honest reviews for
everything you need
to know in the city.

Over 50 destinations
available at all good
bookshops and at
timeout.com/shop

Time Out
Guides

The majority of non-food shops are closed Monday mornings. Many shops shut for at least two weeks in summer (usually in August) and almost all are shut for two or three days around the 15 August public holiday. If you want to avoid finding a particular shop *chiuso per ferie* (closed for holidays), be sure to ring ahead.

Although service is improving, many shop assistants still seem hell-bent on either ignoring or intimidating customers. This is no time for Anglo-Saxon reticence; perfect the essential lines *'mi può aiutare, per favore?'* ('Can you help me, please?') and *'volevo solo dare un' occhiata'* ('I'm just looking') and you're ready for any eventuality.

Prices & paying

Italians bemoan the advent of the penury-inducing euro, and if you last came to Rome with the lira you'll notice that bargains are far harder to find. Home-grown designer names are still a little easier on the wallet here than abroad, however. Bargaining

belongs firmly at the flea market: in shops, prices are fixed.

You should always be given a *scontrino* (receipt). If you aren't, then ask for it: by law, shops must provide one, and they and you are liable for a fine in the (wildly unlikely) event of your being caught without it. Major credit cards are accepted just about everywhere, but do check before getting to a till.

The rules on returning purchases are infuriatingly vague. Faulty goods, obviously, must be refunded or replaced. Many shops will also accept unwanted goods that are returned unused with a receipt within seven days of purchase, though this is not obligatory.

Tax rebates

Non-EU residents are entitled to a sales tax (IVA) rebate on purchases of personal goods worth over €155, if they are bought from a shop with the 'Europe Tax Free' sticker. The shop will give you a receipt and a 'Tax Free Shopping Cheque', which should be stamped by customs before leaving Italy.

Libreria del Cinema p135

Coming Out p113

Nightlife

The injection of funding that
has enlivened Rome's art scene
since the dawn of the millennium
has also had a tangible knock-on
effect on nightlife, turning this
once-sleepy city into a lively
European capital.

In a development that cuts
against this country's reverence
for the well-tried and the traditional,
young, cutting-edge artistic
communities are being given space
to bring their entertainment projects
out of niches. This flurry of activity
seeps into Rome's nightlife, where
dancing to the best international
DJs and hearing the latest bands is
easier than ever. You will, however,
need some inside information to
avoid the Eurotrash dished out by
the plethora of commercial venues.

Where to go, when to go

New compulsory closing times
forcing most *centro storico* bars
to shut at 2am have cancelled
the unwritten 'open until the last
punter stumbles out the door'
rule that long gave Roman nights
their uniquely relaxed feel.

Discos and live venues still stay
open until the small hours, though,
allowing Romans to maintain their
habit of starting the evenings late
and ending them even later.

Rome's nightlife venues tend
to be concentrated mostly around
a few easily accessible areas.

In Testaccio, nightlife action
is concentrated around Monte
Testaccio (p122): you'll be spoilt
for choice – just walk around until
you find the vibe you're after.

The area around via Libetta, off via Ostiense, teems with trendy clubs and is poised to become even more crowded: the city council has slowly begun to develop the whole district as an arts hub.

Fashionistas head for the *centro storico*: spend an evening in the *triangolo della Pace* and you're part of trendy Roman life. The campo de' Fiori area, once another fashionista meeting spot, has become increasingly chaotic and, as the evening progresses, squalid.

Artsy, studenty San Lorenzo is altogether less pretentious: drinks are cheaper, and there's always something interesting going on.

Trastevere has lovely alleys packed with friendly, crowded bars, where English is the lingua franca. Note, though, that around piazza Trilussa, it can get pretty seedy in the wee hours.

Clubbing

When picking a club for the night, bear in mind that many of Rome's mainstream venues serve up commercial house or 1980s retro on Fridays and Saturdays. Established places like Goa (p127), La Saponeria (p127) and Micca Club (p114) offer high-quality DJ sets.

For something alternative try the Brit-pop/punk rock served up by the Beatles-look-alike DJs of Fish & Chips (Fridays, Radio Café, via Principe Umberto 67, www. radiocaferoma.org) or dance the night away at Screamadelica (Circolo degli Artisti, p116), where global live acts are topped by DJs playing rock, pop and indie. On Tuesdays, DJ Andrea Esu and international guests spin their electro-house and tech sounds at L-Ektrica (Akab, p126). Vintage enthusiasts strike gold at Twiggy, Rome's best '60s night, where Italy's top live bands introduce DJs Luzy L and Corry X (for the 2007/8

DON'T MISS: 2009

SHORTLIST

Best for live music
- Auditorium – Parco della Musica (p99)
- *Centri sociali* (p28)
- Circolo degli Artisti (p116)
- Teatro Palladium (p127)

Best mainstream
- Akab (p126)
- Alpheus (p127)
- Goa (p127)
- La Maison (p83)
- La Saponeria (p127)

Best gay
- Coming Out (p113)
- Gay Village (p41)
- Hangar (p108)
- Skyline (p114)

Best gay one-nighters
- Omogenic at Circolo degli Artisti (Fri; p116)
- Phag Off at various venues (for more information visit www.phagoff.org)
- Venus Rising at Goa (women only, last Sun of month; p127)

Best alternative
- Rashomon (p127)
- Rialtosantambrogio (p76)

Best for *aperitivi*
- B-Said (p116)
- Freni e Frizioni (p133)
- Société Lutèce (p82)
- Crudo (p72)

Best late bars
- Crudo (p72)
- Etabli (p82)
- Friends Art Café (p133)
- Salotto 42 (p82)

Best jazz joints
- Alexanderplatz (p150)
- Casa del Jazz (p28)
- The Place (p150)

season at Traffic, via Vacuna 98, but check www.myspace.com/twiggy60sparty for updates).

Going live

Gloriously eclectic programming at the Auditorium – Parco della Musica (p99) has helped seduce music-shy Romans into making live sounds a regular diary fixture.

But Rome's live music scene is also being boosted by a string of smallish clubs. In 2005, the city-sponsored Casa del Jazz (viale di Porta Ardeatina 55, 06 704 731, www.casajazz.it) opened in a villa confiscated from a local mobster. The cool Teatro Palladium (p127) hosts a daring programme too. And City Hall continues to fund the RomaEuropa Festival (p36), the cutting-edge Enzimi festival (www.enzimi.com) and the odd free mega-concert in a grand setting.

Concerts by huge international names are still rare, but when they do happen, it's often in atmosphere-less mega-venues like the Stadio Olimpico (p99) or the PalaLottomatica, the magnificent indoor stadium designed by Pierluigi Nervi for the 1960 Olympics, in the suburb of EUR (p154).

Until very recently, much of Rome's alternative live action centred on *centri sociali* – disused buildings occupied by dissatisfied youth and transformed into spaces for art, music and politics. With more opportunities elsewhere, their importance has waned, but they still have plenty to offer at bargain prices (admission is usually €5).

Summer in the city

Rome gives its best over the long summer: you'll be spoilt for choice between festivals, concerts, open-air cinema, theatre and discos, most of which come under the Estate Romana (p41) umbrella.

Gay Rome

Rome's gay community waited with bated breath over the winter of 2006-7 but parliamentary debate on civil unions eventually ground to a halt – thanks, many suspect, to Vatican intervention.

Gay life in the Italian capital continues to be mainstream, however, with new organisations, venues and facilities popping up. The historic Mario Mieli (www.mariomieli.org) group, flanked by the newer, hyperactive Di'Gay Project (www.digayproject.org), is doing a superb job of adding more social goodies to the shopping trolley.

Likewise, the gay going-out scene continues to diversify and cater for distinct clienteles, with restaurants, pubs, clubs and bars attracting punters of all ages. A proliferation of mixed one-nighters also mirrors the increasing number of places where men and women can have fun under the same roof. Or, for that matter, outdoors: one of the most

The Place p150

notable successes in the Roman calendar is the summer Gay Village (p41). The www.gayvillage.it website is also a great source of year-round events info.

Many gay venues ask for an Arcigay card, which costs €15 for annual membership, though an €8 one-month version is available for out-of-towners. The card can be bought at any participating venue.

Getting in

Getting into Rome's fashionable mainstream clubs can be stressful, no matter how well you're dressed. Intimidating bouncers will block your way, while PR luvvies smirk as they whisk supposed VIPs through the door past lines of frustrated would-be clients. But persistence and patience will get you in eventually.

Clubs and discobars generally charge an entrance fee at weekends but not on weekdays; be aware that on your first visit you will often have to buy a *tessera* (membership card) on top of, or sometimes instead of, the entrance fee. Tickets often include a 'free' drink, but you can expect the drinks you buy thereafter to be pricey. Another popular formula is to grant 'free' admission while forcing you to buy a (generally expensive) drink. To get out again you have to hand a stamped drink card to the bouncer, so hold on to whatever piece of paper staff give you or you'll be forced to pay twice.

Where we haven't specified a price for entrance, admission is free.

Finding out

For details of upcoming events, consult the listings magazines *Trovaroma* (Thursday with *La Repubblica*), *Roma C'è* (Wednesday) or *Zero6* (monthly, free in shops and pubs). Or visit www.romastyle.info, which is good for techno and drum 'n' bass, and www.2night.it or www.musicaroma.it for the latest gigs. Fans of indie and punk rock should take a look at www.myspace.com/romecityrockers and www.pogopop.it (in English, after a fashion).

Gagosian Gallery p33

WHAT'S BEST
Arts & Leisure

It won't bowl you over, and you'll
need to know where to look, but
on the arts front, Rome is hopping.
Generous public funding since the
turn of the millennium has made
the Eternal City a great centre
for the performing arts.

But fine arts too – of the
contemporary, commercial variety
– shifted swiftly up through several
gears late in 2007 when top art
dealer Larry Gagosian opened a
stunning new gallery here.

Music

Rome is now back on the music-
lovers' map of Europe after over
a century of neglect. This is thanks
mainly to the Auditorium – Parco
della Musica (p99).

Inaugurated in 2002, this complex
of exhibition and concert spaces,
designed by Renzo Piano, has
been hugely successful, enticing
Romans of all tastes with a
programme of such extraordinary
breadth it is second only to
New York's Lincoln Center for
the variety of its offerings. This
democratic eclecticism has cast its
spell over citizens who had never
set foot in a classical music venue
in their lives: 2006 saw over a
million presences. Even more
miraculous, in a country where
the arts are traditionally a financial
black hole, the Auditorium is self-
funding and firmly in the black.

But it is not the only venue in
Rome for music. Many of the more
traditional concert halls and
locations have also benefited from
the surge of energy, and many of
them offer high-quality programmes.

Opera is one branch of the
musical arts that continues to
languish, with constipated
programmes and generally
mediocre productions.

But like many other musical
offerings in Rome, the settings
for opera – the Teatro dell'Opera

(p108) and the Baths of Caracalla (p117) – are so glorious that the quality doesn't always matter.

Not that it's always low – for instance, La Stravaganza (06 7707 2842, www.lastravaganzamusica.it) organises delightful chamber music concerts inside the Palazzo Doria Pamphili; during the interval the audience is invited to wander into the adjacent gallery (p78) to enjoy the superb art collection. On Sunday mornings, there are noon recitals in the sumptuous Cappella Paolina of the president's residence, Palazzo del Quirinale (p96). At the church of Sant'Anselmo (piazza Cavalieri di Malta 5) on the Aventine, Benedictine monks sing Gregorian chant evensong daily at 7.15pm.

Check the local press, and look out for wall posters for other such concerts, many of which are free.

Theatre

If you're thinking of an evening at the theatre, don't expect daring performances: the Italian school of drama, with its stiff style imposed by the stuffy dramatic arts academy, still holds sway.

One interesting recent project is the Casa dei Teatri (06 4544 0707, www.casadeiteatri.culturaroma.it), in a palazzo in Villa Pamphili. This centre integrates performances with workshops and research.

Dance

This Cinderella of Italian arts is allowed out of the kitchen more often nowadays, and features in seasonal programmes and festivals such as RomaEuropa (p36).

Galleries

Rome's commercial contemporary art world had been striving for some time to rival Turin and Naples. Now local dealers are wondering whether things have moved too fast.

SHORTLIST

Best overall arts venue
- Auditorium – Parco della Musica (p99)

Arts festivals
- Estate Romana (p41)
- FotoGrafia – Festival Internazionale di Roma (p39)
- RomaEuropa Festival (p36)
- Rome Literature Festival (p41)

Taking to the streets
- Carnevale celebrations (p39)
- Christmas in piazza Navona (p42)
- Gay Village (p41)
- La Notte Bianca (p36)

Perfect summer settings
- Jazz & Image festival in Villa Celimontana (p41)
- Cosmophonies in the Roman theatre at Ostia Antica (p41)
- Roma Incontra il Mondo world music festival in Villa Ada (p41)
- Teatro dell'Opera summer season in the Baths of Caracalla (p41)

Rome & film
- Metropolitan (p33)
- Nuovo Olimpia (p33)
- Cinema – Festa Internazionale di Roma (p37)

Fun for kids
- Bioparco-Zoo (p92)
- Explora – Museo dei Bambini di Roma (p92)
- Time Elevator (p95)

Pampering
- El Spa (p150)
- L'Olfattorio – Bar à Parfums (p91)
- Via Giulia IV (p76)

Cinema – Festa Internazionale di Roma

The indefatigable Larry 'Gogo' Gagosian inaugurated his temple to art dealing (via Francesco Crispi 16, www.gagosian.com) in December 2007 with a glittering bash and a show by Cy Twombly. While welcoming the international attention Gagosian attracts, locals are wondering whether there'll be any market share left for them.

Film

Italian dubbers are recognised as the world's best, but that's no consolation if you like to see films in the original language (*lingua originale* or *versione originale* – VO in listings). That said, you're better served in Rome than in any other Italian city. The Nuovo Olimpia (via in Lucina 16G), just off via del Corso and the Metropolitan (via del Corso 7) have regular VO programming. There are VO screenings at the Alcazar (via Merry del Val 14) and at the Nuovo Sacher (largo Ascianghi 1) on Mondays.

The Casa del Cinema (largo M Mastroianni 1, www.casadelcinema. it) inside Villa Borghese screens an interesting selection of films for free.

Rome's annual film festival, Cinema – Festa Internazionale di Roma (p37), is one to look out for.

Sport

Most Romans have an aversion to physical activity, but they are passionate supporters.

Rome is home to two first-class football clubs: AS Roma (www.as roma.it) and SS Lazio (www.ss lazio.it). The two teams share the Stadio Olimpico (p99) in the Foro Italico complex.

In 2007, a spate of stadium violence prompted tough new measures. Tickets can no longer be bought from the Stadio Olimpico box office: you must buy them from www.listicket.it or from specialist outlets. Tickets are personal (you'll need photo-ID to get into the stadium) and non-transferable.

Though most Romans reserve their enthusiasm for football, the city also has its rugby fans. Since 2000, the national side has been in the Six Nations' Championship, with home games played at the Stadio Flaminio (viale Tiziano, 06 3685 7309, www.federugby.it).

The best guides to enjoying London life

(but don't just take our word for it)

Calendar

Cinema – Festa Internazionale di Roma p37

Kicking back has always come easily to the Romans: the ancients allotted themselves a whopping 150 days each year for R&R. Today's ten annual public holidays are, ostensibly, within the European norm. In fact, the final total usually turns out to be quite a bit more: any holiday that falls midweek is invariably taken as an invitation to *fare il ponte* ('do a bridge') – between the official holiday and the nearest weekend.

Religious holidays (and the Easter week in particular) turn the city centre into a heaving mass of visiting humanity; only Ferragosto (the Assumption) on August 15 shuts the city down. Different districts of Rome hold smaller-scale celebrations of their own

patron saints in their own way, from calorific blowouts to costume parades, to extravagant firework displays.

An embarrassment of cultural riches has been lavished on the city in recent years, striking a happy balance between small-scale, independent festivals and bigger-budget citywide events that make ample use of Rome's endless supply of photogenic venues.

Keep an eye on local press and wall posters for the occasional huge free concert, and also for major exhibitions, which tend to be announced at short notice. The websites of the cultural heritage ministry (www.beni culturali.it), the Rome city council (www.comune.roma.it), the city's

RomaEuropa Festival

information site www.060608.it and the Rome tourist board (www.romaturismo.it) are very useful sources of information.

Dates highlighted in **bold** are public holidays. For information on celebrations to mark the 2000th anniversary of the birth of St Paul, see box p142.

September 2008

Until 30 Nov **The Genius of Leonardo da Vinci**
Sala del Bramante, piazza del Popolo 1

1 Sept-28 Oct **Rome and Egypt, from Myth to History**
Castel Sant'Angelo (p143)

1 Sept-31 Oct **De Chirico and the Museum**
Galleria Nazionale di Arte Moderna (p92).

Mid Sept tbc **La Notte Bianca**
www.lanottebianca.it
Rome's annual all-night party. There are street performances throughout the city, art installations and concerts, plus shops, clubs and museums stay open through the night. At time of press this event was facing possible cancellation.

25 Sept-11 Jan **Giovanni Bellini**
Scuderie del Quirinale (p97)
www.palaexpo.it
Works by the Venetian master.

Late Sept-early Dec
RomaEuropa Festival
Various locations
www.romaeuropa.net
Rome's most prestigious performing arts festival.

October 2008

Ongoing RomaEuropa Festival, Giovanni Bellini, The Genius of Leonardo da Vinci, Rome and Egypt, from Myth to History,

De Chirico and the Museum
(for all, see Sept)

2 Oct-17 Feb **Ruins and
Rebirths in Italian Art**
Colosseum (p57)

11 Oct-6 Jan 2009 **Bill Viola**
Palazzo delle Esposizioni (p101)
Works by the US video artist.

14 Oct-6 Jan 2009 **The Etruscans**
Palazzo delle Esposizioni (p101)
Major exhibit on this sophisticated,
shadowy pre-Roman people.

22-31 **Cinema – Festa
Internazionale di Roma**
Auditorium-Parco della Musica
(p99) and other venues
www.romacinemafest.org
The third edition of Rome's controversial film festival.

Late Oct **Mostra dell'Antiquariato**
Via de' Coronari
This street antique fair is packed with
antique dealers.

November 2008

Ongoing RomaEuropa Festival,
Giovanni Bellini, The Genius
of Leonardo da Vinci (for all,
see Sept); Bill Viola (see Oct);
The Etruscans (see Oct); Ruins
and Rebirths in Italian Art
(see Oct)

1-2 **All Saints/All Souls**
Cimitero del Verano, piazzale
del Verano
Romans visit family graves.

December 2008

Ongoing Giovanni Bellini (see
Sept); Bill Viola (see Oct); The
Etruscans (see Oct); Ruins and
Rebirths in Italian Art (see Oct)

8 Immacolata Concezione
Piazza di Spagna (p88)
Immaculate Conception.

25-26 Natale & Santo Stefano
Nativity scenes in churches and on St
Peter's square (p144); Christmas fair in
piazza Navona.

31 **San Silvestro**
Free concert in piazza del Popolo; much
street partying.

January 2009

Ongoing RomaEuropa Festival,
Giovanni Bellini (see Sept); Bill
Viola (see Oct); The Etruscans
(see Oct);Ruins and Rebirths
in Italian Art (see Oct)

1 Capodanno
New Year's Day.

6 Epifania – La Befana
Piazza Navona (p76)
La Befana, the old witch, brings
Epiphany treats for all the children.

17 **Sant'Eusebio**
Sant'Eusebio, via Napoleone III
Animal lovers have pets blessed.

www.treesforcities.org

Trees for Cities
Charity registration number 1032154

Travelling creates so many
lasting memories.

Make your trip mean something for
years to come - not just for you but
for the environment and for people
living in deprived urban areas.

Anyone can offset their flights,
but when you plant trees with
Trees for Cities, you'll help create
a green space for an urban
community that really needs it.

To find out more visit
www.treesforcities.org

Leave
Your
Mark

Create a green future for cities.

February 2009

Ongoing **Ruins and Rebirths in Italian Art** (see Oct)

13-24 **Carnevale**
Around the city centre
Kids dress up and throw confetti in the run-up to Lent.

3 Feb-10 May **Alexander Calder**
Palazzo delle Esposizioni (p101)
An exhaustive retrospective.

3 Feb-3 May **Charles Darwin 1809-2009**
Palazzo delle Esposizioni (p101)

March 2009

Ongoing Alexander Calder, Charles Darwin 1809-2009 (for both, see Feb).

1 May-18 May **China 21st Century**
Palazzo delle Esposizioni (p101)
Contemporary art from China.

9 **Feast of Santa Francesca Romana**
Monastero Oblate di Santa Francesca Romana, via Teatro di Marcello 32 & 40
Rare opportunity to visit this medieval nunnery; Romans have cars blessed at Santa Francesca Romana church in the Roman Forum.

16 **Palazzo Massimo alle Colonne**
Corso Vittorio Emanuele 141
Once-a-year opening of the patrician palace, 8am-1pm.

19 **Feast of San Giuseppe**
Around via Trionfale
Partying and batter-ball eating marks St Joseph's day.

22 **Maratona della Città di Roma**
Around the city centre
www.maratonadiroma.it
There's a 5km fun-run for those not up to the whole 42km Rome Marathon.

Late Mar **Giornate FAI**
Various locations
www.fondoambiente.it

For one weekend each spring, private and institutional owners of interesting, historic properties reveal their spectacular interiors that are usually off-limits to the public.

April 2009

Ongoing Alexander Calder, Charles Darwin 1809-2009 (for both, see Feb); China 21st Century (see Mar).

6-12 **Holy Week & Easter**
Vatican (p139), Colosseum (p57)
Palm Sunday mass at St Peter's, and Pope's Via Crucis at Colosseum on Good Friday.

April-May **FotoGrafia**
Various locations
www.fotografiafestival.it
International festival of photography.

21 **Natale di Roma**
Campidoglio (p54)
Rome celebrates its 2,762st birthday with an immense display of fireworks.

25 **Liberation Day**

Late Apr **Mostra delle Azalee**
Piazza di Spagna (p88)
Some 3,000 vases of azaleas on the Spanish Steps.

May 2009

Ongoing Alexander Calder, Charles Darwin 1809-2009 (for both, see Feb); China 21st Century (see Mar); FotoGrafia (see Apr).

1 **Primo Maggio**
Piazza San Giovanni
www.primomaggio.com
Trade unions organise this huge, free rock concert for May Day.

May-Sept **Caravaggio/Bacon**
Galleria Borghese
See box p97.

Mid May **Settimana della Cultura**
www.beniculturali.it

PalaExpo

Central Rome's prime exhibition venue – the Palazzo delle Esposizioni (p101) – is back in action after a five-year overhaul. It is bigger, brighter and significantly more technologically advanced. Almost 22,000 people tramped across the gleaming marble floors of this huge pile on via Nazionale in the ten days after it reopened.

Inaugurated in 1883, the palazzo was designed by Pio Piacentini as the cultural hiatus on the new showcase artery lined with offices housing the bureaucratic machinery of recently-united Italy. The timing was bad: this was a low point in Italian architecture, when the Piedmontese rulers had not been long in their new capital and were anything but tuned in to Rome's genius loci. People complained that the building looked aloof at the top of its intimidating staircase; they hated that it has no windows. It was described as bombastic, frivolous and directionless.

The latest €28 million revamp has not only increased exhibition space, but reorganised commercial activities – with a new-look bookshop, a chi-chi restaurant under the glass roof on the top floor and a *caffetteria* in the basement – and has opened up a small garden and created a good-sized cinema. The *caffetteria* looks set to be an instant success; the 400-square-metre bookshop has an excellent selection of arts-related material. But the restaurant is uninvitingly dwarfed by its huge white space – a space which used to house a self-service restaurant each lunch time. And the main ground-floor gallery itself is daunting and impersonal in a pale, high-ceilinged, shiny-floored way.

What remains to be seen is whether the offerings on show at this venue draw the crowds. A good inaugural Mark Rothko retrospective proved a crowd-pleaser, while an exhaustive exhibit on the oeuvre of Stanley Kubrick showed that the upstairs space can now be used to interesting and more intimate effect. The kind of blockbuster 'civilisation' shows staged at Venice's Palazzo Grassi were introduced late in 2008, with a mega-event on the Etruscans.
■ www.palaexpo.it

For one week, all state-owned museums are free and many otherwise closed sites are open. Dates vary from year to year.

Mid May-late June
Rome Literature Festival
Basilica di Massenzio,
Roman Forum (p60)
www.festivaldelleletterature.it
Book launches and readings.

Mid May-late June
Roseto Comunale
Via Valle Murcia/clivo dei Pubblici
Annual opening of Rome's municipal rose garden.

Late May **Piazza di Siena**
Piazza di Siena, Villa Borghese
(p91)
www.piazzadisiena.com
Rome's ultra-smart four-day show-jumping event.

June 2009

Ongoing Roseto Comunale,
Caravaggio/Bacon (for both,
see May).

Early June-end Sept
Estate Romana
Various locations
www.estateromana.comune.roma.it
Piazze, palazzi and parks come alive with music, and films are shown on outdoor screens. Many events are free.

Early June-Aug
Jazz & Image Festival
Villa Celimontana (p108)
www.villacelimontanajazz.com
Jazz concerts beneath the trees of this lovely park.

Mid June-early Aug
Roma Incontra il Mondo
Villa Ada, via di Ponte Salario
www.villaada.org
World music by the lake in this park in the northern suburbs.

Mid June-mid Aug **Fiesta!**
Via Appia Nuova 1245
www.fiesta.it
Latin American music fest at the Capanelle racecourse near Ciampino.

Late June-early Sept **Gay Village**
Venue varies
www.gayvillage.it
A ten-week open-air bonanza with bars, restaurants, live acts, discos, cinema – for boys and girls. Venue moves from year to year: check the website.

Late June-mid Aug **Teatro
dell'Opera Summer Season**
Baths of Caracalla (p177)
www.operaroma.it
Rome's opera company stages grand performances in these Roman ruins.

Late June-early Sept
Cosmophonies
www.cosmophonies.com
Roman Theatre, Ostia Antica (p157)
World music, light entertainment and opera amid the ruins.

29 **Santi Pietro e Paolo**
Basilica di San Paolo fuori
le Mura (p123)
Street fair outside St Paul's basilica and mass at St Peter's for the feast day of Rome's patron saints.

July 2009

Ongoing Caravaggio/Bacon
(see May); Estate Romana, Jazz & Image Festival, Roma Incontra il Mondo, Gay Village, Fiesta!, Teatro dell'Opera Summer Season, Cosmophonies (for all, see June)

Mid July **Festa di Noantri**
Piazza Santa Maria in Trastevere,
piazza Mastai
Two weeks of arts events, street performances and fairground attractions.

August 2009

Ongoing Caravaggio/Bacon (see May); Estate Romana, Jazz & Image Festival, Roma Incontra il Mondo, Gay Village, Fiesta!, Teatro dell'Opera Summer Season, Cosmophonies (for all, see June)

1 **Festa delle Catene**
San Pietro in Vincoli (p104)

The chains that bound St Peter are displayed in a special mass.

5 Festa della Madonna della Neve
Santa Maria Maggiore (p105)
A blizzard of rose petals flutters down on festive mass-goers.

10 Notte di San Lorenzo
San Lorenzo in Panisperna, via Panisperna 90
Nuns distribute bread and candles on this, the night of shooting stars.

15 Ferragosto
Rome closes down for the feast of the Assumption.

September 2009

Ongoing Caravaggio/Bacon (see May); Estate Romana, Gay Village, Cosmophonies (for all, see June)

Early Sept **La Notte Bianca**
www.lanottebianca.it
Rome's annual all-night party. There are street performances throughout the city, plus shops, clubs and museums stay open through the night. At time of press this event was facing possible cancellation.

Sept-Nov **RomaEuropa Festival**
Various locations

www.romaeuropa.net
Rome's most prestigious performing arts festival.

October 2009

Ongoing RomaEuropa Festival (see Sept)

Late Oct **Mostra dell'Antiquariato**
Via de' Coronari
Antique fair in this collector's mecca.

November 2009

Ongoing RomaEuropa Festival (see Sept)

1-2 All Saints/All Souls
Cimitero del Verano
Romans visit family graves.

December 2009

8 Immacolata Concezione
Piazza di Spagna (p88)
Immaculate Conception.

25-26 Natale & Santo Stefano
Nativity scenes in churches; Christmas fair in piazza Navona.

31 San Silvestro
Free concert in piazza del Popolo; much street partying.

Palazzo delle Esposizioni p101

Itineraries

Papal Progress   44

Rome on Film   47

Rome in a Rush   50

St Peter's

Papal Progress

For centuries, popes celebrated their election to the throne of St Peter's with a procession from the Vatican to Rome's cathedral, San Giovanni in Laterano, along a route known as the **via Papalis**. Once performed on horseback, today *il possesso* is carried out in a limousine. Take a day out to follow the five-kilometre (three-mile) route on foot, encountering many of the city's best-known landmarks along the way.

To get the most out of your own procession, it helps to know a bit of Papal history. As medieval Rome spiralled into lawlessness, things got so bad that even the pope left town: in 1309, Clement V moved the papal court to Avignon, where it stayed for nearly a century. Meanwhile, Rome's remaining 17,000 inhabitants camped out in the ruins by the river, while despotic local barons sallied forth from their medieval towers in violent bids for power.

In 1378, Pope Gregory XI bravely decided to give Rome a try again but died almost the moment he returned, causing a schism that led to two rival popes being elected – one who dashed back to Avignon within the year, the other brazening it out in Rome. Attempts to sort out the unholy mess only resulted in the election of a third pope in 1409. It took the Council of Constance (1414) to set things to rights, and Martin V, of the powerful Roman Colonna family, was elected with the mandate of returning the papacy to the Holy City.

At first the popes surveyed the ruins from their HQ in the old Lateran palace (p109). Then Nicholas V (1447-55) got moving. He brought clean water to the city and moved the papacy across the river to the Vatican. But the pope was also the bishop of Rome, and taking possession of Rome's cathedral was a highly potent bit of symbolism.

Early processions became ever more spectacular with hundreds of bishops, priests, monks and representatives of charitable corporations following ornately decorated allegorical chariots.

For your own procession, make an early start, and factor in lunch and a few detours en route. If you rush along without stops, you could probably complete it in three hours but you'd be missing the point. (Remember that San Giovanni in Laterano is open until 6.30pm daily.) Along the way, you'll be seeing the very best of papal Rome, so take your time and prepare to be dazzled.

Start at the steps of **St Peter's** (p144) beneath the balcony from which a newly elected pope still greets the faithful, then walk across the great piazza to look back at the façade: this is not the church that early popes processed from. It was not until 1506 – after the original fourth-century basilica had been repeatedly patched up – that it was decided to demolish the building and start again, using the latest Renaissance techniques. The new St Peter's was not finished until 1626. Another 40 years passed before Bernini put the finishing touches to his dazzlingly theatrical landscaping of the piazza, with its sweeping colonnade.

The broad Fascist-era via della Conciliazione, which leads from the Vatican towards the river, was part of Mussolini's grand urban plan: an entire medieval quarter was swept away to make way for a tricky piece of road widening. The early popes would have trotted (on a white horse, with everyone else on foot) through the narrow tangle of streets, through piazza Scossacavalli.

Straight ahead is the imposing bulk of the medieval **Castel Sant'Angelo** (p143) constructed atop Emperor Hadrian's circular mausoleum. The castle is linked to the Vatican by a secret walkway – *il passetto* – along which the popes could rush when trouble loomed.

The castle overlooks the strategic crossing point of the River Tiber: here, popes exacted a toll from the pilgrims crossing this bridge to St Peter's. Cross at the traffic lights and walk down via del Banco di Santo Spirito, named after the bank founded by Pope Paul V. Goldsmith and raconteur Benvenuto Cellini wrote about his day job working in these ornate premises of the former mint of the Papal States, now a branch of the Banca di Roma.

Turn sharp left before the bank into via dei Banchi Nuovi, a cobbled street where bankers, lawyers, notaries and merchants made and lost fortunes. Now the historic *palazzi* are the ultra-trendy premises of avant-garde dress designers, antiques shops and smart wine bars. Banchi Nuovi segues into via del Governo Vecchio.

At the end of this street (barely a couple of blocks from sensationally beautiful piazza Navona, p76) is an irregular square with a timeworn classical sculpture covered in pieces of inky, handwritten sheets of paper: this is **Pasquino**, the 'talking' statue. Pause for a moment to read the wicked pen-portraits of Italy's rich and powerful.

Turn left off this square up via del Teatro Pace to fill up on great slabs of pizza base filled with whatever takes your fancy at **Lo Zozzone** (p82).

Continue to the right out of piazza Pasquino, past the **Museo di Roma** (p78), and head towards busy corso Vittorio Emanuele, an artery driven through the medieval city after unification in 1870. **Campo de' Fiori** (p65), with its morning market stalls and great wine bars, stands across the other side of the *corso*.

On corso Vittorio, the extremely fine early Renaissance **Palazzo Massimo alle Colonne** (p76) on your left follows the curve of Roman remains beneath the area; the first printing press to reach Italy in 1471 made its owners a fortune when they set up shop at the back of these premises, printing religious tracts and Bibles. The grand domed church on your right is **Sant'Andrea della Valle** (p70) where the first act of Puccini's *Tosca* is set.

Continue into **largo di Torre Argentina** (p69), where you can peer into the central archaeological area before taking via del Plebiscito. Halfway along this street, the **Gesù** (p69) church is a masterpiece of the Baroque period, reflecting the staggering power and wealth of the Company of Jesus (Jesuits) in 17th-century Rome.

Via dell'Aracoeli leads from here to the bottom of Michelangelo's *cordonata* (staircase) up to the **Capitoline** (p54). Take extreme care – and the zebra crossing – to get to it. You may well wonder how the papal steed and the allegorical carts got up the stairs, but a twisting ramp to the right of the *cordonata* still transports VIPs to the mayor's office in Palazzo Senatorio, at the back of the grand piazza. The bronze statue of Marcus Aurelius – emperor and philosopher – that stands in the square is a hideous copy of the second-century original: to see that, you'll have to enter the **Capitoline Museums** (p56), where the bronze is now housed.

Skirt to the left of Palazzo Senatorio, past Romulus, Remus and the she-wolf on a column, and descend the steps towards the **Roman Forum** (p60). You'll need to locate the ticket office in largo della Salaria Vecchia and pay to enter if you wish to stroll along the ancient via Sacra. Some of the temples here have medieval churches foisted upon them, like that of Antoninus and Faustina, now the church of San Lorenzo in Miranda. (Alternatively you can deviate from the papal route, and continue along via dei Fori Imperiali, admiring the Roman Forum from outside the fence.)

At the far end of the Forum (and the via dei Fori Imperiali) stands the **Colosseum** (p57). This 50,000-seater amphitheatre where thousands of Christians met their deaths was consecrated in 1749 by pope Benedict XIV: on Good Friday each year the pope processes around the ruin in a torch-lit *Via Crucis* (Stations of the Cross).

It's about a 15-minute walk from here to San Giovanni, but it's worth stopping en route to explore the exquisite church of **San Clemente** (p109) before you proceed up the long, straight via di San Giovanni in Laterano. Or save your legs and hop on the 117 electric bus, which will take you from the Colosseum to within sight of the end of the *via Papalis* and the benediction loggia of **San Giovanni in Laterano** (p109).

Tourists (unlike pilgrims) often overlook this basilica, which is rather a pity. The history of the building mirrors that of the city itself. Built on a site donated by Emperor Constantine in the fourth century, it has been transformed over the centuries by the greatest craftsmen and artists in the whole of Christendom. Contrast the gleaming expanse of gold leaf and mosaic with the simplicity of the tranquil 12th-century cloisters, and marvel at the ancient octagonal baptistery (legend says Constantine himself was baptised there) and, across the piazza, the extraordinary **Sancta Sanctorum** (p112), where the holiest relics are kept.

RISTORANTE *Antica*
CAFÉ VENETO

LEATHER GOODS

Via Veneto p49

Via Veneto p49

Rome on Film

In the heady, glamorous *dolce vita* days of the 1950s and '60s Rome was known as 'Hollywood on the Tiber'. So down by the river, on the **Ponte di Sant'Angelo**, is where we shall start our three-hour walk. From what is arguably the city's most stunning bridge, you get views of the great papal castle built atop Emperor Hadrian's circular mausoleum, while in the distance the dome of **St Peter's** rises above medieval Borgo.

Peer over the stone balustrade of the bridge, between Bernini's teams of stone angels, and you'll see a surprisingly rural scene: people fishing, cormorants, ducks, rowers and the odd pleasure boat. Until the 1960s Romans swam from a popular bathing station beneath the ancient bridge. In *Accattone*, Pier Paolo Pasolini's juvenile delinquent makes the sign of the cross before diving off the bridge for a dare.

With real life drama going on around them in the street, neo-realist directors saw no reason to film in gloomy studios. As a result, almost every corner of this cinematic city has served as a backdrop to one masterpiece or another. When the American studios piled into post-war Rome to make escapist romantic comedies, or huge historical sword and sandal epics, the city turned into one gigantic cinema lot.

Even today you are likely to stumble across film set paraphernalia on Rome's streets: racks of costumes, coils of cables, banks of lights and a generator or two or a tightly curtained star's trailer. Movie directors dream of filming in Rome and no star can resist spending a few seductive weeks here.

This same seductiveness has helped Rome's new film festival

(p33), which has proved to be enticing to critics and stars alike. To tie in with the festival, a number of panels (with text in Italian and English) about famous made-in-Rome films have sprung up in appropriate locations around town. They're not always easy to find, and are frequently tucked around the corner from where famous films were shot, but the information they provide is fascinating.

For the first panel along our route, cross the embankment as you head south off Ponte di Sant'Angelo and take via del Panico. At the far end of this cobbled street stands the massive bulk of forbidding Palazzo Taverna, chosen by director Jane Campion as the Roman home of heiress Isabel Archer (Nicole Kidman) in *Portrait of a Lady* (1996). The panel is situated just beyond the palazzo's main gateway, at the corner of via di Monte Giordano and via degli Orsini.

Turn right down via degli Orsini towards little piazza dell'Orologio ('clock square', and there is a clock on the palazzo), and left into via del Governo Vecchio with its wine bars and chic boutiques. At the piazza Pasquino end of the street is the excellent cinema bookshop **Libreria Altroquando** (no. 80, www.altroquando.com), where you can stock up on movie memorabilia and screenplays.

Go left into via Santa Maria dell'Anima. Beneath the medieval tower on the corner with via Tor Millina is a panel celebrating *Ieri, Oggi e Domani* (1963), a huge box office hit for director Vittorio De Sica. No red-blooded Italian male could resist the famous scene in which Sofia Loren performs a light-hearted striptease for Marcello Mastroianni in an apartment overlooking **piazza Navona** (p76), which lies on the other side of this block. One of the building's balconies overlooking the piazza was used in the film, though it's not easy to decide which.

Cut across piazza Navona and negotiate the traffic on corso Rinascimento then, keeping the Italian Senate building **Palazzo Madama** to your left, duck down via dei Staderari.

Through piazza Sant'Eustachio and into the via of the same name, there's a panel for Peter Greenaway's 1987 film *Belly of an Architect*. This extraordinary film features a banquet laid out on tables in front of the **Pantheon** (p76) in piazza della Rotonda, just round the corner.

Walk past the Pantheon and head down via dei Pastini: the panel for *L'Eclisse* (*The Eclipse*) is well hidden in the first tiny alleyway on the right, vicolo della Spada D'Orlando. Michelangelo Antonioni's 1962 movie starring Monica Vitti and Alain Delon has memorable scenes set in what used to be Rome's stock exchange, spectacularly inserted into the colonnaded ruins of the Roman temple of the deified Emperor Hadrian in piazza di Pietra, just beyond. On piazza di Pietra, the cinema-themed **Caffè Fandango** (p81) – owned by an Italian producer-distributor – is a good coffee or lunch stop.

Cut down via dei Bergamaschi into **piazza Colonna**, the political heart of Rome, and from here cross via del Corso to admire the elegant shops of the Galleria Alberto Sordi, renamed in honour of the great Roman comic actor who died in 2003. Walk through to the rear of the gallery and out into via dei Sabini to find the next panel, about *La dolce vita*. Having read up on the film, brace yourself for the staggeringly theatrical scene before you as you emerge from via dei Crociferi and come face to face with the **Trevi Fountain** (p95). You will be no less amazed by the spectacle than Marcello Mastroianni was, but chances are no one will be dancing in its waters, as Anita Ekberg did in Federico Fellini's 1959 masterpiece. Resist the temptation to emulate the buxom Swede: wading, swimming and dancing in the fountain are strictly forbidden.

The other film most associated with the city is William Wyler's charming 1953 hit, *Roman Holiday*. But the promised panel explaining Gregory Peck and Audrey Hepburn's Trevi Fountain scene, which is meant to be situated in via della Stamperia on the north-west side of the fountain, was nowhere to be seen as this guide went to press. Never mind, console yourself with an ice-cream around the corner at **Il Gelato di San Crispino** (p98) and prepare yourself for the last part of the walk. Or else duck into the **Cinema Trevi** (vicolo del Puttarello 25) and pick up the programme for its *Cineteca nazionale* screenings. Generally speaking, Italy is a dubber's paradise; foreign films screened in the original language are marked 'VO' (*versione originale)*.

Busy, polluted via del Tritone has a panel for Vittorio De Sica's much-loved 1948 neo-realist Oscar-winner *Bicycle Thieves* (*Ladri di Biciclette*), but it is concealed behind the green news kiosk in front of the stuccoed HQ of the *Il Messaggero* newspaper. The scene where the all-important bicycle is stolen was shot in via del Traforo, which disappears into the cavernous tunnel to your right.

Continue up via del Tritone and into **piazza Barberini** to admire the fine Bernini fountain of the sea god before embarking on a gentle stroll through the very heart of *dolce vita* Rome. The hotels lining broad via Veneto still charge film-star prices: the super-deluxe Excelsior Hotel's 745-square-metre (8,000-square-foot) Cupola suite – with seven terraces as well as its own movie theatre – is rumoured to cost upwards of £20,000 a night. Wannabe movie stars sit in dark glasses at pavement cafés, but these days you're more likely to find tour groups than A-listers lingering along this seen-better-days road.

So try to imagine the boulevard at the height of its fame when the paparazzi were snapping Sofia Loren and Frank Sinatra, Gary Cooper and Ava Gardner (Ava's favourite beauty salon, **Femme Sistina** at via Sistina 75A, is still going strong nearby if you feel like breaking your walk with a little old-style pampering).

Famous watering holes like Doney's (a panel referring to Fellini's 1957 film *Le Notti di Cabiria* stands just on the corner beyond the restaurant), Café de Paris and Harry's Bar are still here. During the film festival, via Veneto buzzes (a little) like the old days when the event's Business Street initiative is held here.

When the glitz palls, walk under the Porta Pinciana arches at the top of the street and cross the busy intersection, making for the entrance to the **Villa Borghese** park (p91), marked by a pair of enormous stone eagles. A handy park map here points you in the direction of various attractions including the superb **Galleria Borghese** (p92) with its world-famous art collection, as well as places to rent bikes and rollerskates, and the zoo.

Alternatively, stop off just inside the park at the gloriously civilised **Casa del Cinema** cinematheque. Reward yourself with a delicious open-air drink and/or lunch (brunch at the weekend) under the umbrella pines at the Casa's **Cinecaffè** (p94) while you mull over your evening's cinema-going plans.

Ara Pacis

Rome in a Rush

If you're on a hectic business trip to the Eternal City, or simply passing through after a stay out in the sticks, don't despair about getting to grips with what Rome has to offer. Clear two to three hours and this remarkably compact metropolis will reveal its secrets.

Understanding what you're looking at is very simple – as long as you remember that Rome experienced three great outbursts of art and architecture, all of which feature on this lightning tour. First came the Classical period (100 BC-AD 300) from which an amazing amount survives, albeit in ruins; next up is the Renaissance (c1420-1527) when a colourful succession of bellicose, megalomaniac, billionaire popes threw their ill-gotten gains into an orgy of exquisite church and palace building; and as a grand finale came the outrageously overblown

Baroque period (c1620-1680), which put fruity festoons on every last theatrical façade.

Get your taxi driver to drop you at the top of the **Spanish Steps** (p88). (Or take Metro A to Spagna, and take the well-hidden lift on the left to the top of the steps.) You've seen it in the movies, but the view of the city from the top of the Spanish Steps is still spectacular: straight ahead is super-smart via Condotti, lined with the flagship stores of Italy's top designers. Flocks of loungers follow the sun as it moves across the staircase. The Spanish Embassy to the Holy See still stands in **piazza di Spagna**. Romantic poet John Keats breathed his last in the pink house at the foot of the Steps, now a museum (p85).

Resist basking in the sun on the Steps, or bunking off with your credit card. Instead, after glancing at the pretty boat-shaped fountain at the bottom of the Steps, turn right into via del Babuino, one of the three prongs of the Tridente district.

At the far end of this upmarket street, lined with antiques shops and galleries, is **piazza del Popolo**, hub of Pope Sixtus V's striking 17th-century urban planning scheme. Before you get there, duck right into picturesque via Margutta, home to a string of galleries.

From a pavement table at **Rosati** (p89), cappuccino in hand, you'll notice that piazza del Popolo holds fine examples of all Rome's artistic periods. In the centre of this great neo-classical square stands an Egyptian obelisk purloined by Emperor Augustus from the Temple of the Sun at Heliopolis. Twin pepperpot Baroque churches mark the start of the Tridente, while the church of **Santa Maria del Popolo** (p85) (you absolutely must dash into it, if only to gawp at the matching pair of paintings by Baroque master Caravaggio) is a Renaissance gem. The mighty gate in the ancient Roman city walls was hastily built to welcome Queen Christina of Sweden in 1655.

Busy via del Corso, the central prong of the Tridente, was where Carnevale horse races were held in papal Rome. Today Roman youth deck themselves out in the low-cost fashion emporia lining this thoroughfare. Rush past them all, stopping only to glimpse at some of Rome's most splendid *palazzi*.

The ultra-aristocratic Ruspoli and Borghese families still live in their grand city palaces. You can often get into **Palazzo Ruspoli** (p85) for exhibitions, but you will have to content yourself with a glimpse of the courtyard of vast 17th-century **Palazzo Borghese** (via Fontanella Borghese). Napoleon Bonaparte's sister, the beautiful Paolina, lived here with her husband Prince Camillo Borghese.

Further down via del Corso is the even more spectacular **Palazzo Doria Pamphili** (p78). You may like to spend an hour exploring its jaw-dropping art collection.

Alternatively, check which way the political wind is blowing in nearby piazza Colonna (named after Marcus Aurelius' immense column, at the centre of the square). The prime minister's office is in 16th-century **Palazzo Chigi** here; nearby in 17th-century **Palazzo Montecitorio** is the Italian lower house of parliament. The obelisk in the centre of the piazza was the needle of the outsized sundial set up here by Emperor Augustus.

It's only a two-minute walk from here to piazza Augusto Imperator. The emperor built a huge circular mausoleum, now sadly stripped of its marble, for himself and his family. By the river is the Richard Meier building housing Augustus' **Ara Pacis** (p85, Altar of Peace); the Imperial family is depicted in stunning, delicate reliefs, and a long Latin inscription lists the scholar-emperor's achievements.

You'll probably be flagging by now, so reward yourself with the remarkably reasonable buffet lunch at **'Gusto** (p88; insist on an outside table). After which – if you still have sufficient time and energy – hop on the 81 bus right outside the restaurant. In the space of about 20 minutes, it will whisk you past those Roman landmarks you haven't yet seen: through **piazza Venezia**, past the **Capitoline** (p54), down to the **Bocca della Verità** (p64), along the side of the **Circus Maximus** (p57) and back up past the **Palatine** (p60) to the **Colosseum** (p57). You can hop off here and head back to your hotel (or the train station, or the airport) feeling that you really have seen (just about) everything.

ristorante settembrini

settembrini is our street

settembrini is a character from "the enchanted mountain"

settembrini is our home, your home

it is our wager and our hope to have made a place that offers prime ingredients in quality dishes at reasonable prices.

one is tempted to say superb dishes but we'll let you be the judge of that.

via Settembrini 27, 00197 Rome
phone: +39 06 3232617
www.ristorantesettembrini.it
closed saturday lunch, sunday all day

SETTEMBRINI
vino e cucina

Rome by Area

Il Centro   **54**

Tridente, Trevi & Borghese   **84**

Esquilino, Celio & San Lorenzo   **100**

The Aventine & Testaccio   **117**

Trastevere & the Gianicolo   **128**

The Vatican & Prati   **139**

Out of Town   **151**

View from the Vittoriano

Il Centro

Centro archeologico

The ancient world's most powerful city started in humble fashion in the eighth century BC, when a group of huts was built on a hill overlooking the Tiber.

Not many centuries later, this hill – the **Palatine** – bristled with magnificent palaces, including the recently opened **House of Augustus** (see box p71), where gem-like frescoes give an idea of the beauty with which the first Roman emperor surrounded himself.

The Palatine overlooked the hustle and bustle of the **Roman Forum** below. It was from here that the Republic – and later the Empire – was run and justice administered, in grandiose buildings around richly decorated public squares. The facing hill

– the **Capitoline** – was Rome's most sacred, with imposing temples. Flanking the Roman Forum, successive emperors strove to assert their own particular importance and munificence in the **Imperial Fora**. Also in this history-packed area, emperors kept public discontent at bay with gory diversions and heart-stopping sports at the **Colosseum** and the **Circus Maximus**.

The Capitoline (Campidoglio) was the site of two major temples, to Jupiter Capitolinus – chunks of which are visible inside the **Capitoline Museums** – and Juno Moneta, 'giver of advice', where the church of **Santa Maria in Aracoeli** now stands.

The splendid piazza that now tops the Capitoline was designed in the 1530s by Michelangelo; the

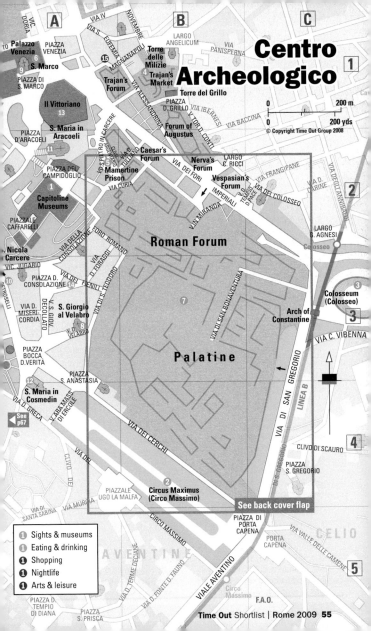

Capitoline Museums

best approach is via the steps called the *cordonata*, also by Michelangelo, with two giant Roman statues of the mythical twins Castor and Pollux at the top. The building directly opposite is Rome's city hall; on either side are the *palazzi* housing the Capitoline museums. The equestrian statue of Marcus Aurelius in the centre is a computer-generated copy; the second-century gilded bronze original is inside the museum.

At the bottom of the *cordonata* is piazza Venezia. Dominating this dizzying roundabout is the **Vittoriano**, a piece of nationalistic kitsch that outdoes anything dreamed up by the ancients.

South of the Capitoline, on low ground by the river, was the *velabrum*, the marshy area where Remus and Romulus were, according to Rome's foundation myth, found floating in a basket

and then suckled by a she-wolf (see box p71). Two delightful Republican-age temples still stand here, and the area is dotted with remains of the *forum boarium* and *forum holitorium* (cattle and vegetable markets) that later occupied this space.

Sights & museums

Capitoline Museums

Piazza del Campidoglio 1 (06 6710 2475/06 0608/www.museicapitolini.org).
Open 9am-8pm Tue-Sun. **Admission** €6.50; €4.50 reductions; extra charge during exhibitions. No credit cards.
Map p55 A2 ❶
Housed in two *palazzi* opposite each other on Michelangelo's piazza del Campidoglio, the Capitoline Museums (Musei capitolini) are the oldest museums in the world, opened to the public in 1734, though the collection was begun in 1471 by Pope Sixtus IV. His successors continued to add ancient scuptures and, later, paintings.

Entry is through the Palazzo dei Conservatori (to the right at the top of the steps). The courtyard contains parts of a colossal statue of Constantine that originally stood in the Basilica of Maxentius in the Roman Forum. Inside, ancient works are mixed with statues by the Baroque genius Gian Lorenzo Bernini.

In a smart new section on the first floor, the second-century statue of Marcus Aurelius has finally been given a suitably grand space. Also here are chunks of the Temple of Jupiter. A much-reproduced fourth-century BC Etruscan she-wolf and suckling twins (added in the Renaissance) is also to be moved to this new wing. A glass dome will provide further exhibition space in the 'Roman Garden' outside.

The second-floor gallery contains paintings by greats such as Titian, Tintoretto and Caravaggio. Across the piazza (or through the underground *Tabularium*, the ancient Capitoline archive building), the Palazzo Nuovo houses one of Europe's greatest collections of ancient sculpture, including the coy *Capitoline Venus*, the *Dying Gaul* and countless portrait busts of emperors and their families.

Circus Maximus

Via del Circo Massimo.
Map p55 B4 ❷
Little of the actual structure remains at the Circus Maximus, ancient Rome's major chariot-racing venue, but it's still possible to visualise the flat base of this long grassy basin as the racetrack, and the sloping sides as the stands. A major restoration, scheduled to begin in late 2008, should make the original layout even easier to 'read'. At the southern end are some brick remains of the original seating (the tower is medieval). The oldest and largest of Rome's ancient arenas, the Circus Maximus hosted chariot races from at least the fourth century BC. It was rebuilt by Julius Caesar to hold as many as 300,000 people. Races involved up to 12 rigs of four horses each; the circus was also flooded for mock sea battles.

Colosseum

Piazza del Colosseo (06 3996 7700).
Open 9am-sunset daily. **Admission** (includes Roman Forum & Palatine) €9; €4.50 reductions; extra charge during exhibitions. No credit cards.
Map p55 C3 ❸
Note: if the queue at the Colosseum is daunting, get your ticket from the Palatine entrance at via di San Gregorio 30 and go straight in.

Built in AD 72 by Emperor Vespasian, *il Colosseo* hosted gory battles between combinations of gladiators, slaves, prisoners and wild animals of all descriptions. Properly called the *Amphitheatrum flavium*, the building was later known as the Colosseum not because it was big, but because of a gold-plated colossal statue, now lost, that stood alongside. The arena was about 500m (a third of a mile) in circumference and could seat over 50,000 people. Nowhere in the world was there a larger setting for mass slaughter. In the 100 days of carnage held to inaugurate the amphitheatre in AD 80, 5,000 beasts perished. Sometimes, animals got to kill people: a common sentence in the Roman criminal justice system was *damnatio ad bestias*, where miscreants were turned loose, unarmed, into the arena. After the fall of the Roman Empire authorities banned games here and the Colosseum became a quarry for stone and marble to build Roman *palazzi*. The pockmarks on the Colosseum's masonry date from the ninth century, when the lead clamps holding the stones together were pillaged. This irreverence didn't stop until the mid-18th century, when the Colosseum was consecrated as a church.

Standing beside the Colosseum, Constantine's triumphal arch was erected in AD 315, shortly before the emperor abandoned the city for Byzantium.

Imperial Fora Museum

Via IV Novembre 94 (06 6992 3521/http://en.mercatiditraiano.it).
Open *Oct-Mar* 9am-4.30pm Tue-Sun. *Apr-Sept* 8.30am-6.30pm Tue-Sun.
Admission €6.50: €4.50 reductions;

A funny thing happened...

In 1997, then-mayor Francesco Rutelli presided over Rome's 'reappropriation' of its most symbolic monument: the **Roman Forum**. Fences and ticket offices were removed, and Romans in droves flocked to what had been the nerve centre of the ancient world's most powerful city.

Psychologically, it was an important moment for the city. For many years after the fall of the Empire in 476, during those Dark Ages when marauding barbarians first breached the walls of *Caput mundi*, the Forum continued to exert a fascination on the locals. For a century or so, it was not only kept up, but embellished: the last significant addition – the column of Phocas – was erected in 608.

But time and Rome's astounding population decline – from well over a million at the height of Empire to just a few thousand in the darkest days – led to a steady crumbling: the hub of the ancient world became a ruin-strewn grassy stretch known as the *campo vaccino* (cow field), where locals gathered through the ages to graze flocks, or for picturesque picnics. Plundered for building materials for centuries, what remained of the Forum was excavated in more scientific fashion from the early 19th century.

In 2007, then-culture minister Rutelli announced that uncontrolled numbers of visitors tramping over the site, with little in the way of security, had caused damage to the remains. Fences would be re-erected, an admission charge re-introduced, well-trained guides would be on offer and the whole area would be adequately signposted... something direly needed in what can appear to be a random pile of crumbly masonry.

When the fences first went back up in spring 2008, there was no sign of these improvements. The change came, however, during an interregnum at city hall. In April 2008 right-winger Gianni Alemanno beat Rutelli in mayoral elections. It remains to be seen whether the new incumbent will carry through the promised improvements.

extra charge during exhibitions.
No credit cards. **Map** p55 B1 ④
When the Roman Forum (p60) became too small to cope with the growing city, emperors combined philanthropy with propaganda and created new fora of their own in what is now known collectively as the *Fori imperiali* (Imperial Fora). Along the via dei Fori Imperiali (sliced cavalierly through the ruins by Mussolini) are five separate fora – each one was built by a different emperor.

Massive excavations in the 1990s unearthed great swathes of this archeological space. It's not easy to interpret the ruins, most of which are visible from street level. A pre-emptive visit to the *fori* model at the visitors' centre (via dei Fori Imperiali, open 9.30am-6.30pm daily) will help. At the time of writing, the visitors' centre had suspended its tours of the lower site.

NEW The best-preserved and unquestionably most impressive part of the complex is Trajan's forum and the towering remains of Trajan's markets behind. Two years of restoration work came to an end in October 2007, giving Trajan's markets a gloriously cleaned-up interior, a beautifully lit collection of marble artefacts and a new name: *il Museo dei fori imperiali*. Moreover, it opened up atmospheric stretches of the ancient streets and medieval buildings surrounding the market itself. Finally, the fora have found a worthy hub.

Entering Trajan's markets from via IV Novembre, the first room is the Great Hall, a large space possibly used for the corn dole in antiquity. To the south of the Great Hall are the open-air terraces at the top of the spectacular Great Hemicycle, built in AD 107. To the east of the Great Hall, stairs lead down to the so-called via Biberatica, an ancient street flanked by well-preserved shops; these were probably *tabernae* (bars), hence the name (*bibere* is Latin for 'to drink'). More stairs lead down through the various layers of the Great Hemicycle, where most of the 150 shops or offices are still in perfect condition, many with doorjambs still

showing the grooves where shutters would have slid into place when the working day was over.

Below the markets, at the piazza Venezia end of via dei Fori Imperiali, is **Trajan's forum**, laid out in the early second century AD. It's dominated by Trajan's column (AD 113), with detailed spiralling reliefs showing victories over Dacia (modern-day Romania). The rectangular foundation to the south of Trajan's column, where several imposing granite columns still stand, was the basilica Ulpia, an administrative building.

Across the road from Trajan's forum, **Caesar's forum** was the first of the *Fori imperiali*, built in 51 BC by Julius Caesar. Three columns of the *Venus generatrix* temple have been rebuilt. Back on the same side as Trajan's forum, **Augustus' forum** was inaugurated in 2 BC. Three columns from the Temple of Mars Ultor still stand, as does the towering wall separating the forum from the sprawling Suburra slum behind. **Nerva's forum** (AD 97) lies mainly beneath via dei Fori Imperiali. On the south side of the road, **Vespasian's forum** (AD 75) was home to the Temple of Pax (Peace), part of which is now incorporated into the church of Santi Cosma e Damiano. Maps placed on a wall here by Mussolini show how Rome ruled the world.

Mamertine Prison

Clivio Argentario 1 (06 679 2902).
Open *Nov-Mar* 9am-5pm daily. *Apr-Oct* 9am-7pm daily **Admission** donation expected. **Map** p55 A2 ⑤
Anyone thought to pose a threat to the security of the ancient Roman state was thrown into the *Carcere mamertino* (Mamertine Prison), a dank, underground dungeon, between the Roman Forum and present-day via dei Fori Imperiali. The prison's most famous inmates, legend has it, were Saints Peter and Paul. Peter head-butted the wall in the ground-level room leaving his features impressed on the rock, and is said to have caused a miraculous well to bubble up.

Santa Maria in Cosmedin p64

ROME BY AREA

Palazzo Venezia Museum

Via del Plebiscito 118 (06 6999 4106). **Open** 8.30am-7.30pm Tue-Sun. **Admission** €4; €2 reductions; extra charge during exhibitions. No credit cards. **Map** p55 A1 ⑥

This collection contains a hotchpotch of anything from terracotta models by Baroque sculptor Gian Lorenzo Bernini for the angels that now grace Ponte Sant'Angelo, to medieval decorative art. Major exhibitions are staged regularly; they often give access to the huge Sala del Mappamondo, used by Mussolini as his office.

Opened in 2006, the lapidarium occupies the upper level of the cloister of the 'secret garden of Paul II'. It houses ancient, medieval and Renaissance sarcophagi, coats of arms, funerary monuments and assorted fragments.

Roman Forum & Palatine

Via di San Gregorio 30/largo della Salaria Vecchia (06 3996 7700). **Open** 9am-1hr before sunset daily. **Admission** (includes Colosseum)

€9; €6.50 reductions; extra charge during exhibitions. No credit cards. **Map** p55 B3 ⑦ **Note:** Letters ⓐ in the text refer to the Roman Forum and Palatine map on the back cover flap.

From March 2008, the Forum and Palatine once again became a single site, visited on the same ticket, which also allows entrance to the Colosseum. We recommend entering from the quieter via di San Gregorio entrance, visiting the Palatine first, then making your way down to the Forum.

However, guided tours (€4.50) of parts of the Forum that are generally off-limits to visitors depart from the largo della Salaria Vecchia ticket office (formerly largo Remo e Romolo, off via dei Fori Imperiali); if you wish to join these, you should book your tour and enter from there.

Palatine

Legend relates that a basket holding twin babes Romulus and Remus was found in the swampy area near the Tiber to the west of here, and suckled

Cardinal Alessandro Farnese, who created a pleasure villa. His gardens – the *Horti farnesiani* ❹ – are still a lovely, leafy – if unkempt – place to wander on a hot day. Beneath the gardens is the *cryptoporticus* ❺, a semi-subterranean tunnel built by Nero.

Roman Forum

During the early years of the Republic, this was an open space with shops and a few temples, and it sufficed; but by the second century BC ever-conquering Rome needed to give an impression of authority and wealth. Out went the food stalls; in came law courts, offices and immense public buildings with grandiose decorations. The *Foro romano* remained the symbolic heart of the Empire.

Descending from the Palatine, the Forum is framed by the Arch of Titus (AD 81 – ❻), built to celebrate the sack of Jerusalem. To the right are the towering ruins of the Basilica of Maxentius ❼, completed in AD 312. Below on the left is the house of the Vestal Virgins ❽. Along the via Sacra ❾, the Forum's high street, are (right) the great columns of the Temple of Antoninus and Faustina ❿; the giant Basilica Emilia (right – ⓚ) – once a bustling place for administration, courts and business; the Curia ⓛ, the home of the Senate, begun in 45 BC by Julius Caesar; and the Arch of Septimius Severus ⓜ, built in AD 203. Beside the arch are the remains of an Imperial rostra ⓝ, from where Mark Antony supposedly asked Romans to lend him their ears.

by a she-wolf in a cave (see box p71). In 753 BC, having murdered his brother, Romulus scaled the Palatine hill and founded Rome. In fact, archeological evidence shows that proto-Romans had settled on *il Palatino* a century or more before that. Later, the Palatine became the Beverly Hills of the ancient city, where movers and shakers built their palaces. On the southern side of the Palatine, overlooking the Circus Maximus, are the remains of vast Imperial dwellings, including Emperor Domitian's *Domus augustana* ❸, with what may have been a private stadium in the garden. Next door, the Museo Palatino ❹ charts the history of the Palatine from the eighth century BC.

🆕 Immediately west of here is the House of Augustus (*Domus augusti*, ❺, four spectacularly frescoed rooms of which were opened to the public in March 2008 (see box p71).

With Rome's decline the Palatine became a rural backwater; in the 1540s, much of the hill was bought by

San Giorgio in Velabro

Via del Velabro 19 (06 6920 4534/ www.oscgeneral.org). **Open** 10am-12.30pm, 4-6.30pm daily. **Map** p55 A3 ❽

This austere little church of the seventh century has 16 Roman columns pilfered from the Palatine and the Aventine hills in its nave, and pieces of an eighth- or ninth-century choir incorporated into the walls. In the apse is a much-restored 13th-century fresco of St George. Outside to the left is the

ROME BY AREA

Vittoriano p64

Arco degli Argentari, built in AD 204; it was a gate on the road between the main Forum and the *forum boarium* (cattle market) along which money-changers (*argenteri*) plied their trade.

San Marco

Piazza San Marco (06 679 5205).
Open 4-7pm Mon; 8.30am-noon, 4-7pm Tue-Sun. **Map** p55 A1 ⑨
Founded, tradition says, in 336 on the site of the house where St Mark the Evangelist stayed, this church was rebuilt by Pope Paul II in the 15th century when the neighbouring Palazzo Venezia was constructed, and given its Baroque look in the mid-18th century. Remaining from its earlier manifestations are the 11th-century bell tower, and the ninth-century mosaic of Christ in the apse. In the portico is the gravestone of Vanozza Catanei, mother of the notorious Cesare and Lucrezia Borgia.

San Nicola in Carcere

Via del Teatro di Marcello 46 (06 6830 7198). **Open** 7am-7pm Mon-Sat; 9am-7pm Sun. **Map** off p55 A3 ⑩
The 12th-century San Nicola was built over three Roman temples, dating from the second and third centuries BC; a guide (donation appreciated) takes you down to these. On the outside of the church, six columns from the Temple of Janus can be seen on the left; the ones on the right are from the Temple of Spes (Hope).

Santa Maria in Aracoeli

Piazza del Campidoglio 4 (06 6798 8441). **Open** *Nov-Mar* 9.30am-12.30pm, 2.30-5.30pm daily. *Apr-Oct* 9am-12.30pm, 3-6.30pm daily.
Map p55 A2 ⑪
Up a daunting flight of steps, the Romanesque Aracoeli ('altar of heaven') stands on the site of an ancient temple to Juno Moneta. The current basilica-form church was designed in the late 13th century. The first chapel on the right has scenes by Pinturicchio from the life of St Francis of Assisi's helpmate St Bernardino (1486). To the left of the altar, a round chapel contains relics of St Helena, mother of the Emperor Constantine. At the back of the transept, the Chapel of the Holy Child contains a much-venerated disease-healing *bambinello*, which is often whisked to the bedside of moribund Romans.

I Sapori della Legalità

Santa Maria in Cosmedin & the Mouth of Truth

Piazza della Bocca della Verità (06 678 1419). **Open** *Oct-Mar* 9.30am-5pm daily. *Apr-Sept* 9.30am-6pm daily. **Map** p55 A3 ⑫

Built in the sixth century and enlarged in the eighth, Santa Maria was embellished with a glorious Cosmati-work floor, throne and choir in the 11th-13th centuries. In the sacristy is a fragment of an eighth-century mosaic of the Holy Family, brought here from the original St Peter's. The church is better known as the *bocca della verità* (the mouth of truth), after the great stone mask of a man with a gaping mouth on the portico wall – probably an ancient drain cover. Anyone who lies while their hand is in the mouth will have that hand bitten off, according to legend. It was reportedly used by Roman husbands to determine the fidelity of their wives. On the little green opposite stand the first-century BC Temples of Hercules (round) and Portunus (square).

Vittoriano

Piazza Venezia (06 699 1718). **Open** *Monument* 9.30am-4.30pm daily. *Museo Centrale del Risorgimento* 9.30am-6.30pm daily. *Complesso del Vittoriano* (06 678 0664) 9.30am-7.30pm Mon-Thur; 9.30am-11.30pm Fri-Sat; 9.30am-8.30pm Sun. **Admission** varies. **Map** p55 A1 ⑬

Variously known as 'the wedding cake' and 'the typewriter', this eyesore is a monument to united Italy, constructed between 1885 and 1911. You can climb the steps (free) for a good view over the city, or check out the exhibitions – mainly of 19th- and 20th- century art – held regularly in the gallery along the left side of the monument as you look at it. Along the right side, a door leads to a space that hosts exhibits on Italian history, and a collection of memorabilia from the Unification struggle.

NEW Also through this entrance – and best of all – is a brand new lift (€7, €3.50 reductions) that whizzes you up to the very top of the monument for an

Shopping

I Sapori della Legalità

NEW *Via del Foro di Traiano 84 (06 6992 5262)/www.isaporidellalegalita.it)*. **Open** 10am-6.30pm Mon-Fri. Closed Aug. No credit cards. **Map** p55 A1 ⑮

Tucked away beneath Trajan's forum, this shop may look like any upmarket food emporium, with delicious olive oil, wine and organic foodstuffs. What sets it apart is that everything is produced by co-operatives of young people on land confiscated from organised crime outfits.

The Ghetto & Campo de' Fiori

From the earliest of ancient times, the area in the great loop of the River Tiber was the *campus martius* (field of war), where Roman males did physical jerks to stay fighting fit. As time went on, the area became packed with theatres providing low brow fun for ancient Romans. After barbarian hordes rampaged through Rome in the fifth and sixth centuries, the area fell into ruin. By the late Middle Ages, it was densely populated and insalubrious.

That part of the *campus martius* that today stretches south from busy corso Vittorio Emanuele (aka corso Vittorio) to the Tiber saw its fortunes improve when the pope made the Vatican – just across the river – his main residence in the mid-15th century. Nowadays, its tightly wedged buildings, narrow cobbled alleys and mixture of graceful Renaissance columns and chunky blocks of ancient travertine form the perfect backdrop to everyday Roman streetlife.

The area is one of contrasts: **campo de' Fiori** – with its lively morning market and livelier partying crowds at night – stands

unmissable, breathtaking 360-degree panorama across the whole of Rome and far beyond... from the only spot where the spectacle isn't marred by the Vittoriano itself. There's a (very expensive) café on one of the lower terraces.

Eating & drinking

San Teodoro

Via dei Fienili 49-51 (06 678 0933). **Meals served** 12.45-3.15pm, 8-11.30pm Mon-Sat. Closed 1wk Dec, 2wks Jan; 1wk Easter. €€€€. **Map** p55 A3 ⑭

Of a summer's evening, there are few more pleasant places in Rome for an alfresco meal than this seafood-oriented restaurant around the back of the Forum, in a pretty residential piazza. Come prepared to splash out, though. Some dishes are pure *cucina romana*; others, like the *tonnarelli* San Teodoro (with shrimps, courgettes and cherry tomatoes) are lighter and more creative. In summer, opens Sundays too.

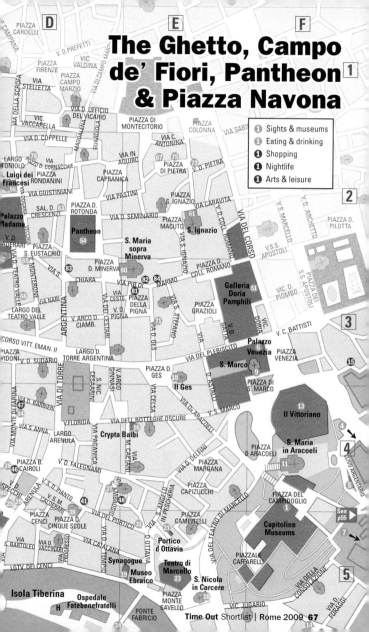

next to solemn, dignified **piazza Farnese** with its grand Palazzo Farnese, partly designed by Michelangelo. Top-end antique dealers in via Giulia rub along with craftsmen plying their trades in streets with names (via dei Leutari – lutemakers; via dei Cappellari – hatmakers) that recall the jobs of their medieval ancestors.

In the south-east, **largo Argentina** is a polluted transport hub with a chunk of ancient Rome at its heart: visible when you peer over the railings are columns, altars and foundations from four temples, dating from the mid-third century BC to c100 BC.

On the southern side of the square lies the **Ghetto**: its picture-postcard winding alleys mask a sorrowful history. Rome's Jews occupy a unique place in the history of the diaspora, having maintained a presence in the city uninterrupted for over 2,000 years. The Ghetto was walled off from the rest of the city in 1556, and remained that way until the 1870s. In piazza Mattei stands the beautiful, delicate Turtle Fountain, erected overnight in the 1580s, though the turtles may have been an afterthought.

Sights & museums

Crypta Balbi

Via delle Botteghe Oscure 31 (06 678 0167). **Open** 9am-7.45pm Tue-Sun. **Admission** €7; €3.50 reductions; extra charge during exhibitions; see p12 Museo Nazionale Romano. No credit cards. **Map** p67 E4 ⑯

The Crypta Balbi – the foyer of the Theatre of Balbus – combines the best of the ancient with state-of-the-art technology and is packed with displays, maps and models that explain (in English) Rome's evolution from a bellicose pre-Imperial era, to early Christian times and on through the dim Middle Ages.

Galleria Spada

Piazza Capo di Ferro 13 (06 683 2409/www.galleriaborghese.it). **Open** 8.30am-7.30pm Tue-Sun. **Admission** €5; €2.50 reductions. No credit cards. **Map** p66 C4 ⑰

This gem of a palace – alas, showing signs of neglect – was acquired by art collector Cardinal Bernardino Spada in 1632; the walls are crammed with paintings. There are some impressive names here: Domenichino, Guercino, Guido Reni plus the father-daughter Gentileschi duo, Orazio and Artemisia. The main attraction of the museum, however, is the Borromini Perspective, where perspective trickery makes a 9m-long (30ft) colonnade look much longer.

Il Gesù

Piazza del Gesù (06 697 001/www.chiesadelgesu.org). **Open** *Church* 7am-12.30pm, 4-7.30pm daily. *Loyola's rooms* 4-6pm Mon-Sat; 10am-noon Sun. **Map** p67 E3 ⑱

The Gesù, built in 1568-84, is the flagship church of the Jesuits, and was designed to involve the congregation as closely as possible in services, with a nave unobstructed by aisles. One of Rome's great Baroque masterpieces – *Triumph in the Name of Jesus* by Il Baciccia (1676-79) – decorates the ceiling of the nave. On the left is the ornate chapel of Sant'Ignazio (1696). Above the altar is what was long believed to be the biggest lump of lapis lazuli in the world; in fact, it's covered concrete. Outside the church, at piazza del Gesù 45, you can visit St Ignatius's rooms.

Jewish Museum of Rome

Lungotevere Cenci (06 6840 0661/www.museoebraico.roma.it). **Open** *Mid Sept-mid June* 10am-5pm Mon-Thur, Sun; 9am-2pm Fri. *Mid June-mid Sept* 10am-7pm Mon-Thur, Sun; 9am-4pm Fri. **Admission** €7.50; €3 reductions. No credit cards. **Map** p67 E5 ⑲

As well as luxurious crowns, Torah mantles and silverware, the Museo ebraico presents vivid reminders of the persecution suffered by Rome's Jews at various times through history: copies of the 16th-century papal edicts that banned Jews from many activities, and heart-rending relics from the concentration camps. Recently refurbished and extended, the museum now displays exquisite carvings from long-gone Roman synagogues.

Museo Barracco

Corso Vittorio 166A (06 6821 4105/ http://en.museobarracco.it). **Open** 9am-7pm Tue-Sun. **Admission** €3; €1.50 reductions; extra charge during exhibitions. No credit cards. **Map** p66 C3 ⑳

This small collection of mainly pre-Roman art was amassed in the first half of the 20th century. Don't miss the copy of the *Wounded Bitch* by the fourth-century BC sculptor Lysippus, on the second floor.

Portico D'Ottavia

Via Portico D'Ottavia. **Map** p67 E5 ㉑
Great ancient columns and a marble frontispiece, held together with rusting iron braces, now form part of the church of Sant'Angelo in Pescheria, but they were originally the entrance of a massive colonnaded square (portico) containing temples and libraries, built in the first century AD by Emperor Augustus and dedicated to his sister Octavia. A walkway (open 9am-6pm daily) has been opened through the *forum piscarium* – the ancient fish market; it continues past a graveyard of broken columns and capitals to the Teatro di Marcello, passing by three towering columns that were part of the Temple of Apollo (433 BC).

Sant'Andrea della Valle

Corso Vittorio 6 (06 686 1339). **Open** 7.30am-12.30pm, 4.30-7.30pm daily. **Map** p66 C3 ㉒
Designed in 1524 by Giacomo della Porta, this church was handed over to Carlo Maderno who stretched the design upward, creating a dome that is the highest in Rome after St Peter's. Puccini set the opening act of *Tosca* in the chapel on the left.

Theatre of Marcellus

Via Teatro di Marcello. **Map** p67 E5 ㉓
The Teatro di Marcello is one of the strangest and most impressive sights in Rome – a Renaissance palace grafted

Marcus Aurelius in the Capitoline Museums p56

Legendary leg-up

House of Augustus p61

The Capitoline Wolf

Throughout Rome's history, anyone aspiring to power needed a legend on their side to lend legitimacy.

Rome's first emperor, Augustus (reigned 27 BC-AD 14), was already well set up, with a family tree descending from Rome's mythical founder Romulus (Aeneas, Venus and Mars featured too). Just to drive home the point, Augustus happened to discover the very cave where the she-wolf nursed babes Remus and Romulus: and as luck would have it, the cave turned out to be right beneath his home on the **Palatine**. In an artistic PR exercise aimed at stressing his role as the founder of a new Rome, Augustus had the cave-home of the city's original founder magnificently decorated.

Both Augustus' residence and the cave – known as the **Lupercal** – hit headlines recently. In spring 2008, four rooms of the house were opened to the public after lengthy restoration. The frescoes – discovered in the 1970s – are astoundingly fresh, colourful and detailed. In Augustus' upstairs study, fauns laugh amid stylised

vegetation, and tiny gems twinkle. Open from 11am daily, the house is included in the Forum ticket.

The inauguration came a couple of months after the triumphant announcement by then-culture minister Francesco Rutelli of the discovery of the Lupercal. A probe sent into the bowels of the Palatine hill had hit a hollow. A camera on a cable revealed a circular room, some six metres (20 feet) in diameter, with a brightly decorated vault. Visitable until the 16th century, after which it had been left to decay, the Lupercal is well documented; the shells in the newly discovered cave tally with those described five centuries ago.

The Lupercal will be dug out and reopened, presumably with its entrance just metres from the new HQ of Italy's Democratic Party, of which Rutelli is a leading light. But this time round, the legend-based magic didn't work: close to Rome's founders the Democrats may be, but in April 2008 Rutelli lost his battle to become mayor, and the Democrats were beaten in general elections.

ROME BY AREA

on to an ancient theatre. Julius Caesar began building the theatre, but it was finished in 11 BC by Augustus, who named it after his favourite nephew. Originally, it had three tiers and seated up to 20,000 people. Abandoned in the fourth century AD, it was turned into a fortress in the 12th century and then into a palazzo in the 16th by the Savelli family.

Tiber Island & Ponte Rotto
Map p67 D5 ㉔

When the last Etruscan king was driven from Rome, the Romans uprooted the wheat from his fields and threw it in baskets into the river. Silt accumulated and formed an island where Aesculapius, the Roman god of medicine, founded a sanctuary in the third century BC. That's what the legend says, and the island has always had a vocation for public health. Today a hospital occupies the north end. The church of San Bartolomeo is built over the original sanctuary; the columns in the nave are from that earlier building. Remains of the ancient building can also be seen from the riverside footpath, from where there's also a fine view over the *ponte rotto* (broken bridge). This stands on the site of the *Pons aemilius*, Rome's first stone bridge, built in 142 BC. It was rebuilt many times before 1598, when they gave up trying. To the east of the bridge is a tunnel in the embankment: the gaping mouth of the city's great *cloaca maxima* sewer, built in the sixth century BC.

Eating & drinking

See also p81 Casa Bleve.

Alberto Pica
Via della Seggiola 12 (06 686 8405).
Open *Jan-Mar, Oct, Nov* 8.30am-2am Mon-Sat; *Apr-Sept, Dec* 8.30am-2am Mon-Sat; 4.30pm-2am Sun. Closed 2wks Aug. No credit cards. **Map** p67 D4 ㉕
Horrendous neon lighting, surly staff and some very good ice-cream are the hallmarks of this long-running bar: *riso alla cannella* (cinnamon rice) is particularly delicious.

Ar Galletto
Piazza Farnese 102 (06 686 1714).
Meals served 12.15-3pm, 7.15-11pm Mon-Sat. Closed 10 days Aug. €€€. **Map** p66 C4 ㉖
With a ringside view of stately piazza Farnese, Ar Galletto serves unpretentious Roman dishes without the inflated prices charged by other restaurants around here. Dishes like *penne all'arrabbiata* or *spaghetti alle vongole* are appetising. There are tables on the square in summer.

Bartaruga
Piazza Mattei 9 (06 689 2299/ www.bartaruga.it). **Open** 6pm-midnight Mon-Thur, Sun; 6pm-2am Fri, Sat. No credit cards. **Map** p67 D4 ㉗
This baroque locale in peach and midnight blue with divans and candelabra is the haunt of the beautiful, the eccentric and those too entranced by the lovely square outside to move on elsewhere. Staff can be surly.

Bernasconi
Piazza Cairoli 16 (06 6880 6264).
Open 7am-8.30pm Tue-Sun. Closed Aug. No credit cards. **Map** p67 D4 ㉘
It's well worth fighting your way inside this cramped, inconspicuous bar for unbeatable chewy, yeasty *cornetti*.

Bruschetteria degli Angeli
Piazza B Cairoli 2 (06 6880 5789).
Open 12.30-3.30pm, 7.30pm-1am daily. Closed 2wks Aug. €. **Map** p67 D4 ㉙
The star turns here are the heavenly house *bruschette* (average €8) with various toppings from red chicory and bacon to grilled courgettes and mozzarella. There's also pasta, grilled steaks and a good range of draught beers.

Crudo
Via degli Specchi 6 (06 683 8989/ www.crudoroma.it). **Open** *Bar & lounge* 7.30pm-2am Mon-Sat; **meals served** 12.30-3.30pm, 8-11.30pm Mon-Fri; 8-11.30pm Sat. Closed Aug. **Map** p67 D4 ㉚
With a dazzling designer interior with art installations, plasma screens and DJs, Crudo offers some of the best *aperitivi* in town, plus glam dining (€€€).

Da Giggetto

Via Portico d'Ottavia 21A-22 (06 686 1105/www.giggettoalporticodottavia.it).
Meals served 12.30-3pm, 7.30-11pm Tue-Sun. Closed 2wks July. **€€€.**
Map p67 E5 ③

This old standby in the Ghetto serves up decent versions of Roman-Jewish classics like *carciofi alla giudia* (fried artichokes) and fried *baccalà* (salt cod). The atmosphere is warm and bustling, with large tables of tourists enjoying the ambience and the plentiful helpings.

Ditirambo

Piazza della Cancelleria 75 (06 687 1626/www.ristoranteditirambo.it).
Meals served 7.30-11.30pm Mon; 1-3pm, 7.30-11.30pm Tue-Sun. Closed 3wks Aug. **€€€. Map** p66 C3 ②

This funky trattoria serves up good-value pan-Italian dishes based on fresh, mainly organic ingredients. The chef specialises in traditional fare with a creative kick, as in the excellent baby squid with a purée of *cicerchie* beans or the veal silverside braised in coffee.

Forno Campo de' Fiori

Vicolo del Gallo 14 (06 6880 6662).
Open 7.30am-2.30pm, 5-8pm Mon-Sat. Closed 2wks Aug. No credit cards.
Map p66 C3 ③

This bakery does the best takeaway sliced pizza in the campo de' Fiori area. Its plain pizza bianca base is delicious in itself, but check out the one with *fiori di zucca* (courgette flowers) too.

Gloss

Via del Monte della Farina 43 (06 6813 5345/www.glossroma.it).
Open 7pm-2am Tue-Sun. Closed Aug. No credit cards. **Map** p67 D4 ④

This inviting bar offers an *aperitivo*-hour buffet (from 7pm) and a wide range of cultural offerings, including ever-changing art displays. Music comes live, or courtesy of DJs.

Il Goccetto

Via dei Banchi Vecchi 14 (06 686 4268). **Open** 6.30pm-midnight Mon; 11.30am-2pm, 6.30pm-midnight Tue-Sat. Closed 1wk Jan, 3wks Aug.
Map p66 B3 ⑤

Morning market in Campo de' Fiori

One of the more serious *centro storico* wine bars, with dark wood-clad walls and a cosy, private-club feel. Wine is the main point here, with a satisfying range by the glass from €3.

Il Pagliaccio

Via dei Banchi Vecchi 129A (06 6880 9595/www.ristoranteilpagliaccio.it).
Meals served 8-10.30pm Mon, Tue; 1-2.30pm, 8-10.30pm Wed-Sat. Closed 1wk Jan, 2wks Aug. **Map** p66 B3 ⑥

Though its first Michelin star in 2007 has pushed prices up somewhat, chef Anthony Genovese's restaurant still offers one of the best-value gourmet dinners in Rome. A risk-taking approach is clearly illustrated in an *antipasto* of lobster in black pepper and cocoa sauce. But his skill is equally evident in less pyrotechnic dishes like the lamb with salsify and winter greens. Leave plenty of space for the excellent desserts.

CASINA VALADIER

Restaurant, lounge bar, live music

a charming place in the heart of rome,
romantic and trendy

OPEN ALL DAYS FROM 10.00 TO 2.00 PM

VILLA BORGHESE - PIAZZA BUCAREST - 00187 ROME
PH. + 39 06 69922090 FAX. + 39 06 6791280
INFO@CASINAVALADIER.IT

La Vineria

Campo de' Fiori 15 (06 6880 3268).
Open 8.30am-2am Mon-Sat. Closed
2wks Aug. **Map** p66 C4 ③⑦

The longest-running wine bar on the
campo, La Vineria is where Romans
flock to chat and plan the evening
ahead over good wines by the glass.
Glasses are very small and start from
just €1.50.

Le Piramidi

Vicolo del Gallo 11 (06 687 9061/
www.cucinaraba.com). **Open** 10am-
midnight Tue-Sun. Closed Aug. **€.**
No credit cards. **Map** p66 C4 ③⑧

Le Piramidi makes for a welcome
change from takeaway pizza if you're
just in the mood for a quick snack.
The range of Middle Eastern takeaway fare is small, but it's all fresh,
cheap and tasty.

Sora Margherita

Piazza delle Cinque Scole 30 (06
687 4216). **Meals served** 12.30-
2.30pm Tue-Thur, Sun; 12.30-2.30pm,
8- 9.30pm Fri, Sat. Closed Aug. **€€.**
No credit cards. **Map** p67 D5 ③⑨

This rustic hole-in-the-wall trattoria is
not for health freaks, but no one
argues with serious Roman Jewish
cooking at these prices. The classic
pasta and meat dishes on offer include
a superlative *pasta e fagioli* (pasta
with beans), *tonnarelli cacio e pepe*
(pasta with cheese and pepper) and
ossobuco washed down with rough-
and-ready house wine. On Friday and
Saturday evenings, you have to book
for one of two sittings.

Shopping

Borini

Via dei Pettinari 86 (06 687 5670).
Open 3.30-7.30pm Mon; 9.30am-1pm,
3.30-7.30pm Tue-Sat. Closed 3wks Aug.
Map p66 C4 ④⓪

Franco Borini's shop is busily chaotic,
with piles of shoes inside peeling walls.
His elegant but durable footware
follows fashion trends religiously but
thankfully comes at prices that won't
make you gasp.

Forno del Ghetto

Via Portico d'Ottavia 1 (06 687
8637). **Open** 7am-2pm, 3.30-7.30pm
Mon-Thur; 8am-2pm Fri; 7.30am-5pm
Sun. Closed 3wks Aug & Jewish
holidays. No credit cards.
Map p67 D4 ④①

This tiny shop has no sign but is
immediately recognisable by the line
of slavering regulars outside. Among
lots of other goodies, they come here
for the unforgettable damson and
ricotta tart.

Ibiz

Via dei Chiavari 39 (06 6830 7297).
Open 9.30am-7.30pm Mon-Sat. Closed
2wks Aug. **Map** p66 C4 ④②

Ibiz bags are made by hand in the on-
site workshop: look on as you mull
over which of the handbags, briefcas-
es, backpacks and leather accessories
you want to take home.

Ilaria Miani

Via Monserrato 35 (06 683 3160/
www.ilariamiani.it). **Open** 4.30-8pm
Mon; 10.30am-1.30pm, 4.30-8pm
Tue-Sat. **Map** p66 B3 ④③

Interior designer Ilaria Miani's country-
chic furniture and *objets* grace many of
Italy's most stylish homes. Pick some
up for yourself in her richly coloured
retail space.

Laboratorio Marco Aurelio

Via del Pellegrino 48 (06 686 5570/
www.marcoaurelio.it). **Open** 11am-9pm
Tue-Sat. **Map** p66 C3 ④④

This jewellery designer creates stunning pieces, many inspired by ancient
Roman styles, on site in hammered and
wrought silver.

Loco

Via dei Baullari 22 (06 6880
8216). **Open** 3.30-8.30pm Mon;
10.30am-8pm Tue-Sat. Closed 2wks
Aug. **Map** p66 C3 ④⑤

If you like your shoes avant-garde, this
small copper and wood decorated store
is the place. From classy to wild and
eccentric, its pieces are always one step
ahead of the flock.

ROME BY AREA

Momento

Piazza Cairoli 9 (06 6880 8157).
Open 10.30am-7.30pm Mon-Sat;
noon-7.30pm Sun. **Map** p67 D4 **46**

The poshest of princesses and her
boho cousin will be equally awed by
the collection of clothes and accessories at this treasure trove. There's
something here for the fearless and for
the colourful, and all at very
approachable prices.

Spazio Sette

Via dei Barbieri 7 (06 686 9747/
www.spaziosette.com). **Open** 3.30-
7.30pm Mon; 9.30am-1pm, 3.30-7.30pm
Tue-Sat. Closed 3wks Aug.
Map p67 D4 **47**

A stalwart of the Roman design circuit since it opened in the 1970s,
Spazio Sette is a coolly chic treasure
trove of kitchenware, table decorations, rugs, furniture and lights occu-
pying three floors of a delightful
17th-century palazzo.

Nightlife

Rialtosantambrogio

Via Sant'Ambrogio 4 (06 6813
3640/www.rialtosantambrogio.org).
Open times & days vary. Closed
July-mid Sept. **Admission** free-€7.
No credit cards. **Map** p67 E4 **48**

This *centro sociale* (squat) in the
Ghetto hosts performances, art
exhibitions, live music and disco
nights along with cutting-edge electronica DJs and VJs, especially at the
weekend. It's a meeting point for a
radical crowd.

Arts & leisure

Via Giulia IV

Via Giulia 4 (06 687 7449). **Open**
9am-7.30pm Mon-Sat. Closed 3wks
Aug. **Map** p66 B4 **49**

This gorgeous spa frequented by
Rome's beautiful people offers a
mouth-watering range of massage
and beauty treatments for both men
and for women, plus there's a ham-
mam and hairdressing available. By
appointment only.

The Pantheon & Piazza Navona

Like its counterpart to the
south (**The Ghetto & Campo
de' Fiori** p65), this area of
picturesque alleys in the loop of
the river north of corso Vittorio
Emanuele was part of the ancient
campus martius.

After the Empire fell, the *campus*
was prime construction territory
and every medieval wall tells a tale
of primitive recycling: grand *palazzi*
were built from stolen marble;
humbler souls constructed their
little houses among the ruins.
It's still a democratic area, where
mink-coated contessas mingle
with pensioners, craftsmen and
tradesmen. After dark, smart
restaurants, hip bars and,
increasingly, tourist-trap rip-offs,
fill to bursting, especially around
Santa Maria della Pace.

Two squares – both living links
to ancient Rome – dominate the
district: **piazza della Rotonda** –
home to the Pantheon – and
magnificent **piazza Navona**.

West of piazza Navona, piazza
Pasquino is home to a truncated
classical statue; for centuries,
Romans have pinned satirical
verse (pasquinades) to this
sculpture. Further north, elegant,
antiques-shop-lined via dei
Coronari was once the haunt
of pilgrim-fleecing rosary-
makers (*coronari*).

When corso Vittorio was
hacked through the medieval
fabric in the 1870s, only the most
grandiose of homes were spared:
Palazzo Massimo at no 141, with
its curved façade following the
stands in Domitian's *odeon*
(small theatre), is one.

To the east of the Pantheon,
Galleria Doria Pamphili contains
one of Rome's finest art collections,

What you don't see

Roman Forum

Rome's ancient remains – from the **Roman Forum** to the **Colosseum**, the **Domus Aurea** to the **Pantheon** – are jaw-droppingly imposing and magnificently humbling. For the average 21st-century visitor, these shattered remains, in pitted travertine and time-sculpted brick, are what the ancient city is all about.

In fact, the picture they give is utterly misleading. Ancient Rome couldn't have been more different.

If the Forum feels packed and noisy to you on a busy day in high season, try this exercise: in your mind's eye, imagine that concentrated here are the offices of state, law courts, major temples, banks and just about everything needed to ensure the smooth working of a city of a million people or more. To get anything done in the highly centralised state, ancients converged here, not only from the city but from all over the Republic and later the Empire. It must have been difficult to move or breathe. The noise must have been deafening.

Now, remove the grass and trees, and fill in every empty space with masonry. Imposing steps lead up to buildings designed to instill awe. Towering statues follow you with staring eyes (so much so that you may not even notice the eyes of an army of official informers, watching your every move). And all of it – buildings and statues – is painted in the kind of gaudy colours that nowadays only grace outlandish Indian temples. There's not a square inch of white to be seen.

Lastly, forget what your guide book tells you. Despite ancient maps and reams of ancient writing, pinpointing the exact locations of Roman buildings is an imprecise science. Consensus is rare. As British School at Rome director Andrew Wallace-Hadrill wrote in the *TLS* in 2001: 'controversy rages over just what is where: the famous buildings known from ancient writings are constantly relocated [...] The Basilica Aemilia shunts round the Forum like an old goods train, and we wait in vain for Augustus' famed Parthian arch to alight in its definitive place.'

ROME BY AREA

while the charmingly rococo **piazza Sant'Ignazio** looks like a stage set. In neighbouring piazza di Pietra, the columns of the Temple of Hadrian can be seen embedded in the walls of Rome's ex-stock exchange.

Sights & museums

Chiesa Nuova/Santa Maria in Vallicella

Piazza della Chiesa Nuova (06 687 5289/www.chiesanuova.net). **Open** *Apr-Oct* 8am-noon, 4.30-7.30pm daily. *Nov-Mar* 8am-noon, 4-7pm daily. **Map** p66 B2 ⑤⓪

Filippo Neri (1515-95) was a wealthy Florentine who abandoned commerce to live among the poor in Rome. He founded the Oratorian order in 1544. In 1575, work began on the order's headquarters, the Chiesa Nuova. Neri wanted a large, simple building; the walls were covered with the exuberant frescoes and multicoloured marbles only after his death. Pietro da Cortona painted the *Assumption of the Virgin* (1650) in the apse, Rubens the *Virgin and Child* (1608) over the altar.

Doria Pamphilj Gallery

Via del Corso 305 (06 679 7323/ www.doriapamphilj.it). **Open** 10am-5pm daily. **Admission** €8; €5.70 reductions. No credit cards. **Map** p67 F3 ⑤①

The entrance to this magnificent private gallery is through state apartments planned in the mid-16th century. The main galleries are situated around the central courtyard. Velázquez's portrait of the Pamphilj Pope Innocent X is the highlight of the collection; there's also a splendid bust by Bernini of the same pontiff next to it. At the end of the Galleria degli Specchi are four smaller rooms ordered by century. In the 17th-century room, Caravaggio is represented by the *Rest on the Flight into Egypt* and the *Penitent Magdalene*; the 16th-century room includes Titian's shameless *Salome* and a *Portrait of Two Men* by Raphael.

Museo di Roma

Palazzo Braschi, via di San Pantaleo 10 (06 6710 8346/www.museodiroma. comune.roma.it). **Open** 9am-7pm Tue-Sun. **Admission** €6; €4.50 reductions; extra charge during exhibitions. No credit cards. **Map** p66 C3 ⑤②

A rotating collection recounts the evolution of the city from the Middle Ages to the early 20th century. Sculpture, clothing, furniture and photographs help to put the city's monuments in a human context.

Palazzo Altemps

Piazza Sant'Apollinare 46 (06 687 2719). **Open** 9am-7.45pm Tue-Sun. **Admission** €7; €3.50 reductions; extra charge during exhibitions; see p12 Museo Nazionale Romano. No credit cards. **Map** p66 C1 ⑤③

The 15th- to 16th-century Palazzo Altemps houses part of the state-owned stock of Roman treasures: gems of classical statuary purchased from the Boncompagni-Ludovisi, Altemps and Mattei families. The Ludovisis liked 'fixing' statues: an *Athena with Serpent* (room 9) was revamped in the 17th century by Alessandro Algardi, who also 'improved' the *Hermes Loghios* in room 19. Room 21 has the Ludovisi Throne, the museum's greatest treasure, a fifth-century BC work from Magna Grecia... though some believe it to be a fake.

Pantheon

Piazza della Rotonda (06 0608). **Open** 8.30am-7.30pm Mon-Sat; 9am-6pm Sun; 9am-1pm public holidays. **Map** p67 D2 ⑤④

The Pantheon was built by Hadrian in AD 119-128 as a temple to the most important deities; the inscription on the pediment records a Pantheon built 100 years before by General Marcus Agrippa (which confused historians for centuries). Its fine state of preservation is due to the building's conversion to a church in AD 608, though its bronze cladding was stolen over the centuries: part is now in Bernini's *baldacchino* in St Peter's. The bronze doors are, in fact the original Roman ones. Inside, the Pantheon's glory lies in its dimensions. The diameter of the hemispherical dome is exactly equal to the height of the building. At the centre of the dome is the oculus, a circular hole 9m (30ft) in diameter, a symbolic link between the temple and the heavens. Until the 18th century the portico was used as a marketplace: supports for the stalls were inserted into the notches that today are still visible in the columns.

Piazza Navona

Map p66 C2 ⑤⑤

This tremendous theatrical space owes its shape to an ancient athletics stadium, built in AD 86 by Emperor Domitian. Just north of the piazza, at piazza di Tor Sanguigna 16, remains of the original arena are visible from the street. The piazza acquired its current form in the mid-17th century. The central fountain of the Four Rivers, finished in 1651, is one of the most extravagant masterpieces designed by Bernini. Its main figures represent the longest rivers of the four continents known at the time; Ganges of Asia, Nile of Africa, Danube of Europe and Plata of the Americas, all with appropriate flora. The figure of the Nile is veiled, because its source was unknown.

San Luigi dei Francesi

Piazza San Luigi dei Francesi (06 688 271). **Open** 10am-12.30pm, 3.30-7pm Mon-Wed, Fri-Sun; 10am-12.30pm Thur. **Map** p67 D2 ⑤⑥

Completed in 1589, San Luigi/St Louis is the church of Rome's French community. In the fifth chapel on the left are Caravaggio's spectacular scenes from the life of St Matthew (1600-02). But make sure you don't overlook the lovely frescoes of St Cecilia by Domenichino (1615-17), in the second chapel on the right.

Sant'Agnese in Agone

Piazza Navona (06 6819 2134/ www.santagneseinagone.org). **Open** 9am-noon, 4-7pm Tue-Sat; 10am-1.30pm, 4-8pm Sun. **Map** p66 C2 ⑤⑦

Legend says that teenage St Agnes was cast naked into the stadium of Domitian around AD 304 when she refused to renounce Christ and marry a powerful local. Her pagan persecutors chopped her head off (the implausibly small skull is still here), supposedly on the exact spot where the church now stands. Begun in 1652, the church was given its splendidly fluid concave façade by Borromini.

Sant'Agostino

Piazza Sant'Agostino (06 6880 1962). **Open** 7.45am-noon, 4-7.30pm daily. **Map** p66 C1 ⑤⑧

This 15th-century church has one of the earliest Renaissance façades in Rome, made of travertine filched from the Colosseum. Inside, the third column on the left bears a fresco of Isaiah by Raphael (1512). In the first chapel on the left is Caravaggio's depiction of the grubbiest pilgrims ever to present themselves at the feet of the startlingly beautiful *Madonna of the Pilgrims* (1604).

Santa Maria della Pace

Arco della Pace 5 (06 686 1156). **Open** 10am-noon, 4-6pm Mon-Sat; 10am-noon Sun. **Map** p66 C2 ⑤⑨

Built in 1482, Santa Maria della Pace was given its theatrical Baroque façade by Pietro da Cortona in 1656. Just inside the door is Raphael's *Sybils* (1514). There's a beautifully harmonious cloister by Bramante, his first work after arriving in Rome in the early 16th century; exhibitions are often held here (for information, see www.chiostrodelbramante.it).

Santa Maria sopra Minerva

Piazza della Minerva 42 (06 679 3926/ www.basilicaminerva.it). **Open** 8am-1pm, 3-7pm daily. **Map** p67 E3 ⑥⓪

Rome's only Gothic church was built on the site of an ancient temple of Minerva in 1280. Its best works of art are Renaissance: on the right of the transept is the Carafa chapel, with frescoes by Filippino Lippi (1457-1504). Also here is the tomb of the Carafa

Casa Bleve

Pope Paul IV (1555-59), famous for enclosing the Jewish Ghetto and having loincloths painted on the nudes of Michelangelo's *Last Judgement* in the Sistine Chapel. A bronze loincloth was also ordered to cover Christ's genitals on a work here by Michelangelo, a Christ holding up a cross. The *Madonna and Child*, an earlier work believed by some to be by Fra Angelico, is in the chapel to the left of the altar, close to the artistic monk's own tomb. The father of modern astronomy, Galileo Galilei, who dared suggest that the earth revolved around the sun, was tried for heresy in the adjoining monastery in 1633. In the square in front of the church is a charming marble elephant bearing an obelisk on its back, by Bernini.

Sant'Ignazio di Loyola

Piazza Sant'Ignazio (06 679 4406/ www.chiesasantignazio.org). **Open** 8am-12.15pm, 3-7.15pm daily. **Map** p67 E2 ⑥

Sant'Ignazio was begun in 1626 to commemorate the canonisation of St Ignatius, founder of the Jesuits. Trompe l'oeil columns soar above the nave, and architraves by Andrea Pozzo open to a cloudy heaven. When the monks next door claimed that a dome would rob them of light, Pozzo simply painted a dome on the ceiling. The illusion is fairly convincing if you stand on the disc set in the floor of the nave. Walk away, however, and it collapses.

Sant'Ivo alla Sapienza

Corso Rinascimento 40 (06 686 4987). **Open** 10am-noon Sun. **Map** p67 D3 ⑥
In this crowning glory of Borromini's tortured imagination, the concave façade is countered by the convex bulk of the dome, which terminates in a bizarre corkscrew spire. Inside, the convex and concave surfaces on the walls and up into the dome leave you feeling like someone spiked your cappuccino. Opens, erratically, at other times too.

Eating & drinking

See also **Friends Art Café** (p133).

Armando al Pantheon

Salita de' Crescenzi 31 (06 6880 3034).
Meals served 12.30-2.45pm, 7.15-10.45pm Mon-Fri; 12.30-3pm Sat. Closed Aug. **€€**. **Map** p67 D2 ⑥⑨

Armando is a welcome find just yards from the Pantheon: simple, no-frills fare, such as *fettucine all'Armando* (with peas, mushrooms and tomatoes) or *ossobuco,* is served by the delightful owners, at excellent prices. The only concessions to changing times are some vegetarian and gluten-free dishes.

Bar della Pace

Via della Pace 5 (06 686 1216).
Open 4pm-3am Mon; 8.30am-3am Tue-Sun. **Map** p66 C2 ⑥④

Eternally à la mode, this bar has warm, antiques- and flower-filled rooms for the colder months and (pricey) pavement tables beneath the trademark ivy-clad façade.

Bar Sant'Eustachio

Piazza Sant'Eustachio 82 (06 6880 2048/www.santeustachioilcaffe.it).
Open 8.30am-1am Mon-Thur, Sun; 8.30am-1.20am Fri, Sat. No credit cards. **Map** p67 D3 ⑥⑤

This is one of the city's most famous coffee bars and its walls are plastered with celebrity testimonials. The coffee is quite extraordinary, if expensive. Try the *gran caffè*: the *schiuma* (froth) can be slurped out afterwards with spoon or fingers.

Caffè Bernini

NEW *Piazza Navona 44 (06 6819 2998/www.caffebernini.com).* **Open** 9.30am-2am daily. **Map** p66 C2 ⑥⑥

Hordes of hawkers and a plethora of tourist rip-off eateries can make a visit to glorious piazza Navona a trial. So full marks to the recently relaunched Caffè Bernini where the pan-Med food is good and fairly priced (for the area), and sitting outside for a coffee or *aperitivo* is an affordable pleasure.

Caffè Fandango

Piazza di Pietra 32-33 (06 4547 2913/www.caffefandango.it).
Open 11am-midnight Tue-Thur; 11am-1am Fri, Sat; 11am-9pm Sun. **Map** p67 E2 ⑥⑦

Owned by one of Italy's leading independent film distributors, this café is distinctly movie-themed, with scattered memorabilia plus film-related books and DVDs on sale.

Casa Bleve

Via del Teatro Valle 48-49 (06 686 5970/www.casableve.it). **Meals served** 1-3pm, 7.30-10pm Tue-Sat. **€€€**. **Map** p67 D3 ⑥⑧

The main room of this elegant wine bar is a huge colonnaded roofed-in courtyard in a palazzo near the Pantheon. The buffet offers a vast choice of cheese, cured meat, smoked fish and salads, and there's an impressive selection of wines. The first Bleve off-licence/eaterie in the Ghetto (via Santa Maria del Pianto 9-11, open 8am-10.30pm Tue-Fri, 8am-8pm Sat) has a more intimate vibe.

Da Francesco

Piazza del Fico 29 (06 686 4009).
Meals served *Apr-Oct* 11.50am-3pm, 7pm-12.30am Mon, Wed-Sun; 7pm-12.30am Tue. *Nov-Mar* 11.50am-3pm, 7pm-12.30am Mon, Wed-Sun. **€€**. No credit cards. **Map** p66 B2 ⑥⑨

Da Francesco is the genuine *centro storico* pizzeria article. They serve tasty pizzas and a range of competent, classic dishes in a warm, traditional ambience. The service is brisk but friendly. There's little point making reservations because bookings can sometimes go astray.

Da Vezio

Via Tor di Nona 37 (06 683 2951).
Open 7am-8pm Mon-Sat. No credit cards. **Map** p66 B1 ⑦⓪

Vezio Bagazzini's legendary neighbourhood bar in the Ghetto is no longer, but this dyed-in-the-wool Communist has moved his Marxist-Leninist souvenirs and photos to new premises in pretty, artsy via Tor di Nona.

Enoteca Corsi

Via del Gesù 87-88 (06 679 0821).
Meals served noon-3.30pm Mon-Sat.
Closed Aug. **€**. **Map** p67 E3 ⓸
The menu changes daily at this 1940s
wine shop – you'll find it written up
on the board at the entrance. Dishes
follow the traditional Roman culinary
calendar – potato *gnocchi* on
Thursdays and stewed *baccalà* (salt
cod) on Fridays.

Etabli

*Vicolo delle Vacche 9 (06 687
1499/www.etabli.it).* **Open** 6pm-2am
Tue-Sat; noon-4pm, 6pm-2am Sun.
Map p66 B2 ⓶
This new-ish locale in the super-chic
triangolo della pace area is already
drawing Rome's bright young things
with its pared-back decor, twiddly
chandeliers and deep armchairs
around the fireplace. The welcome is
suave-warm, the feeling intimate. In
one room light meals are served at
appropriate times; there's a restaurant
(**€€€**) upstairs.

La Caffettiera

Piazza di Pietra 65 (06 679 8147).
Open 7am-9pm Mon-Sat; 8am-9pm
Sun. **Map** p67 E2 ⓷
Politicians from the nearby parliament
buildings lounge in the sumptuous tea
room of this temple to Neapolitan goodies, while lesser mortals bolt coffees at
the bar. The rum babà reigns supreme,
but ricotta-lovers rave over the
crunchy *sfogliatella*.

Lo Zozzone

*Via del Teatro Pace 32 (06 6880
8575).* **Open** *July-Mar* 9am-9pm Mon-
Fri; 9am-11pm Sat. *Apr-June* 9am-9pm
Mon-Fri; 9am-11pm Sat; 11am-9pm
Sun. Closed Aug. **€**. No credit cards.
Map p66 C2 ⓸
The 'dirty old man' (that's what the
name means) serves Rome's best *pizza
bianca ripiena* – which, as a sign
explains, is 'White Pizza With Any
Thing You Like Inside'. Fillings range
from classics like prosciutto and mozzarella to exotic combinations. Pay
at the till for a standard slab (€3.50);

then join the receipt-waving hordes
to get served. In summer, it also opens
on Sundays.

Salotto 42

*Piazza di Pietra 42 (06 678 5804/
www.salotto42.it).* **Open** 10am-2am
Tue-Sat; 10am-midnight Sun. Closed
Aug. **Map** p67 E2 ⓹
Incredibly comfortable chairs and
sofas give a cosy feel during the day,
when a smörgåsbord of nibbles is
available. By night, the sleek room
becomes a gorgeous cocktail bar with
a great soundtrack and excellent cocktails. There's a selection of books on
fashion, art and design.

Société Lutèce

*Piazza di Montevecchio 17 (06 6830
1472/www.societe-lutece.it).* **Open**
6pm-2am Tue-Sun. Closed 2wks Aug.
Map p66 C2 ⓺
Société Lutèce is popular with eclectic
Roman hipsters, the bar's cramped
quarters often cause a spill-over into
the small piazza. The *aperitivo* buffet
(from 7.30pm) is plentiful and the vibe
is decidedly laid-back.

Stardust

Via dell'Anima 52 (06 686 8986).
Open 7pm-2am daily. No credit cards.
Map p66 C2 ⓻
Moaning neighbours mean that this
former stalwart of the Trastevere
nightlife scene has had to drop the vol-
ume since its move to the *centro*. It continues, however, to function as bistro
from 7-10pm and bar/pub thereafter,
with bartenders (quietly) playing anything from Cuban jazz to Euro-rap and
Czech polkas.

Trattoria

*Via del Pozzo delle Cornacchie 25 (06
6830 1427).* **Meals served** 12.30-3pm,
7.30-11pm Mon-Sat. Closed 2wks Aug.
€€€. **Map** p67 D2 ⓼
Ebullient Sicilian chef Filippo La
Mantia takes Sicilian standards like
caponata or *pasta alla Norma* and
gives them his own creative twist.
There's a €15-a-shot lunchtime cous-
cous bar (noon-3pm Mon-Sat).

Shopping

Ai Monasteri

*Corso Rinascimento 72 (06 6880 2783/
www.aimonasteri.it).* **Open** 10am-1pm,
3.30-7.30pm Mon-Wed, Fri, Sat; 10am-
1pm Thur. Closed Aug. **Map** p66 C2 ⑦
This richly perfumed old shop, founded in 1894, sells jams, chocolates, cos-
metics and cure-all potions produced
by religious orders around Italy.

Arsenale

*Via del Governo Vecchio 64 (06 686
1380/www.patriziapieroni.it).* **Open**
3.30-7.30pm Mon; 10am-7.30pm
Tue-Sat. Closed 2wks Aug.
Map p66 C2 ⑧
Patrizia Pieroni's wonderful garments
make for great window displays – not
to mention successful party conversa-
tion pieces – and have been going
down well with the Roman boho-chic
luvvy crowd for years.

Ditta G Poggi

*Via del Gesù 74-75 (06 679 3674/
www.poggi1825.it).* **Open** 9am-1pm,
4-7.30pm Mon-Sat. Closed 2wks Aug.
Map p67 E3 ⑧
This wonderfully old-fashioned shop
has been selling paints, brushes, canvases and artists' supplies of every
description since 1825.

Le Tartarughe

*Via Pie' di Marmo 17 (06 679
2240).* **Open** 3.30-7.30pm Mon;
10am-7.30pm Tue-Sat. Closed 3wks
Aug. **Map** p67 E3 ⑧
Designer Susanna Liso's sumptuous
classic-with-a-twist creations range
from cocktail dresses to elegant work-
wear, all in eye-catching colours. For
gorgeous accessories, head across the
road to no.33.

Maga Morgana

*Via del Governo Vecchio 27 (06 687
9995).* **Open** 10am-7.30pm Mon-Sat.
Map p67 D3 ⑧
Designer Luciana Iannace's quirky
one-of-a-kind women's clothes include
hand-knitted sweaters, skirts and
dresses. More knitted and woollen
items are sold down the road at no.98.

Moriondo & Gariglio

*Via del Piè di Marmo 21 (06 699
0856).* **Open** 9am-7.30pm Mon-Sat.
Closed Aug. **Map** p67 E3 ⑧
This fairytale chocolate shop with
beautiful gift boxes is especially lovely close to Christmas, when you will
have to fight to get your hands on
the excellent marrons glacés. See
box p134.

Nightlife

See also **Friends Art Café** (p133),
Salotto 42 (p82), **Société Lutèce**
(p82), and **Stardust** (p82).

Anima

*Via Santa Maria dell'Anima 57
(347 850 9256).* **Open** 6pm-4am daily.
Map p66 C2 ⑧
With improbably baroque gilded
mouldings, this small venue has a
buzzing atmosphere and serves really good drinks. It caters for a mixed
crowd of all ages and nationalities.
Expect to hear hip hop, R&B, funk,
soul and reggae.

Bloom

*Via del Teatro Pace 30 (06 6880
2029).* **Open** 7pm-3am Mon, Tue,
Thur-Sat. Closed Aug.
Map p66 C2 ⑧
A restaurant, bar and disco (generally
on Friday and Saturday), Bloom is
cooler than ice: eat sushi, sip a cocktail,
dance or simply relax and join your
fashionable fellow guests checking out
each others' outfits.

La Maison

*Vicolo dei Granari 3 (06 683 3312/
www.lamaisonroma.it).* **Open** 11pm-
4am Wed-Sat. Closed June-Sept.
Map p66 C2 ⑧
One of the clubs of choice of Rome's
fashion victims, La Maison is dressed
to impress. Huge chandeliers, dark red
walls and curvy sofas give it an opulent, courtly feeling. Surprisingly, the
place is not snobbish, the music on
offer is not banal and the atmosphere
is buzzing. The doormen are sometimes picky, however.

ROME BY AREA

Via Condotti

Tridente, Trevi & Borghese

The Tridente

For the Grand Tourist of the 18th century, this wedge-shaped warren *was* Rome. Thousands of English 'milords' took lodgings in and around piazza di Spagna. Here they found English banks and English shops; trusted guides were employed when venturing beyond the familiar streets.

Even today there are visitors who never make it further than the Tridente's plethora of glorious fashion retailers.

The whole area was built as a showpiece. At the head of the wedge is **piazza del Popolo**. It was given its oval form by architect Giuseppe Valadier in the early 19th century.

Leading out centrally from the square is the Tridente's principal thoroughfare, via del Corso, which passes high-street clothing retailers en route to the towering column of Marcus Aurelius (piazza Colonna) – which was built between AD 180 and 196 to commemorate the victories on the battlefield of that most intellectual of Roman emperors – and piazza Venezia.

Via Ripetta veers off down the riverside, leading to Augustus' **mausoleum** and the **Ara Pacis**.

The third street, chic via del Babuino, runs past a series of tempting antique and designer stores to the **Spanish Steps**.

Parallel to via del Babuino, tucked right below the Pincio hill, is via Margutta, fondly remembered as the focus of the 1960s art scene and 'home' to Gregory Peck in the 1953 classic *Roman Holiday*. Fellini, too, lived on this artsy alley.

Criss-crossing the three main arteries are streets such as via Condotti that have given Rome its reputation as a major fashion centre.

Sights & museums

Ara Pacis Museum
Via Ripetta/lungotevere in Augusta (06 0608/www.arapacis.it). **Open** 9am-7pm Tue-Sun. **Admission** €6.50; €4.50 reductions; extra charge during exhibitions. No credit cards.
Map p86 A2 ❶

The *Ara pacis augustae* ('Augustan Altar of Peace') was inaugurated in 9 BC to celebrate the security that the Emperor Augustus' victories had brought. The altar was rebuilt in the early 20th century from fragments amassed through a long dig and a trawl through the world's museums. The altar itself sits inside an enclosure carved with delicately realistic reliefs. The upper band shows the ceremonies surrounding the dedication of the altar. The carved faces of Augustus and his family have all been identified. The monument now resides in a container designed by Richard Meier, inaugurated to much fanfare and even more controversy in 2006.

The forlorn brick cylinder next door in piazza Augusto Imperatore was originally a mausoleum covered with marble pillars and statues, begun in 28 BC. Augustus was laid to rest in the central chamber on his death in AD 14. The whole square is due for a grand refurbishment.

Keats-Shelley Memorial House
Piazza di Spagna 26 (06 678 4235/ www.keats-shelley-house.org). **Open** 9am-1pm, 3-6pm Mon-Fri; 11am-2pm, 3-6pm Sat. **Admission** €4. No credit cards. **Map** p86 C3 ❷

The house at the bottom of the Spanish Steps where the 25-year-old John Keats

died of tuberculosis in 1821 is crammed with mementos: a lock of Keats's hair and his death mask, an urn holding tiny pieces of Shelley's charred skeleton, and copies of documents and letters.

Palazzo Ruspoli-Fondazione Memmo
Via del Corso 418 (06 687 4704/ www.fondazionememmo.com). **Open** times vary. **Admission** varies. No credit cards. **Map** p86 B3 ❸

The palace of one of Rome's old noble families is used for touring exhibitions of art, archaeology and history. The basement rooms often host photo exhibitions; admission is sometimes free.

San Lorenzo in Lucina
Piazza San Lorenzo in Lucina 16A (06 687 1494). **Open** 9am-8pm daily. **Map** p86 B4 ❹

This 12th-century church – built on the site of an early Christian place of worship – incorporates Roman columns into its exterior. The 17th-century interior has Bernini portrait busts, a kitsch 17th-century *Crucifixion* by Guido Reni and a monument to French artist Nicolas Poussin, who died in Rome in 1665. In the first chapel on the right is a grill, reputed to be the one on which St Lawrence was roasted to death.

Santa Maria del Popolo
Piazza del Popolo 12 (06 361 0836). **Open** 7am-noon, 4-7pm Mon-Sat; 7.30am-1.30pm, 4.30-7.30pm Sun. **Map** p86 B1 ❺

According to legend, Santa Maria del Popolo occupies the site where the hated Emperor Nero was buried. In 1099, Pope Paschal II built a chapel here to dispel demons still believed to haunt the spot. In 1472, Pope Sixtus IV rebuilt the chapel as a church. In the apse are Rome's first stained-glass windows (1509). The apse was designed by Bramante, while the choir ceiling and first and third chapels in the right aisle were frescoed by Pinturicchio. The Chigi Chapel was designed by Raphael for wealthy banker Agostino Chigi, and features Chigi's horoscope. The church's most-gawped-at possessions, however,

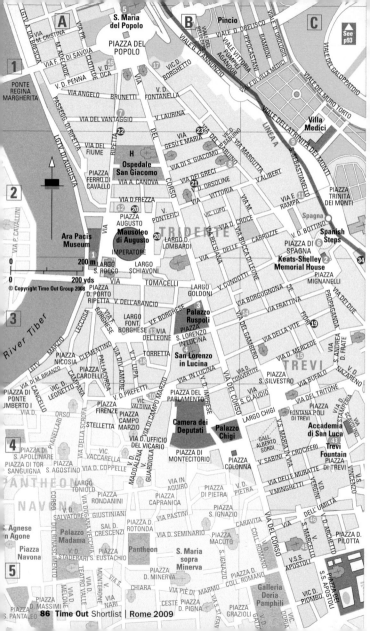

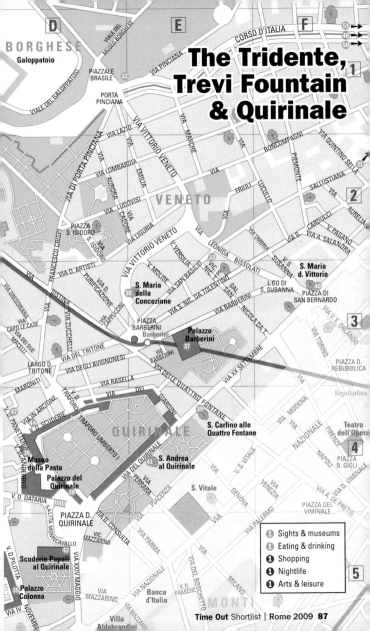

The Tridente, Trevi Fountain & Quirinale

are the two masterpieces by Caravaggio to the left of the main altar, showing the stories of Saints Peter and Paul.

Spanish Steps & Piazza di Spagna

Map p86 C2 ⑥

Piazza di Spagna has been considered a compulsory stop for visitors to Rome since the 18th century. The square takes its name from the Spanish Embassy, but is most famous for the Spanish Steps (Scalinata di Trinità dei Monti), an elegant cascade down from the church of Trinità dei Monti. The steps (completed in 1725) were, in fact, funded by a French diplomat. At the foot of the stairs is a boat-shaped fountain, the *barcaccia*, designed in 1627 by either Gian Lorenzo Bernini or his less-famous father Pietro.

Eating & drinking

Buccone

Via Ripetta 19-20 (06 361 2154/ www.enotecabuccone.com). **Open** *Shop* 9am-8.30pm Mon-Thur; 9am-midnight Fri, Sat. **Meals served** 12.30-3pm, 7.30-10.30pm Mon-Sat. Closed 3wks Aug. €€. **Map** p86 B1 ⑦

Originally – and still – a bottle shop, Buccone squeezes tables between its high wooden shelves at meal times. The fare – a few pasta dishes, meaty seconds and creative salads – is simple but good, the prices very reasonable.

Caffè Canova-Tadolini

Via del Babuino 150A (06 3211 0702/ www.museoateliercanovatadolini.it). **Open** 8am-8.30pm Mon-Sat. Closed 3wks Aug. **Map** p86 B2 ⑧

Once the studio of 19th-century sculptor Antonio Canova, this café has tables among its sculpture models and a refined and elegant old-world feel.

Ciampini al Café du Jardin

Viale Trinità dei Monti (06 678 5678). **Open** *Apr-mid May, mid Sept-mid Oct* 8am-8pm daily. *Mid May-mid Sept* 8am-1am Mon, Tue, Thur-Sun. Closed mid Oct-Mar. **Map** p86 C2 ⑨

This open-air café near the top of the Spanish Steps is surrounded by lovely creeper-curtained trellises, with a pond in the centre. There's a spectacular view, especially at sunset.

Da Gino

Vicolo Rosini 4 (06 687 3434). **Meals served** 1-2.45pm, 8-10.45pm Mon-Sat. Closed Aug. €€. No credit cards. **Map** p86 B4 ⑩

In a hard-to-find lane just off piazza del Parlamento, this neighbourhood *osteria* champions the lighter side of the local tradition in dishes like *tonnarelli alla ciociara* (pasta with mushrooms and tomatoes), and pasta and chickpeas in ray sauce; desserts include an excellent tiramisù.

GiNa

Via San Sebastianello 7A (06 678 0251/www.ginaroma.com). **Open** 11am-8pm daily. Closed 2wks Aug. **Map** p86 C2 ⑪

This bright and artsy light-lunch and dinner bar is a rather good option for snacking by the Spanish Steps. The menu is homely: a couple of soups, four or five daily pasta dishes, a range of creative and gourmet salads, wine by the glass or bottle. You can also order a gourmet picnic hamper.

'Gusto

Piazza Augusto Imperatore 9 (06 322 6273/www.gusto.it). **Open** *Wine bar* 11am-2am daily. **Meals served** *Pizzeria* 12.45-3pm, 7.30pm-1am daily. *Restaurant* 12.45-3pm, 7.45pm-midnight daily. €€-€€€. **Map** p86 B2 ⑫

'Gusto is a multi-purpose, split-level pizzeria, restaurant and wine bar, with a kitchen shop and bookshop next door. The ground-floor pizza and salad bar is always packed; upstairs, the more expensive restaurant applies oriental techniques to Italian models, though not always convincingly. The wine bar out back is buzzing and stylish, with a good selection of wines by the glass and nibbles. Around the corner at via della Frezza 16, the mod-*osteria* L'Osteria is part of the same outfit. **NEW** 'Gusto's newest outpost – 'Gusto al 28 – is a minimal-chic fish restau-

Caffè Canova-Tadolini

rant and wine bar at piazza Augusto Imperatore 28.

Matricianella

Via del Leone 4 (06 683 2100/ www.matricianella.it). **Meals served** 12.30-3pm, 7.30-11pm Mon-Sat. Closed 3wks Aug. **€€€**. **Map** p86 B3 ⑬
This is a friendly, bustling place with great prices. The Roman imprint is most evident in classics such as the *bucatini all'amatriciana* (pasta with spicy sausage sauce) or *abbacchio a scottadito* (thin strips of lamb), but there are plenty more creative options. The well-chosen wine list is a model of honest pricing. Book ahead.

Palatium

Via Frattina 94 (06 6920 2132). **Open** 11am-11pm Mon-Sat. Closed 2wks Aug. **€€**. **Map** p86 C3 ⑭
Though it's backed by the Lazio regional government, this wine bar and eaterie is more than a PR exercise. It gives punters the chance to go beyond the Castelli romani clichés to explore lesser-known local vintages such as Cesanese or Aleatico. There's a generous *aperitivo* buffet from 3pm to 7.30pm, after which Palatium switches into restaurant mode, offering light creative dishes made with local ingredients.

Pizza Ciro

Via della Mercede 43 (06 678 6015). **Meals served** 11am-2am daily. **€**. **Map** p86 C3 ⑮
This may look like a modest, touristy pizza parlour, but Ciro is, in fact, one enormous eating factory. The pizzas are not at all bad, and *primi* such as *tubetti alla Ciro* (pasta with rocket and mussels) provide a decent alternative.

Rosati

Piazza del Popolo 4/5A (06 322 5859). **Open** 7am-11pm daily. **Map** p86 A1 ⑯
Frequented by Calvino and Pasolini, this bar's interior has remained unchanged since 1922. Try the *Sogni romani* cocktail: orange juice with liqueurs in red and yellow – the colours of the city.

Stravinskij Bar

Via del Babuino 9 (06 328 881/06 689 1694/www.hotelderussie.it). **Open** 10am-midnight daily. **Map** p86 B1 ⑰
Inside the swanky De Russie hotel, this chic bar has an inside area with comfy

Trevi in our hearts

Trevi Fountain

The Roman attitude to the city's iconic landmarks is as fiercely proud as it is flexible. Indeed, what better way of showing your pride than to express yourself through your unique heritage... sometimes in surprising ways.

If, in any other city in the world, someone lobbed a tin of paint into a rococo masterpiece, he or she would be vilified by the public and hounded by the media. But when, in 2007, a self-styled 'futurist artist' turned the waters of the **Trevi Fountain** a striking shade of scarlet, opinions were split. Half the city traipsed over in the moonlight to toss a coin into the opaque waters, and exclaim about how the bright colour brought out the stark white of the splendid sculpted background.

Aesthetics really matter to Romans: even what could be construed as pure vandalism may, here, be recognised as a fleeting act of artistic homage to a much-revered object of supreme beauty. The regular varnishing of the toenails on the huge marble foot tucked just around the corner from **via Pie' di Marmo** ('marble foot street') in via Santo Stefano del Cacco is a case in point.

Less damaging, but equally indicative of how Romans consider their beloved monuments as part of everyday life, are the city's 'talking' statues: Pasquino in the **piazza Pasquino**; the river god Marforio in **piazza del Campidoglio**; Madame Lucrezia outside the church of **San Marco** (p63); the so-called baboon in **via del Babuino**. Through the centuries these ancient statues were covered in scraps of paper bearing lampoons against the powers that be... ie the pope and his cronies. Today the pope still features in the doggerel taped to Pasquino, but Italy's politicians come in for a written horse-whipping too.

January 2008 saw Rome's 'futurist' strike again, this time at another of Rome's famous sites. Accomplices helped him launch half a million coloured balls down the **Spanish Steps**, prompting not fury but delight from morning commuters who immortalised the moment with mobile-phone cameras and improvised the odd multi-hued football match.

armchairs and a fabulous patio where tables are surrounded by orange trees.

Vic's

Vicolo della Torretta 60 (06 687 1445).
Meals served 12.30-3pm Mon; 12.30-3pm, 7.30-10.30pm Tue-Sat. **€**. No credit cards. **Map** p86 B3 ⑱
This wine and salad bar offers a range of creative salads such as radicchio, pine nuts, sultanas and parmesan. Pared-back Roman *osteria* decor, charming service and a fairly priced wine list.

Shopping

The Tridente is Rome's chic shopping area *per eccellenza*.
In this wedge you'll find the big names of Italian fashion: Prada, Fendi, Gucci, Dolce & Gabbana…

Anglo-American Book Co

Via della Vite 102 (06 679 5222/ www.aab.it). **Open** 3.30-7.30pm Mon; 10am-7.30pm Tue-Sat. Closed 2wks Aug. **Map** p86 C3 ⑲
A good selection of books in English.

La Soffitta Sotto i Portici

Piazza Augusto Imperatore (06 3600 5345). **Open** 9am-sunset 1st & 3rd Sun of mth. Closed Aug. **Map** p86 B2 ⑳
Street market with collectibles of all kinds, ranging from magazines to jewellery, at non-bargain prices. There's a multilingual information desk too.

The Lion Bookshop

Via dei Greci 36 (06 3265 4007).
Open 3.30-7.30pm Mon; 10am-7.30pm Tue-Sun. **Map** p86 B2 ㉑
This friendly shop is a great place for contemporary fiction and children's books. Closed on Sunday in June-Oct.

L'Olfattorio – Bar à Parfums

Via Ripetta 34 (06 361 2325/ www.olfattorio.it). **Open** 11am-2.30pm, 3.30-7.30pm Tue-Sat. Closed Oct. **Map** p86 B1 ㉒
'Bartender' Maria will awaken your olfactory organs and guide you towards your perfect scent. Paradise for perfume-lovers.

TAD

Via del Babuino 155A (06 3269 5131/ www.taditaly.com). **Open** noon-7.30pm Mon; 10.30am-7.30pm Tue-Fri; 10.30am-8pm Sat. **Map** p86 B1 ㉓
The concept behind this 'concept store' is that you can shop for clothes, shoes, flowers, household accessories, CDs, mags and perfumes, get your hair done, eat fusion Thai-Italian and drink – all in one super-cool place. Opens on Sunday afternoons in summer.

Villa Borghese & Via Veneto

The area now occupied by the verdant Villa Borghese gardens has always been green. Ancient aristocrats built sprawling villas north and north-east of the city centre. Noble families and monastic orders continued the tradition right up until the 1800s.

When Rome became the capital of Italy in 1871, most of the impressive estates were carved up to build pompous *palazzi*. Only Villa Borghese was saved from post-Unification property speculators. It is now the city's most central public park, with one of Rome's great art repositories – the superb **Galleria Borghese** – at its heart, and one of Rome's greatest views – from the Pincio, over piazza del Popolo to the dome of St Peter's.

Descending south from the park, via Vittorio Veneto (known simply as via Veneto) was the haunt of the famous and glamorous in the *dolce vita* years of the 1950s and '60s. These days, it's home to insurance companies, luxury hotels and visitors wondering where the stars and paparazzi went.

At the southern end of via Veneto is piazza Barberini. In ancient times, erotic dances were performed here to mark the coming of spring. The square's magnificent centrepiece, Bernini's Triton fountain, was once

in open countryside. Now he sits –
his two fish-tail legs tucked beneath
him on a shell supported by four
dolphins – amid thundering
traffic.The bees around him are
the Barberini family emblem.

Sights & museums

Bioparco-Zoo

*Piazzale del Giardino Zoologico 20
(06 360 8211/www.bioparco.it).* **Open**
Nov-Mar 9.30am-5pm daily. *Apr-Oct*
9.30am-6pm daily. **Admission** €8.50;
€6.50 reductions. **Map** p93 D1 ㉔
Slightly more sprightly since its
makeover from 'zoo' to 'biopark', this
will keep your kids happy for an after-
noon. Next door – and accessible
through the zoo – is the Museo Civico
di Zoologia di Roma, with sections on
biodiversity and extreme habitats.

Explora – Museo dei Bambini di Roma

*Via Flaminia 82 (06 361 3776/www.
mdbr.it).* **Open** sessions at 10am, noon,
3pm, 5pm Tue-Sun. **Admission** €6;
€7 3-12s. **Map** p93 A2 ㉕
This children's museum provides good
educational fun for under-12s. The 3pm
and 5pm sessions on Thursday after-
noon cost €5 for all. Booking essential.

Galleria Borghese

*Piazzale Scipione Borghese 5 (06 841
3979/www.galleriaborghese.it).* **Open**
9am-7pm Tue-Sun. **Admission** €8.50;
€5.25 reductions; extra charge during
exhibitions. **Map** p93 E2 ㉖
Note: Booking (€2) is obligatory.
Begun in 1608, the Casino Borghese was
designed to house the art collection of
Cardinal Scipione Borghese, Bernini's
greatest patron. The interior decoration
(1775-90) was restored in the 1990s. A
curved double staircase leads to the
imposing entrance salon, with fourth-
century AD floor mosaics showing gladiators fighting wild animals. In Room 1
is Antonio Canova's 1808 waxed marble figure of Pauline, sister of Napoleon
and wife of Prince Camillo Borghese, as
a topless *Venus*; Prince Camillo thought
the work so provocative that he forbade

even the artist from seeing it after completion. Rooms 2-4 contain some wonderful sculptures by Gian Lorenzo
Bernini: the *David* (1624) in room 2 is a
self-portrait of the artist; room 3 houses
his *Apollo and Daphne* (1625); room 4
his *Rape of Proserpine* (1622). Room 5
contains important pieces of classical
sculpture, including a Roman copy of a
Greek dancing faun and a sleeping hermaphrodite. Bernini's *Aeneas and
Anchises* (1620) dominates room 6, while
room 7 has an Egyptian theme: included among the classical statues is a second-century Isis. The six Caravaggios
in room 8 include the *Boy with a Basket
of Fruit* (c1594) and the *Sick Bacchus*
(c1593), believed to be a self-portrait.

Upstairs, the picture gallery holds a
surfeit of masterpieces. Look out for:
Raphael's *Deposition* and Pinturicchio's
*Crucifixion with Saints Jerome and
Christopher* (room 9); Lucas Cranach's
Venus and Cupid with Honeycomb
(room 10); and Rubens's spectacular
Pietà and *Susanna and the Elders*
(room 18). Titian's *Venus Blindfolding
Cupid* and *Sacred and Profane Love*,
recently restored but still difficult to
interpret, are the stars of room 20,
which also contains a stunning *Portrait
of a Man* by Antonello da Messina.
Event highlights Caravaggio/Bacon:
From the Galleria Borghese's ongoing
'ten great artists in ten years' programme, 2009 is dedicated to these two
masters (May-Sept 2009). Box p97.

Galleria Nazionale d'Arte Moderna e Contemporanea

*Viale delle Belle Arti 131 (06 3229
8221/www.gnam.arti.beniculturali.it).*
Open 8.30am-7.30pm Tue-Sun.
Admission €6.50; €3.25 reductions;
extra charge during exhibitions.
No credit cards. **Map** p93 C2 ㉗
This collection begins with the 19th
century: an enormous statue of
Hercules by Canova dominates room 4
of the left wing; in the Palizzi room are
views of Rome before the dramatic
changes to the urban landscape in the
late 19th century. The 20th-century
component includes works by de

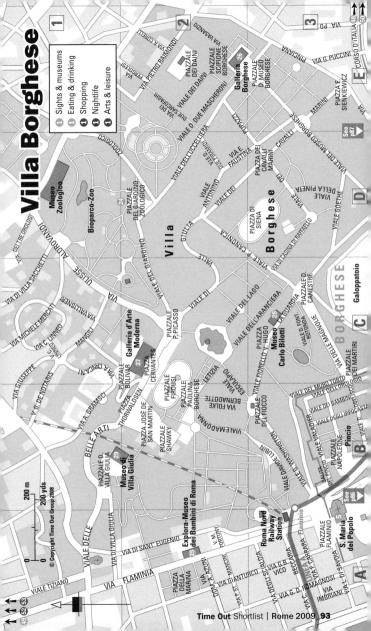

Villa Borghese

Legend:
- 1 Sights & museums
- 1 Eating & drinking
- 1 Shopping
- 1 Nightlife
- 1 Arts & leisure

Map labels:

Museo Zoologico

Bioparco-Zoo

PIAZZALE DEI DAINI

PIAZZALE SCIPIONE BORGHESE

Galleria Borghese 26

PIAZZA D. MUSEO BORGHESE

See p87

PIAZZA E. SIENKIEWICZ

VIA PO

CORSO D'ITALIA

PINCIANA

VIA G. PUCCINI

VIA VASANZIO

VIA PIETRO RAIMONDI

VIA FERDELLESI

VIA P. COBELLI

VIALE D. DUE MASCHERONI

VIALE DELL'UCCELLIERA

VIALE DEI DUE PONTI

PIAZZALE DEL GIARDINO ZOOLOGICO

VIA DELLE TRE MADONNE

VIALE DEI CAVALLI MARINI

PIAZZA DEI CAVALLI MARINI

VIA DELL'OROLOGIO

VIALE DI VALLE GIULIA

Villa Borghese

PIAZZA DI SIENA

VIALE P. CANONICA

VIA DI CASINA DI RAFFAELLO

VIALE GOETHE

VIALE DELLA PINETA

Galleria d'Arte Moderna 27

PIAZZALE P. PICASSO

Museo Carlo Bilotti 28

VIALE DELL'ARANCIERA

PIAZZA FIORELLO T. HUGO

Galoppatoio

BORGHESE

VIA MICHELE MERCATI

VIA C. LINNEO

VIA CANOVA?

PIAZZALE BOLIVAR

PIAZZA THORWALDSEN

PIAZZALE FIRDUSI

PIAZZALE JOSÉ DE SAN MARTIN

PIAZZALE SHAWKY

VIALE DELL'ESCLAPIO

VIA F. BERNADOTTE

VIA DELLE MAGNOLIE

PIAZZALE DEI MARTIRI

Museo di Villa Giulia 29

PIAZZALE DI VILLA GIULIA

BELLE ARTI

VIA A. GRAMSCI

PIAZZALE DELLE BELLE ARTI

VIALE WASHINGTON

VIALE DEL MURO TORTO

Pincio 1

PIAZZALE NAPOLEONE I

See p86

Explora-Museo dei Bambini di Roma 25

Roma Nord Railway Station

VIALE DELLE BELLE ARTI

VIA DI SANT'EUGENIO

VIA DI VILLA GIULIA

PIAZZALE FLAMINIO

S. Maria del Popolo 5

VIA FLAMINIA

VIALE TIZIANO

PIAZZA DELLA MARINA

VIA DEGLI SCIALOIA

VIA G.B. VICO

VIA CARRARA

LINEA Flaminio

200 m

200 yds

© Copyright Time Out Group 2008

Chirico, Modigliani, Morandi and Marini. International stars include *The Three Ages* by Klimt and *The Gardener* and *Madame Ginoux* by Van Gogh. Cézanne, Braque, Rodin and Henry Moore are also represented.

Museo Carlo Bilotti

Viale Fiorello La Guardia (06 8205 9127/06 0608/www.museocarlo bilotti.it). **Open** 9am-7pm Tue-Sun. **Admission** €4.50; €2.50 reductions; extra charge during exhibitions. No credit cards. **Map** p93 C3 ㉘

Opened in 2006, this museum houses the collection of billionaire art tycoon Carlo Bilotti: Giorgio de Chirico, Larry Rivers, Jean Dubuffet and Andy Warhol all feature.

Museo Nazionale di Villa Giulia

Piazzale di Villa Giulia 9 (06 322 6571/06 8205 9127/www.villa borghese.it). **Open** 8.30am-7.30pm Tue-Sun. **Admission** €4; €2 reductions. No credit cards. **Map** p93 B1 ㉙

This collection, in a villa designed by Michelangelo and Vignola for Pope Julius III in the mid 1500s, records the pre-Roman peoples of central Italy, and the sophisticated, mysterious Etruscans in particular. The Etruscans went well prepared to their graves, and most of the collection comes from excavations of tombs: the museum has hundreds of vases, pieces of furniture and models of buildings made to accompany the dead. In the courtyard, stairs descend to the nymphaeum; in an adjacent room is the sixth-century BC terracotta *Apollo of Veio*. In the garden there is a reconstruction of an Etruscan temple and a café.

Santa Maria della Concezione

Via Vittorio Veneto 27 (06 487 1185). **Open** *Church* 7am-noon, 3-7pm daily. *Crypt* 9am-noon, 3-6pm Mon-Wed, Fri-Sun. **Admission** *Crypt* donation expected. **Map** p87 E3 ㉚

Commonly known as *i cappuccini* (the Capuchins) after the long-bearded, brown-clad Franciscan sub-order to which it belongs, this Baroque church's attraction lies in the crypt: the skeletons of over 4,000 monks have been dismantled and arranged in swirls and curlicues through four chapels. Ribs hang from the ceiling in the form of chandeliers, and inverted pelvic bones make the shape of hour-glasses – a reminder (as a notice states) that 'you will be what we now are'. Though it's officially closed on Thursday, you may find the crypt open then too.

Eating & drinking

Cantina Cantarini

Piazza Sallustio 12 (06 485 528). **Meals served** 12.30-2.45pm, 7.30-11pm Mon-Sat. Closed 3wks Aug, 2wks Dec-Jan. €€€. **Map** p87 F2 ㉛

This good-value high-quality trattoria is meat-based for the first part of the week, then turns fishy thereafter. The atmosphere is as *allegro* as seating is tight – though outside tables take off some of the pressure in summer.

Cinecaffè – Casina delle Rose

Largo M Mastroianni 1 (06 4201 6224/www.cinecaffe.it). **Open** *Oct-May* 9am-7pm daily. *June-Sept* 10am-7pm Mon, Sun; 10am-midnight Tue-Sat. Closed 2wks Aug. **Map** p87 D1 ㉜

This ultra-civilised café at the via Veneto end of Villa Borghese serves excellent coffee, drinks and wallet-friendly light lunches to office workers, tourists and cinema aficionados.

Moma

NEW *Via San Basilio 42-43 (06 4201 1798).* **Open** 7.30am-12.30am Mon-Sat. Meals served 12.30-3pm, 8-11.30pm. **Map** p87 E2 ㉝

As the name suggests, this busy, tiny café/wine bar/restaurant (€€€) is aiming for a New York ambience. Tiny overall, there's a bar area downstairs and seating upstairs. The lunchtime snack-sized gourmet salads and hot dishes – some on edible 'plates' of crunchy pastry – make a pleasant change from the usual bar sandwich.

Nightlife

Gregory's

Via Gregoriana 54 (06 679 6386/
www.gregorysjazzclub.com). **Open**
7pm-2am Tue-Sun. Closed Aug.
Map p86 C3 ❸❹
This cosy little venue oozes jazz culture
from every pore: top live acts from
Tuesday to Saturday.

Trevi Fountain & Quirinale

The *acqua vergine* that feeds the
Trevi Fountain is said to be Rome's
best, but don't try drinking straight
from the fountain: it's full of coins
and chlorine. The surrounding
medieval streets conceal many
other testimonies to the importance
of water in the city: from the
'miraculous' well in the church of
Santa Maria in Via (via Mortaro 24),
from where cupfuls of healing liquid
are still dispensed, to the Città
d'Acqua (vicolo del Puttarello 25),
where the *acqua vergine* can be
heard rushing below a recently
excavated ancient Roman street.

The Trevi district was a service
area for the **Quirinal palace**, home
to popes, kings and now the Italian
president: here were the printing
presses, bureaucratic departments
and service industries that oiled
the machinery of the Papal States.
Aristocratic families, such as the
Barberinis and Colonnas, built their
palaces close by; their art collections
are now on view to the public.

Another fine collection lurks
inside the Accademia di San Luca
(piazza dell'Accademia 77) but the
gallery has been *in restauro* for
years, with no reopening date set.
In the meantime, you'll have to settle
for a peek at Borromini's glorious
spiral staircase in the courtyard.

For an altogether more 21st-
century take on the Eternal City,
catch the 45-minute flight-simulator
projection on Rome's history at
Time Elevator (via dei SS Apostoli
20, from €17, €15 reductions).

Sharing the Quirinal hill with the
president's palace are two of Rome's
finest small Baroque churches, **San
Carlino** and **San Andrea**, and a
crossroads with four fountains
(1593) representing river gods.

Sights & museums

Galleria Colonna

Piazza SS Apostoli 66 (06 678 4350/
www.galleriacolonna.it). **Open** 9am-
1pm Sat. Closed Aug. **Admission** €7;
€5.50 reductions. No credit cards.
Map p87 D5 ❸❺
This splendid six-room gallery was
completed in 1703 for the Colonna family, whose descendants still live in the
palace. The immense frescoed ceiling of
the mirrored Great Hall pays tribute to
family hero Marcantonio Colonna, who
led the papal fleet to victory against the
Turks in the Battle of Lepanto in 1571.
The gallery's most famous picture is
Annibale Caracci's earthy peasant *Bean
Eater*, but don't miss Bronzino's wonderfully sensuous *Venus and Cupid*.

Museo Nazionale delle Paste Alimentari

Piazza Scanderbeg 117 (06 699
1120/www.pastainmuseum.it).
Open closed for restoration as this
guide went to press; due to reopen by
end 2008. **Map** p87 D4 ❸❻
This museum is dedicated to pasta-
making: rolling and cutting techniques,
the equipment and the selection of
ingredients. There's a gift shop with all
kinds of pasta-related items.

Palazzo Barberini – Galleria Nazionale d'Arte Antica

Via delle Quattro Fontane 13 (06 481
4591/bookings 06 32 810/www.galleria
borghese.it). **Open** 9am-7.30pm Tue-
Sun. **Admission** €5; €2.50 reductions.
No credit cards. **Map** p87 E3 ❸❼
This vast Baroque palace, built by the
Barberini Pope Urban VIII, houses one

The view from the Pincio p91

of Rome's most important art collections. Top architects like Maderno, Bernini and Borromini queued up to work on this pile, which was completed in just five years (1627-33). Highlights of the collection include Filippo Lippi's *Madonna* (with possibly the ugliest Christ-child ever painted); an enigmatic portrait by Raphael of a courtesan believed to be his mistress; a *Nativity* and *Baptism of Christ* by El Greco; Tintoretto's *Christ and the Woman taken in Adultery*; Titian's *Venus and Adonis*; Caravaggio's *Judith beheading Holofernes* and the beautiful *Narcissus*, a Holbein portrait, *Henry VIII Dressed for his Wedding to Anne of Cleves*; a Bernini bust and painted portrait of Pope Urban VIII; and a self-assured self-portrait by Artemisia Gentileschi.

Palazzo del Quirinale

Piazza del Quirinale (06 46 991/www.quirinale.it). **Open** 8.30am-noon Sun. Closed late June-early Sept. **Admission** €5. No credit cards. **Map** p87 D4 ㉝

The popes still hadn't finished the new St Peter's when (in 1574) they started building a summer palace on the Quirinale hill. In case an elderly pope died on his hols and had to be replaced, the Cappella Paolina was built as a replica of the Vatican's Sistine Chapel minus the Michelangelos. On Sunday mornings, when parts of the presidential palace open to the public, you may be fortunate enough to catch one of the midday concerts held in this chapel.

San Carlino alle Quattro Fontane

Via del Quirinale 23 (06 488 3109/www.sancarlino-borromini.it). **Open** 10am-1pm, 3-6pm Mon-Fri; 10am-1pm Sat; noon-1pm Sun. **Map** p87 E4 ㊲

This was Borromini's first solo piece (1631-41), and the one he was most proud of. The oval dome is remarkable: its geometrical coffers decrease in size towards the lantern to give the illusion of added height; hidden windows make the dome appear to float in mid-air.

Santa Maria della Vittoria

Via XX Settembre 17 (06 4274 0571). **Open** 8.30am-noon, 3.30-6pm Mon-Sat; 3.30-6pm Sun. **Map** p87 F3 ㊵

This early Baroque church, designed by Carlo Maderno, holds one of Bernini's

ROME BY AREA

most famous works. *The Ecstasy of St Teresa*, in the Cornaro chapel (fourth on the left), shows the Spanish mystic floating on a cloud in a supposedly spiritual trance after an androgynous angel has pierced her with a burning arrow. The result is more than a little ambiguous.

Sant'Andrea al Quirinale

Via del Quirinale 29 (06 474 4872). **Open** 8.30am-noon, 3.30-7pm Mon-Fri; 9am-noon, 4-7pm Sat, Sun. **Map** p87 E4 ㉛

Pope Alexander VII (1655-67) was so pleased with Bernini's design for this dazzling little church, built out of pale pink marble, that it became in effect the chapel of the Quirinale palace across the road. It is cunningly designed to create a sense of grandeur in such a tiny space. The star turn is a plaster St Andrew floating through a broken pediment on his way to heaven.

Scuderie Papali al Quirinale

Via XXIV Maggio 16 (06 696 270/ www.scuderiequirinale.it). **Open** during exhibitions only 10am-8pm Mon-Thur, Sun; 10am-10.30pm Fri, Sat. **Admission** varies. **Map** p87 D5 ㊷

The former stables of the Quirinal palace, this large exhibition space was magnificently reworked by architect Gae Aulenti, who took care to preserve the original features. There is a breathtaking view of Rome's skyline from the rear staircase as you leave. Credit cards accepted for phone bookings only.

Trevi Fountain

Piazza di Trevi. **Map** p86 C4 ㊸

Anita Ekberg made this fountain famous when she plunged in wearing a strapless black evening dress in Fellini's classic *La dolce vita*. Now, wading is strictly forbidden. Moreover, the sparkling water is full of chlorine (there's a chlorine-free spout hidden at the back of the fountain to the right). The *acqua vergine* was the finest water in the city, brought by Emperor Agrippa's 25km (15.5-mile) aqueduct to the foot of the Quirinal hill. The fountain as we know it was designed by

Bacon with your Caravaggio?

In its ongoing 'ten great artists in ten years' programme the **Galleria Borghese** has dedicated 2009 to Caravaggio... and Francis Bacon. That this gallery would want to showcase its six magnificent works by Caravaggio is understandable. But where does Francis Bacon fit in?

You won't find many Bacons in Rome's public collections: one of his 45-odd studies based on Velázquez's *Pope Innocent X* is in the modern religious art gallery in the **Vatican Museums** (p145).

Bacon's links with Rome are tenuous: in the months he spent in Rome in 1954, Bacon studiously avoided seeing Velázquez's work. Yet the idea of Bacon and Caravaggio side by side is compelling. Separated by four centuries, these two men – both moody and troubled – erupted on to their contemporary art scenes and rocked the status quo by exploring their own grim realities in a whole new idiom.

It's tempting, as well, to try to draw parallels. If Bacon failed to see Velázquez's *Innocent X*, did he perhaps see Caravaggio's *David with the Head of Goliath* in the Galleria Borghese? In this work, the older, more desperate Caravaggio is said to have portrayed himself in the severed head, its eyes lifeless and its mouth gaping open. Gaping, in fact, much like the pope's in Bacon's versions of *Innocent*.

ROME BY AREA

Nicolo Salvi in 1762. It's a rococo extravaganza of sea horses, conch-blowing tritons, craggy rocks and flimsy trees. Nobody can quite remember when the custom started of tossing coins in to ensure one's return to the Eternal City. The money goes to the Red Cross.

Eating & drinking

Al Presidente

Via in Arcione 94-95 (06 679 7342/ www.alpresidente.it). **Meals served** 1-3pm, 8-11pm Tue-Sun. Closed 3wks Jan, 3wks Aug. **€€€€**. **Map** p87 D4 ㉔
This restaurant under the walls of the Quirinal palace is one of the few really reliable addresses in this largely *menu turistico*-dominated area. The creative Italian menu is strong on fish: among the *primi* is a delicious asparagus and squid soup, while one of the highlights of the *secondi* is the fish and vegetable millefeuille. A light buffet-style lunch (€€€) is served Tue-Sat. Outside tables.

Antica Birreria Peroni

Via San Marcello 19 (06 679 5310/ www.anticabirreriaperoni.it). **Meals served** noon-midnight Mon-Sat. Closed 2wks Aug. **€-€€**. **Map** p86 C5 ㉕
This long-running *birreria* is the perfect place for a quick lunch or dinner. Service is rough-and-Roman but friendly, and the food is good and relatively cheap. Sausage is the main act, with three types of German-style *wurstel* on offer.

Da Michele

Via dell'Umiltà 31 (349 252 5347/ www.michelepizza.it). **Open** Oct-Mar 8am-6pm Mon-Thur, Sun; 10am-3pm Fri, Sun. *Apr-Sept* 8am-10pm Mon-Thur, Sun; 10am-3pm Fri. Closed Jewish holidays; 10 days Pesach (usually Apr). No credit cards. **Map** p86 C5 ㉖
Recently relocated from the Ghetto, Da Michele (ex-Zi' Fenizia) does over 50 flavours of takeaway pizza: all kosher, and all dairy-free.

Il Gelato di San Crispino

Via della Panetteria 42 (06 679 3924/ www.ilgelatodisancrispino.com).

Open noon-12.30am Mon, Wed, Thur, Sun; noon-1.30am Fri, Sat. Closed 3wks Jan. No credit cards. **Map** p87 D4 ㉗
Il Gelato di San Crispino serves what many consider to be the best ice-cream in Rome – or the world. Flavours change according to what's in season – in summer the *lampone* (raspberry) and *susine* (yellow plum) are fabulous. No cones here – only tubs are allowed. Open daily from mid March to mid September.

Heading north

North from Villa Borghese, well-heeled suburbs fill the area that stretches between the **Villa Torlonia** and Villa Ada public parks. By the river, a vibrant sport and arts hub is springing to life: rugby is played in the Stadio Flaminio, and football across the Tiber at the **Stadio Olimpico**; while the new **Auditorium** seethes with music-related activity.

Sights & museums

MACRO

Via Reggio Emilia 54 (06 6710 70400/ www.macro.roma.museum). **Open** 9am-7pm Tue-Sun. **Admission** €1. No credit cards. **Map** off p87 F1 ㉘
Rome's contemporary art scene was given a boost in the 1990s with the opening of this gallery in a striking converted brewery. This space will grow to cover 10,000sq m (107,500sq ft), thanks to an extension designed by architect Odile Decq, due for inauguration during the 2008 Notte Bianca (p36). Shows spill over into MACRO-Future inside the Mattatoio (p121) in Testaccio.

MAXXI

Via Guido Reni 2F (06 321 0181/ www.maxxi.darc.beniculturali.it). **Open** scheduled to reopen spring 2009. **Map** off p93 A1 ㉙
Works to transform this huge former army barracks into the Museo delle arti del XXI secolo (MAXXI), to a striking design by Zaha Hadid, entered their final stage in spring

2008. The grand opening is tentatively scheduled for spring 2009.

Villa Torlonia

*Via Nomentana 70 (06 8205 9127/ 06 0608/www.museivillatorlonia.it).***Open Park** dawn-sunset daily. *Museums etc* Nov-Feb 9am-4.30pm Tue-Sun; Mar, Oct 9am-5.30pm Tue-Sun; Apr-Sept 9am-7pm Tue-Sun. **Admission** €6.50; €3 reductions; extra charge during exhibitions. No credit cards. **Map** off p87 F1 ⑩

With its lush park and scattered attractions, Villa Torlonia is a pleasant place to pass a hot day. Once home of the Torlonia family, and wartime residence of Benito Mussolini, the villa was bought by the city council 30 years ago and has been *in restauro* since. Open to the public are the art nouveau *Casina della civette* with its collection of stained glass and *boiseries*; the *Casino nobile* with its frescoes and plaster mouldings; the *Casino dei principi*, which houses exhibitions; the faux-medieval villa, home to the Technotown activity centre (06 8205 9127/www.technotown.it); and the Limonaia restaurant and tea room.

Eating & drinking

Osteria dell'Arco

Via G Pagliari 11 (06 854 8438). **Meals served** 12.30-3pm, 8-11pm Mon-Fri; 7.30-11pm Sat. Closed 2wks Aug. €€€. **Map** off p87 F1 ⑪

This nouveau-rustic *osteria* serves creative Italian cuisine at excellent prices. Follow a smoked tuna and swordfish starter with pasta with cuttlefish and broccoli, or anglerfish fillets with artichoke. Near the MACRO gallery (p98).

Arts & leisure

Auditorium – Parco della Musica

Via P de Coubertin 15 (06 80 242/ box office 06 808 2058/www. auditorium.com). **Map** off p93 A1 ⑫

Rome's huge new facility is the world's second-most successful performing arts centre (after New York's Lincoln Centre), thanks to an eclectic pro-

gramme and reasonable prices. Guided tours of the complex cost €9 (€5 reductions; no credit cards): times change frequently so call ahead (06 8024 1281) or check the website.

Event highlights Rome's Film Festival will be held here and at venues around the city on 2-11 Oct 2008.

Foro Italico & Stadio Olimpico

Piazza de Bosis/via del Foro Italico. **Map** off p93 A1 ⑬

An obelisk 36m (120ft) high, with the words *Mussolini Dux* carved on it, greets visitors to the Foro Italico, a sports complex conceived in the late 1920s. The avenue leading west of the obelisk is paved with mosaics of good Fascists doing sporty Fascist things. The same avenue is now trampled on by the hoards that visit the Stadio Olimpico to watch Roma (www.asroma.it) and Lazio (www.sslazio.it) football teams play. Tickets cost €10-€100 (no credit cards).

Villa Borghese p91

Palazzo delle Esposizioni

Esquilino, Celio & San Lorenzo

Monti & Esquilino

In ancient times, present-day Monti was the giant Suburra slum where streets ran with effluent and inhabitants died of insomnia. The Esquiline hill, on the other hand, was where the rich and powerful had their gardens and villas.

Nowadays, the alleyways of Monti – north-east of the Forum, between *vie* Nazionale and Cavour – are still noisy and bustling, the only difference being that this area is seriously hip. Up on the Esquiline hill, on the other hand, the solid *palazzi* built after Italy was unified in the 1870s look as if they have seen better days.

Via Nazionale is a traffic artery lined by carbon-copy high street shops; half way down, the huge **Palazzo delle Esposizioni** showcase reopened in late 2007 after lengthy restoration; the pretty **Villa Aldobrandini** park, up a flight of steps at the south-western end, has wonderful views over the city. It's very popular with tramps.

If you've come to Rome on a budget package, chances are you'll end up in a hotel on the Esquilino, around Termini railway station. It may come as a shock. For despite heroic efforts by the municipal authorities to convince us that a 'renaissance' is under way here, the Esquilino's grimy *palazzi* and questionable after-dark denizens may not be what you expected of the Eternal City. But there are charms and attractions.

Piazza Vittorio Emanuele II – the city's biggest square and known simply as piazza Vittorio – was given a new lease of life in the 1980s by a revamp of the central gardens and the arrival of a multi-ethnic community; the food market that moved a few years ago from the piazza into a nearby ex-barracks bursts with exotic produce and smells. Then there are vast basilicas (**Santa Maria Maggiore**), intimate mosaic-encrusted churches (**Santa Prassede**), Roman artefacts (**Palazzo Massimo**) and a magnificent post-war railway station building at Termini.

To the south, on Colle Oppio, Nero fiddled in his **Domus Aurea**, entertaining his guests with his Imperial twanging. Nowadays this stretch of green is peopled by Roman mums and their offspring during the day, and some very dubious characters after dark.

Sights & museums

Baths of Diocletian
Via Enrico de Nicola 78 (06 3996 7700). **Open** 9am-7.45pm Tue-Sun. **Admission** €7; €3.50 reductions; extra charge during exhibitions (see p12). No credit cards. **Map** p102 C1 **1**
Diocletian's baths were the largest in Rome when they were built in AD 298-306, covering over a hectare (2.5 acres) and able to accommodate 3,000 people. A convent complex, designed by Michelangelo, was built around the largest surviving chunk of the baths in the 1560s. It now contains a collection of stone inscriptions that is sufficiently low-key to allow you to focus on the massive bath buildings themselves and on Michelangelo's 16th-century restoration of the place, including its splendid central cloister. (Round the corner, the church of Santa Maria degli Angeli in piazza della Repubblica, and the Aula Ottagona at via Romita 8, were also part of the structure.)

Domus Aurea
Via della Domus Aurea 1 (06 3996 7700). **Open** by appointment only for guided tours 10am-4pm Tue-Fri. **Map** p102 B3 **2**
Note: though crumbling masonry shut the Domus down in 2005, guided tours (€4.50) now allow visitors to view the frescoes and plaster mouldings from restorers' scaffolding. The monument was due to reopen fully in late 2008.
In the summer of AD 64, fire devastated a large part of central Rome. Afterwards, anything unsinged east of the Forum was knocked down to make way for Emperor Nero's Domus Aurea (Golden House). Its main façade faced south and was entirely clad in gold; inside, every inch not faced inlaid with gems was frescoed by Nero's pet aesthete Fabullus. The moment Nero died in AD 68, however, work was begun to eradicate every vestige of the hated tyrant. So thorough was the cover-up job that for decades after its frescoes were rediscovered in 1480, no one realised it was the Domus Aurea that they had stumbled across.

Museo Nazionale d'Arte Orientale
Via Merulana 248 (06 487 4415). **Open** 8.30am-2pm Mon, Wed, Fri, Sat; 9am-7pm Tue, Thur, Sun. Closed 1st & 3rd Mon of mth. **Admission** €4; €2 reductions. No credit cards. **Map** p102 C3 **3**
This impressive collection of oriental art includes artefacts from the Near East, such as pottery, gold, votive offerings, some from the third millennium BC – 11th- to 18th-century painted fans from Tibet, sacred sculptures, and some Chinese pottery from the 15th century.

Palazzo delle Esposizioni
Via Nazionale 194 (06 3996 7500/ www.palaexpo.it). **Open** 10am-8pm Tue-Thur, Sun; 10am-10.30pm Fri, Sat. **Admission** €6; €4.50 reductions. **Map** p102 A2 **4**

ROME BY AREA

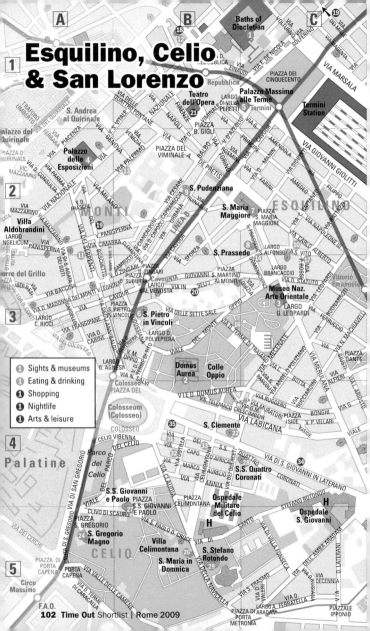

Esquilino, Celio & San Lorenzo

A **B** **C**

Baths of Diocletian

1

S. Andrea al Quirinale

Palazzo del Quirinale

Repubblica

Teatro dell'Opera **21**

Palazzo Massimo alle Terme **5** Termini

Termini Station

Palazzo delle Esposizioni **4**

PIAZZA DEL VIMINALE

2

Villa Aldobrandini

MONTI

S. Pudenziana **3**

S. Maria Maggiore **7**

S. Maria Maggiore

ESQUILINO

S. Prassede **8**

Largo Alfonso **10**

Museo Naz. Arte Orientale **15**

Vittorio Emanuele

LINEA B

S. Pietro in Vincoli **6**

3

Largo C. Ricci

PIAZZA DANTE

Domus Aurea **2**

Colle Oppio

Colosseum (Colosseo)

COLOSSEO

S. Clemente **22**

4

Palatine

Parco del Celio

S. Celio Vibenna

35

31

33

34

S.S. Quattro Coronati

S.S. Giovanni e Paolo **27**

Ospedale Militare del Celio

H

Ospedale S. Giovanni

S. Gregorio Magno **24**

H

Villa Celimontana

S. Stefano Rotondo **29**

26

S. Maria in Domnica

CELIO

5

Circo Massimo

PORTA CAPENA

F.A.O.

PIAZZA DI PORTA METRONIA

- **1** Sights & museums
- **1** Eating & drinking
- **1** Shopping
- **1** Nightlife
- **1** Arts & leisure

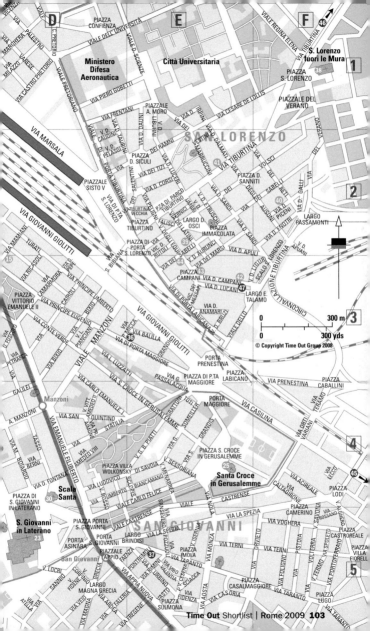

Pedal power

With some 425,000 parking fines handed out each year in the city – and empty parking places like gold dust – it's a wonder that locals use their cars in Rome at all.

City hall is doing much to dissuade them: permit-only zones are being extended, night bus services are being improved, construction work is forging ahead on a third underground train line. And Romans are being encouraged to get pedalling.

A network of urban cycle paths has been crawling slowly off the drawing board for years, though it's under-used. (A map of cycle paths can be downloaded from the BiciRoma site.) Even what should be a cycle-packed haven – the path runs for over 35 kilometres (22 miles) straight through the heart of the city along the banks of the Tiber is rarely used except by Sunday strollers.

With its latest two-wheeled venture – bike-sharing – city hall hopes to change this. In a pilot scheme launched in 2008, 500 bicycles were placed around the city centre. To use the bikes, pedallers must deposit €30 at a **PIT tourist office** (p187), obtain a top-up swipecard that's used to unlock any bike. Each first half-hour of use is free, after which €1 is deducted from your card for every 30 minutes. Bikes can be left at the rack nearest your destination.

■ www.biciroma.it
■ www.roma-n-bike.com

This imposing purpose-built 19th-century exhibition space reopened in 2008 after a major restoration (see box p40). Note that the ticket price can go as high as €12.50, depending on how many shows are on. Work by US video artist Bill Viola will be on display here between 11 Oct 2008 and 6 Jan 2009

Palazzo Massimo alle Terme

Largo di Villa Peretti 1 (06 480 201/ bookings 06 3996 7700). **Open** 9am-7.45pm Tue-Sun. **Admission** €7; €3.50 reductions; extra charge during exhibitions (see p12). No credit cards. **Map** p102 C1 ⑤

In the basement of Palazzo Massimo – home to a large chunk of the Museo Nazionale Romano collection – is an extensive collection of coins, Roman luxuries, descriptions of trade routes and audio-visual displays. On the ground and first floors are busts of emperors – including a magnificent Augustus – and lesser mortals. The first floor begins with the age of Vespasian (AD 69-79): his pugilistic bust is in Room 1; room 5 has a gracefully crouching Aphrodite from Hadrian's Villa at Tivoli; in room 7 is a peacefully sleeping hermaphrodite, a second-century AD copy of a Greek original. On the second floor, rare wall paintings from assorted villas have been reassembled, including a stunning garden scene from Livia's Villa near Rome. Room 10 contains Botero-like, larger-than-life (megalographic) paintings, and room 11 has dazzlingly bright marble intarsio works.

San Pietro in Vincoli

Piazza di San Pietro in Vincoli 4A (06 9784 4952). **Open** 7am-12.30pm, 3.30-6pm daily. **Map** p102 B3 ⑥

Built in the fifth century but reworked many times since, this church is dominated by the monument to Pope Julius II, with Michelangelo's imposing Moses (1515). Julius wanted a much grander tomb but died too soon to oversee it; his successors were less ambitious. As a result, the mighty Moses (in a bad trans-

Baths of Diocletian p101

lation of the Old Testament, the Hebrew word for 'radiant' was mistaken for 'horned') is wildly out of proportion, and infinitely better than the rest, by Michelangelo's students. Pilgrims come here for the chains. Eudoxia, wife of Emperor Valentinian III (445-55), was given a set of chains said to have been used to shackle St Peter in Jerusalem; with others used on the saint in the Mamertine Prison, they are now conserved in a reliquary on the main altar.

Santa Maria Maggiore

Piazza Santa Maria Maggiore (06 483 195). **Open** *Church* 7am-7pm daily. *Museum* (06 483 058) 9am-6pm daily. *Loggia* (guided tours only; booking obligatory) 9am & 1pm daily. **Admission** *Church* free. *Museum* €4. *Loggia* €3. No credit cards. **Map** p102 C2 ⑦

Local tradition says a church was built on this spot in around AD 366; documents place it almost 100 years later. The church was extended in the 13th and 18th centuries. Inside, above the columns of the nave, restored fifth-century mosaics show scenes from the Old Testament. In the apse, 13th-century mosaics show Christ crowning Mary Queen of Heaven. The Virgin theme continues in fifth-century mosaics on the triumphal arch. The ceiling in the main nave is said to have been made from the first shipment of gold from the Americas. In the 16th and 17th centuries two chapels were added: the first was the Cappella Sistina (last chapel on the right of the nave), designed by Domenico Fontana for Sixtus V (1585-90); directly opposite is the Cappella Paolina, a Greek-cross chapel, designed in 1611 by Flaminio Ponzio for Paul V to house a ninth-century icon of the Madonna on its altar. To the right of the main altar, a plaque marks the burial place of Baroque genius Gian Lorenzo Bernini. In the loggia, high up on the front of the church (tours leave from the baptistry; call ahead to check they're taking place), are glorious 13th-century mosaics that decorated the façade of the old basilica, showing the legend of the foundation of Santa Maria Maggiore.

Santa Prassede

Via Santa Prassede 9A (06 488 2456). **Open** 7.30am-noon, 4-6.30pm Mon-Sat; 8am-noon, 4-6.30pm Sun. **Map** p102 C2 ⑧

ROME BY AREA

Doozo

This church is a ninth-century scale copy of the original St Peter's. Artists from Byzantium made the rich, exotic mosaics. In the apse, Christ is being introduced to St Praxedes by St Paul on the right, while St Peter is doing the honours on the left for her sister St Pudenziana. The mosaic on the triumphal arch shows the heavenly Jerusalem, with palm-toting martyrs heading for glory. Off the right-hand side of the nave is the chapel of San Zeno, a dazzling swirl of blue and gold mosaics, punctuated with saints, animals and depictions of Christ and his mother. The wall and ceiling mosaics are ninth century; the jolly Mary in the niche above the altar is 13th century. In a room to the right is a portion of column said to be the one that Jesus was tied to for scourging.

Santa Pudenziana
Via Urbana 160 (06 481 4622). **Open** 9am-noon, 3-6pm Mon-Sat; 9am-noon, 3-6pm Sun. **Map** p102 B2 ⑨
The mosaic in the apse of Santa Pudenziana dates from the fourth century and is a remarkable example of the continuity between pagan and Christian art, depicting Christ and the apostles as wealthy Roman citizens wearing togas, against an ancient Roman cityscape.

Eating & drinking

Agata e Romeo
Via Carlo Alberto 45 (06 446 6115/ www.agataeromeo.it). **Meals served** 12.30-2.30pm, 7.30-10.30pm Mon-Fri. Closed 3wks Aug 2wks Dec-Jan. €€€€. **Map** p102 C2 ⑩
Agata Parisella was the first chef to demonstrate that Roman cuisine could be refined without sacrificing its wholesome essence. The ravioli stuffed with oxtail, for example, is a tribute to the traditional use of less prestigious cuts of meat. Agata's husband, Romeo Caraccio, presides over the dining room and extensive wine list. The decor is elegant but welcoming; the bill is steep.

Al Vino al Vino
Via dei Serpenti 19 (06 485 803). **Open** 10.30am-2.30pm, 5.30pm-1am daily. Closed 2wks Aug. **Map** p102 A3 ⑪
This friendly hostelry offers some 500 wines, with more than 25 available by the glass. But its speciality is *distillati*:

grappas, whiskeys and other strong spirits. There's Sicilian-inspired food to soak it all up.

Dagnino

Galleria Esedra, via VE Orlando 75 (06 481 8660/www.pasticceriadagnino. com). **Open** 7am-11pm daily. **Map** p102 B1 ⑫

Genuine 1950s decor sets the scene for this café-pasticceria that is a corner of Sicily in Rome. If it's Sicilian and edible, it's here: ice-cream in buns, crisp *cannoli siciliani* filled with ricotta cheese, and shiny green-iced cassata.

Doozo

Via Palermo 51-53 (06 481 5655). **Meals served** 12.30-3pm, 8-11.30pm Tue-Sat. Closed 2wks Aug. €€€. **Map** p102 B2 ⑬

This Japanese newcomer on a quiet street parallel to via Nazionale is spacious and cultured, with tables spilling into a gallery, bookshop and a lovely little Zen garden. There's good sushi, sashimi, tempura and karaage chicken served in bento boxes.

Hang Zhou

Via San Martino ai Monti 33 (06 487 2732). **Meals served** noon-3pm, 7-midnight daily. Closed Aug. €€. **Map** p102 C3 ⑭

Hang Zhou rises above most of Rome's dull Chinese eateries not so much for the food – which is quite acceptable – but because it's colourful, friendly and incredibly good value. No bookings are taken, so be prepared to queue.

Indian Fast Food

Via Mamiani 11 (06 446 0792). **Open** 11am-4pm, 5-10.30pm Mon-Sat; noon-4pm, 5-10.30pm Sun. €. No credit cards. **Map** p103 D3 ⑮

This Indian takeaway is just off piazza Vittorio. You can eat in too, accompanied by Indian music videos.

L'Altro Mastai

NEW *Via delle Terme Traiane 4A (06 6830 1296/www.laltromastai.it).* **Meals served** noon-3pm, 7.30-11.30pm Tue-Sat. Closed 3wks Aug. €€€€. **Map** p102 B3 ⑯

Talented chef Fabio Baldassare shifted in autumn 2008 from his *centro storico* home to larger premises, replete with a glorious garden, overlooking Nero's Domus Aurea (p101). He continues to serve an ever changing menu that is worth splashing out for – not a place for a quick snack, but if you have the time, budget and appetite, you're in for a treat. The wine list is satisfyingly vast, the desserts are to die for.

Trattoria Monti

Via di San Vito 13A (06 446 6573). **Meals served** 12.45-2.30pm, 7.45-10.45pm Tue-Sat; 12.45-2.30pm Sun. Closed 3wks Aug. €€€. **Map** p102 C3 ⑰

The cuisine, like the family that runs the place, is from the Marches region – so meat, fish and game all feature on the menu. Vegetarians are well served by a range of *tortini* (pastry-less pies). Make sure you book in the evening.

Shopping

The Monday-Saturday morning food market once known simply as 'piazza Vittorio' has moved into more salubrious premises in via Lamarmora: stalls stock the usual Italian fresh produce, cheese and meats, supplemented by halal meat and spices as well as some exotic fabrics and household goods.

Feltrinelli International

Via VE Orlando 84 (06 482 7878). **Open** 9am-8pm Mon-Sat; 10.30am-1.30pm, 4-8pm Sun. **Map** p102 B1 ⑱

An excellent range of fiction, non-fiction, magazines and guidebooks in English and other languages.

Le Gallinelle

Via del Boschetto 76 (06 488 1017). **Open** 4-7.30pm Mon; 10am-2pm, 4-7.30pm Tue-Sat. Closed 2wks Aug. **Map** p102 A2 ⑲

Vintage and ethnic garments are reworked by Wilma Silvestri and her daughter Giorgia in their funky shop. There are also classic linen suits for men and women.

Nightlife

Hangar

*Via in Selci 69A (06 488 1397/www.
hangaronline.it).* **Open** 10.30pm-2.30
am Mon, Wed-Sun. Closed 3wks Aug.
No credit cards. **Map** p102 B3 ⑳
American John Moss has been at the
helm of Rome's oldest gay bar since it
opened over two decades ago. Hangar
maintains its friendly but sexy atmosphere whether half full (occasionally
midweek) or packed (at weekends and
for porn-video Monday and striptease
Thursday). The venue also boasts a
small dark area.

Arts & leisure

Teatro dell'Opera di
Roma-Teatro Costanzi

*Piazza B Gigli 1 (06 4816 0255/
www.operaroma.it).* **Map** p102 B1 ㉑
The lavish late 19th-century *teatro all'
italiana* interior is quite a surprise after
the Mussolini-era angular grey façade
and its esplanade with tacky potted
palms. The acoustics vary considerably:
the higher (cheaper) seats aren't great,
so splash out on a box.

Celio & San Giovanni

After Emperor Constantine
legalised Christianity in the
fourth century, he donated land
on which the basilica of **San
Giovanni in Laterano** was
built: ground-breaking in that it
brought the new religion out into
the open; but fence-sitting in that
then, this neighbourhood was
about as far as you could get
from the city's centre of power
without exiting through its walls.

If the San Giovanni area fell prey
to property developers in the late
19th century, the Celio – a haven
for an elite of a bucolic bent in
ancient times – remains lush and
unkempt. It gives a glimpse of what
ancient, early Christian and
medieval Rome were like. From

the remains of ancient aqueducts
near the verdant and lovely **Villa
Celimontana** park, to frescoes
of martyrs in the church of **Santo
Stefano Rotondo**, this area has
a bit of everything.

Around Villa Celimontana is a
slew of ancient churches, including
Santi Giovanni e Paolo with its
excavated Roman houses beneath.

The tight grid of streets south-
east of the Colosseum is home
to the fascinating church of **San
Clemente**, and **Santi Quattro
Coronati**, which is blessed with
several extraordinary frescoes.

Further east, amid traffic,
smog and drab post-Unification
apartment buildings are some
of Christianity's most important
churches – including Vatican-
owned San Giovanni itself –
and a host of fascinating minor
ancient remains.

To the south of the basilica
are the sunken brick remains of
the Porta Asinaria, an ancient
gate in the third-century AD
Aurelian Wall. A park follows
the ancient wall north to **Santa
Croce in Gerusalemme** which
is surrounded by a panoply of
easily-visible Roman ruins: through
the opening in the Aurelian Walls
to the right of the church is the
Amphitheatrum Castrum (now
home to the monks' veggie garden,
see box p110), and part of the
Circus Varianus; the Baths of
Helena, of which you can see only
the cistern; and the monumental
travertine archway built by
Emperor Claudius in the first
century AD to mark the triumphal
entrance of the aqueducts into
the city.

North-east of here, outside the
walls, is the up and coming boho-
chic Pigneto district (see box p115),
tucked in the wedge between vie
Prenestina and Casilina.

The gates at Santa Croce p111

Sights & museums

San Clemente

Via San Giovanni in Laterano (06 774 0021). **Open** 9am-12.30pm, 3-6pm Mon-Sat; noon-6pm Sun. **Admission** *Church* free. *Excavations* €5; €3.50 reductions. No credit cards.
Map p102 B4 ㉒

This 12th-century basilica is a 3D time line. In the main church, the *schola cantorum* (choir), with its exquisite carving and mosaic decorations, survives from the fourth-century structure. The apse mosaic is 12th century: from the drops of Christ's blood springs the vine representing the Church, which swirls around peasants in their daily tasks, Doctors of the Church and a host of animals. In the chapel of St Catherine of Alexandria, frescoes by Masolino (c1430) show the saint praying as her torturers prepare the wheel on which she was stretched to death (later giving her name to a firework). From the sacristy, steps lead down to the fourth-century basilica. From there, a stairway descends to an ancient Roman alley. On one side is a second-century Roman *insula* (apartment building) containing a site where the Persian god Mithras was worshipped. On the other side are rooms of a Roman house used for meetings by early Christians.

San Giovanni in Laterano

Piazza San Giovanni in Laterano 4 (06 6988 6433). **Open** *Church* 7am-6.30pm daily. *Baptistry* 8am-12.30pm, 4-7pm daily. *Cloister* 9am-6pm daily. *Lateran Museum* 9am-noon Mon-Sat. **Admission** *Church* free. *Cloister* €2. *Museum* €4. No credit cards.
Map p103 D5 ㉓

San Giovanni and the Lateran palace were the papal headquarters until they were moved across the river to the Vatican in the 15th century. Constantine gave the plot of land to Pope Melchiades to build the church in 313. Little remains of the original basilica. The interior was revamped by Borromini in 1646. The façade, with its huge statues of Christ, the two Johns (Baptist and Evangelist) and Doctors of the Church, was added in 1735. A few treasures from earlier times survive: a 13th-century mosaic in the apse, a fragment of a fresco attributed to Giotto (behind the first column on the right) showing Pope Boniface VIII announcing the first Holy Year in 1300,

Secret garden

The garden at Santa Croce

Through artist Jannis Kounellis's stunning new gates to the *orto* (vegetable garden) of **Santa Croce in Gerusalemme** (p111) lies a vision of Eden: Cistercian monks from the neighbouring monastery tend rows of flowers and vegetables, or collect fruit from trees espaliered against the ancient brick walls.

Climb to the monastery's terrace and the scene is even more celestial: swathes of lavender and sage, Swiss chard and wild strawberry plants occupy perfect circular beds. Tidy pathways shaded by climbing roses, kiwi and grape vines slice the garden into four neat segments: from above you can clearly see that the paths form a cross at whose centre is a pool of spring water used to irrigate the crops

Monks have been growing vegetables here for centuries. Disturbed 14-year-old Syrian-born Emperor Heliogabalus (reigned AD 218-222) built himself an en suite mini-Colosseum that was scarcely finished before the teenage despot was swept from power. A century later Helena, the mother of Emperor Constantine, resided in the palace, placing her Holy Land souvenirs in a shrine here that, over time, turned into the great basilica and monastery of Santa Croce in Gerusalemme.

In 2004 architect Paolo Pejrone oversaw a redesign of the garden. Unveiled in November 2007, the gates designed by the Greek-born, Kounellis are delightful vine-like wrought-iron creations, plump with chunks of fruity coloured glass.

Visitors are welcome but only by prior arrangement. Check the monastery website for details of organised garden tours given by enthusiastic young volunteers, and call 06 701 4769 (ext. 103) to book your place. Don't forget to bring along your basket to stock up at the tiny organic garden shop run by the green-fingered monks.
■ www.basilicasantacroce.com

and the Gothic *baldacchino* over the main altar. Off the left aisle is the 13th-century cloister; a small museum contains vestments and some original manuscripts of music by Palestrina. The north façade was designed in 1586 by Domenico Fontana, who also placed Rome's tallest Egyptian obelisk outside. Also on this side is the octagonal baptistry that Constantine had built. The four chapels surrounding the font have mosaics from the fifth and seventh centuries.

San Gregorio Magno

Piazza di San Gregorio Magno 1 (06 700 8227). **Open** 9am-noon, 3.30-6pm daily. **Map** p102 A5 ㉔
This Baroque church stands on the site of the home of one of the most remarkable popes, Gregory I (the Great; 590-604), who spent his 14-year pontificate vigorously reorganising the Church. In a chapel on the right is a marble chair dating from the first century BC, said to have been used by Gregory as his papal throne. Also here is the tomb of Tudor diplomat Sir Edward Carne, who visited Rome several times to persuade the pope to annul the marriage of Henry VIII and Catherine of Aragon, so that the king could marry Anne Boleyn. Outside stand three small chapels (open 10am-12.30pm Tue, Thur, Sat, Sun; closed Aug), behind which are the remains of shops that lined this ancient road, the *clivus scauri*. To the right of the church is a shop selling monk-made soaps and assorted other goodies.

Santa Croce in Gerusalemme

Piazza Santa Croce in Gerusalemme 12 (06 701 4769/www.basilicasantacroce. com). **Open** *Church* 7am-12.45pm, 2.30-7pm Mon-Sat; 8am-12.45pm, 2.30-7pm Sun. *Chapel of the Relics* 8am-12.30pm, 2.30-6.30pm daily. **Map** p103 E4 ㉕
Founded in 320 by St Helena, mother of Emperor Constantine (who legalised Christianity in 313), this church was rebuilt in the 12th century, and again in 1743-44. Helena had her church constructed to house relics she brought back from the Holy Land: three chunks of Christ's cross, a nail, two thorns from his crown and the finger of St Thomas – allegedly, the very one that the doubting saint stuck into Christ's wound. All of these are displayed in a chapel at the end of a Fascist-era hall at the left side of the nave. The vegetable garden (see box p110), kept by the monks of the adjoining monastery, can be visited by appointment.

Santa Maria in Domnica

Via della Navicella 10 (06 7720 2685). **Open** 8.30am-12.30pm, 4.30-7pm daily. **Map** p102 B5 ㉖
The carved wood ceiling and porticoed façade date from the 16th century but Santa Maria in Domnica – known as the *navicella* (little ship), after the Roman statue that stands outside – is a ninth-century structure containing one of Rome's most charming apse mosaics. What sets this lovely design in rich colours apart is that Mary and Jesus look cheerful: the cherry-red daubs of blush on their cheeks give them a healthy glow.

Santi Giovanni e Paolo

Piazza Santi Giovanni e Paolo 13 (church 06 700 5745/excavations 320 799 6971/www.caseromane.it). **Open** *Church* 8.30am-noon, 3.30-6pm daily. *Excavations* 10am-1pm, 3-6pm Mon, Thur-Sun. **Admission** *Church* free. *Excavations* €6; €4 reductions. No credit cards. **Map** p102 B5 ㉗
Traces of the original fourth-century church can still be seen in the 12th-century façade on piazza Santi Giovanni e Paolo, which is overlooked by a 12th-century bell tower. An 18th-century revamp left the church's interior looking like a banqueting hall. Round the corner in Clivio Scauro is a door leading to labyrinthine excavations: from four different buildings – including the house of fourth-century martyrs John and Paul – and dating from the first century AD on, the 20-odd excavated rooms include some evidently used for secret Christian worship. Call ahead for tours in English.

Arancia Blu p114

Santi Quattro Coronati

Via dei Santi Quattro 20 (06 7047 5427). **Open** *Church & cloister* 10-11.45am, 4-5.30pm Mon-Sat; 9.30-10.30am, 4-5.45pm Sun. *Oratory* 9.30am-noon, 3.30-5.45pm daily. **Map** p102 C4 ㉘

A fourth-century church here was rebuilt as a fortified monastery in the 11th century; the outsized apse is from the original church. The church has an upper-level *matronium*, where women sat during religious functions. There is a beautiful cloister (from the early 13th century). In the oratory next to the church (ring the bell and ask for the key) are frescoes, also painted in the 13th century as a defence of the popes' temporal power. They show a pox-ridden Constantine being healed by Pope Sylvester, crowning him with a tiara and giving him a cap to symbolise the pope's spiritual and earthly authority.

Santo Stefano Rotondo

Via di Santo Stefano Rotondo 7 (06 421 191). **Open** *Oct-Mar* 9.30am-12.30pm, 3-5pm Tue-Sat; 9.30am-12.30pm Sun. *Apr-Sept* 9am-noon, 4-6pm Tue-Sat; 9.30am-12.30pm Sun. **Map** p102 B5 ㉙

One of the very few round churches in Rome, Santo Stefano dates from the fifth century. The church is exceptionally beautiful, with its Byzantine-inspired simplicity. The 34 horrifically graphic frescoes of martyrs being boiled, stretched and slashed, added in the 16th century, disturb the atmosphere somewhat.

Scala Santa & Sancta Sanctorum

Piazza di San Giovanni in Laterano (06 772 6641). **Open** *Scala Santa* Oct-Mar 6.15am-noon, 3-6pm daily Apr-Sept 6.15-noon, 3.30-6.30pm daily. *Sancta Sanctorum* (booking obligatory) Oct-Mar 10.30-11.30am, 3-4pm Mon, Tue, Thur-Sun; 3-4pm Wed. Apr-Sept 10.30-11.30am, 3.30-4.30pm Mon, Tue, Thur-Sun; 3.30-4.30pm Sun. **Admission** *Scala Santa* free. *Sancta Sanctorum* €3.50. No credit cards. **Map** p103 D4 ㉚

Tradition says that these are the stairs that Jesus climbed in Pontius Pilate's house before being sent to his crucifixion. They were brought to Rome in the fourth century by St Helena, mother of the Emperor Constantine. A crawl up the Scala Santa has been a fixture on every serious pilgrim's list ever since.

come, good renditions of Roman favourites and a small, well-priced wine list. Service can be very slow.

Luzzi
Via San Giovanni in Laterano 88 (06 709 6332). **Meals served** noon-3pm, 7pm-midnight Mon, Tue, Thur-Sun. Closed 2wks Aug. €€ **Map** p102 B4 ❸❸
On busy nights (and most are) this neighbourhood trat is the loudest and most crowded 40 square metres in Rome. Perfectly decent pizzas, pasta dishes and *secondi*, which, on our last visit, included an excellent baked lamb (*abbacchio*) with potatoes. The outside tables operate all year round.

Shopping

Immediately outside the Roman walls by the basilica of San Giovanni, via Sannio is home each morning, from Monday to Friday, and all day Saturday to three long corridors of stalls piled high with new and second-hand low-priced clothes.

Soul Food
Via San Giovanni in Laterano 192-194 (06 7045 2025). **Open** 10.30am-1.30pm, 3.30-8pm Tue-Sat. Closed 2wks Aug. **Map** p102 C4 ❸❹
This vintage record shop is a record collector's heaven: indie, punk, beat, exotica, lounge, rockabilly and more.

Nightlife

Coming Out
Via San Giovanni in Laterano 8 (06 700 9871/www.comingout.it). **Open** 11am-2am daily. **Map** p102 B4 ❸❺
This teeming pub offers beers, cocktails and a reasonably wide range of snacks to a predominantly youthful crowd of gay men and women. It's a good place to meet before heading off in search of something a bit more frantic or upbeat. However, there is karaoke here on Wednesdays and live music on Thursdays. Unfortunately, the pub was the object of an arson attack early in 2008.

At the top of the Holy Stairs (but also accessible by non-holy stairs to the left) is the pope's private chapel, the Sancta Sanctorum. In a glass case on the left wall is a fragment of the table on which the Last Supper was supposedly served. The exquisite 13th-century frescoes in the lunettes and on the ceiling are attributed to Cimabue.

Eating & drinking

Café Café
Via dei Santi Quattro 44 (06 700 8743). **Open** 11am-1am daily. Closed 2wks Aug. € **Map** p102 B4 ❸❶
A café, yes, but also a perfect spot for lunch – with soups, salads and pasta dishes – after a stomp around the Colosseum. There's a brunch buffet from 11.30am to 4pm on Sundays. Opens daily in summer.

Il Bocconcino
Via Ostilia 23 (06 7707 9175). **Meals served** 12.30-3.30pm, 7.30-11.30pm Mon, Tue, Thur-Sun. Closed 3wks Aug. €€. **Map** p102 B4 ❸❷
This trat near the Colosseum looks like it's been around for generations but it's a recent addition, with a friendly wel-

Micca Club

*Via Pietro Micca 7A (06 8744 0079/
www.miccaclub.com).* **Open** 10pm-4am
Thur-Sat; 6pm-2am Sun. Closed May-
mid Sept. **Admission** free Thur, Sun;
€5 Fri, Sat; €10 special events.
Map p103 E3 ㊱

A huge spiral staircase leads down to
this cavernous underground venue
with one of Rome's most eclectic
nightlife programmes, ranging from
live acts and international DJ sets to
serious jazz. There's a music-fuelled
Sunday vintage market from 6pm.

Skyline

*Via Pontremoli 36 (06 700 9431/
www.skylineclub.it).* **Open** 10.30pm-
4am daily. **Map** p103 E5 ㊲

This ever-popular gay club has become
even more *the* place to be since its
recent move to new, larger premises.
The crowd is relaxed and mixed, with
constant movement between the bar
areas, the video parlour and the cruisy
cubicle and dark areas. Hosts naked
parties on Mondays.

San Lorenzo

San Lorenzo has a history of
rebellion. It was planned in the
1880s as a working-class ghetto,
with few public services or
amenities. Unsurprisingly, it
soon developed into Rome's
most politically radical district.

These days it retains some of its
threadbare, jerry-built, working-
class character. But it's more
radical-chic than just plain radical:
a constant influx of artists and
students mingles with the few
surviving salt-of-the-earth locals.

Along the north-east side is the
vast Verano cemetery, with the
basilica of **San Lorenzo fuori
le Mura** by its entrance.

To the north-west, the **Città
universitaria** (the main campus
of Europe's biggest university, La
Sapienza), with buildings designed
in the 1930s by Marcello Piacentini

and Arnaldo Foschini, shows the
Fascist take on the architecture
of higher education.

Sights & museums

San Lorenzo fuori le Mura

Piazzale del Verano 3 (06 491 511).
Open *Oct-Mar* 8am-12.30pm, 4-7pm
daily. *Apr-Sept* 7.30am-12.30pm, 4-
8pm daily. **Map** p103 F1 ㊳

This basilica was donated by
Constantine to house the remains of St
Lawrence after the saint met his fiery
end on a griddle. Rebuilt in the sixth
century, it was later united with a
neighbouring church. Bombs plunged
through the roof in 1943, making San
Lorenzo the only Roman church to suf-
fer war damage, but it was painstak-
ingly reconstructed by 1949. On the
right side of the 13th-century portico
are frescoes from the same period,
showing scenes from the life of St
Lawrence. Inside the triumphal arch
are sixth-century mosaics.

Eating & drinking

Arancia Blu

Via dei Latini 55-65 (06 445 4105).
Meals served 8.30pm-midnight Mon-
Sat; 12.30-3pm, 8.30pm-midnight Sun.
€€. **Map** p103 E2 ㊴

This vegetarian restaurant has shaken
off its previously rather earnest macro-
biotic origins and become a stylish
urban bistro with a great wine list;
good-value meat-free fare in a space
with a jazzy, alternative feel. The pota-
to-filled ravioli topped with pecorino
cheese and mint is excellent; the large
cheese selection and well-priced wine
list are pluses.

Bar à Book

*Via dei Piceni 23 (06 4544 5438/www.
barabook.it).* **Open** 4pm-midnight Tue-
Thur; 4pm-2am Fri, Sat; 11am-8pm
Sun. Closed Aug. **Map** p103 F2 ㊵

With its long wooden central table and
shelves piled high with books, this café
in artsy San Lorenzo looks like the
design-conscious study of an eccentric
1960s-loving academic. In fact, it's the

Pigneto fare

Primo

In the last couple of years Il Pigneto, just east of Porta Maggiore, has achieved that critical mass of bars, restaurants and trendsters that turns a below-the-radar district hip.

Squeezed between via Casilina and via Prenestina, Il Pigneto is a mix of houses and low-rise 1960s condominiums. Its proximity to the San Lorenzo stockyards meant that the area suffered heavy wartime bombing. When development came it was piecemeal. The anarchic, bohemian feel of the place attracted arty types like Pier Paolo Pasolini (much of his first film, *Accattone*, was shot here).

Today, partly-pedestrianised via del Pigneto – the central thoroughfare, and home to a morning market from Monday to Saturday – is lined with cool bars like **Pigneto 41** (yes, it's at no.41; closed Sun). Pick of the new restaurants is bustling Slow Food-inspired **Primo** (46, 06 701 3827, www.primoalpigneto. it, closed Mon). Round the corner,

book-lined wine bar **Il Tiaso** (via Perugia 20, 333 284 5283) is deliciously laid-back: like many Pigneto watering-holes, it makes for a refreshing contrast from the *centro storico*, where similar bars can be snooty and overpriced.

Via del Pigneto, and the district itself, is sliced in two by a rail cutting. The area to the east of the pedestrian bridge has more modern *palazzi* than the western triangle. Two of the area's most interesting new restaurants are here. Before its 2007 makeover, **Bar Necci** (via Fanfulla da Lodi 68, 06 9760 1552, www.necci1924. com, open daily) was an old blokes' bar; now it's a shabby-chic brunch, lunch and dinner hangout, with quality creative Italian cooking from personable English chef Ben.

A little further along the main drag, the **Locanda dell'Interprete** (via del Pigneto 207, 334 392 3468, www.locandainterpreter. com, closed Sun) offers good-value gourmet Italian cuisine in a room decorated with curious Stonehenge fantasy murals.

ROME BY AREA

latest creation of the people who own Tram Tram, a restaurant just round the corner (via dei Reti 44, closed Mon, €€) that serves excellent creative Roman and Puglian specialities. In the bar, *aperitivi* come with a DJ on Saturdays from 7.30pm.

B-Said
Via Tiburtina 135 (06 446 9204/ www.said.it). **Open** 10am-midnight Mon-Sat. Closed 2wks Aug. **Map** p103 E2 ④
Said has been producing exquisite chocolate in this factory in San Lorenzo since 1923. But its industrial-chic tea room-restaurant, with a fire-place, comfy armchairs and glassed-over courtyard, is a recent addition. Chocolate pops up in unexpected places on the full lunch menu (€€); from 7.30pm, €10 will get you a decent glass of wine plus anything you like from a buffet of delicious quiches and salads.

Cribbio!
NEW *Via dei Campani 65 (06 490 217).* **Meals served** 8.30pm-midnight Tue-Sun. Closed 2wks Aug. **Map** p103 E3 ④
A recent addition to San Lorenzo's thriving eating scene, Cribbio! serves interesting versions of some local favourites, including a great *tonnarelli cacio e pepe* (pasta with cheese and pepper) and a wonderful tuna tartare. Service can be a little frosty.

Marcello
Via dei Campani 12 (06 446 3311). **Meals served** 7.30-11.30pm Mon-Fri. Closed 3wks Aug. **€**. No credit cards. **Map** p103 E3 ④
Inside this anonymous-looking trat hordes of hungry students wolf food down at old wooden tables. Alongside offal specialities like tripe and *pajata* are light and more creative dishes such as *straccetti ai carciofi* (strips of veal with artichokes).

Uno e Bino
Via degli Equi 58 (06 446 0702). **Meals served** 8.30-11.30pm Tue-Sun. Closed 2wks Aug. **€€€**. **Map** p103 E3 ④

An elegantly minimalist Italian restaurant with one of the best quality-price ratios in Rome. With such pared-back decor, the place needs to be full to work properly. Chef Giovanni Passerini has moved to Paris but the team he assembled continues to produce his audacious combinations of vegetables and herbs with fish, meat and game. Book well in advance.

Nightlife

Circolo degli Artisti
Via Casilina Vecchia 42 (06 7030 5684/www.circoloartisti.it). **Open** 9.30pm-1am Tue-Thur for concerts only; 9pm-4.30am Fri, Sat; 7pm-midnight Sun. Closed Aug. **Admission** from €6, depending on event. No credit cards. **Map** off p103 F4 ④
This is Rome's most popular venue for small- and medium-scale bands from international alternative music circuits. There's a popular gay night on Fridays. On Saturdays (admission free after midnight), 'Screamadelica' offers top-quality concerts by some of Europe's best alternative artists and emerging Italian bands.

La Palma
Via G Mirri 35 (06 4359 9029/www. lapalmaclub.it). Closed for restoration at time of going to press, due to reopen summer 2008. **Map** off p103 F1 ④
Beyond San Lorenzo, La Palma is an oasis in a post-industrial landscape, offering good concerts and quality DJ sets. The schedule is eclectic, though very jazz-focused. In the summer, it hosts a jazz festival in a spacious courtyard with restaurant.

Locanda Atlantide
Via dei Lucani 22B (06 4470 4540/ www.locandatlantide.it). **Open** 9.30pm-3am Tue-Sun. Closed mid June-Sept. **Admission** free-€10. No credit cards. **Map** p103 E3 ④
An unpretentious venue hosting an array of events ranging from concerts and DJ acts to theatrical performances. It pulls an alternative crowd. Extra charge for concerts.

View from Parco Savello

The Aventine & Testaccio

Aventine & Caracalla

The Aventine hill is a leafy, quietly
monied place first colonised by
King Ancius Marcius in the seventh
century BC. The foreigners and
other undesirables who had fled
here from the river port below were
driven out when the hill was set
aside for plebeians in 456 BC.
And here the plebeians remained,
building temples and villas.

The Aventine is a lovely place
for a walk. The delightful Parco
Savello – still surrounded by the
crenellated walls of a 12th-century
fortress of the Savello family –
has dozens of orange trees and
a spectacular view over the city,
especially at sunset. In nearby
piazza Cavalieri di Malta, peek
through the keyhole of the priory
of the Knights of Malta to enjoy the
surrealistic surprise designed by
Gian Battista Piranesi: a telescopic
view of the dome of St Peter's.

Across busy viale Aventino
is the similarly well-heeled San
Saba district and, beyond the
white cuboids of the UN's Food
and Agricultural Organisation,
the giant **Baths of Caracalla**.

Sights & museums

Baths of Caracalla
*Viale delle Terme di Caracalla 52
(06 0608).* **Open** 9am-2pm Mon; 9am-
1hr before sunset Tue-Sun. **Admission**

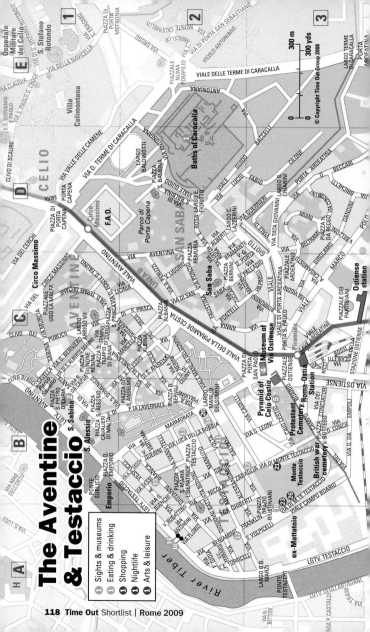

The Aventine & Testaccio

- ① Sights & museums
- ① Eating & drinking
- ① Shopping
- ① Nightlife
- ① Arts & leisure

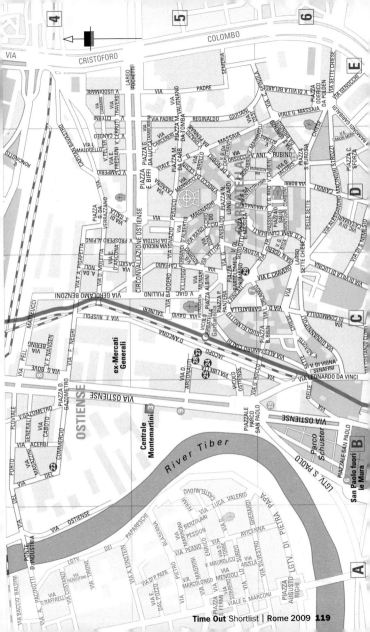

€6 (includes Tomb of Cecilia Metella & Villa dei Quintili); €3 reductions. No credit cards. **Map** p118 D2 ❶

The high-vaulted ruins of the Terme di Caracalla are peaceful today, but were anything but tranquil in their heyday, when up to 1,600 Romans could sweat it out in the baths and gyms. You can get some idea of their original splendour from the fragments of mosaic and statuary that litter the site.

The baths were built between AD 213 and 216. The two cavernous rooms down the sides were the gymnasia, where Romans engaged in such strenuous sports as toss-the-beanbag. There was also a large open-air *natatio* (pool), saunas and baths of varying temperatures, as well as a library, a garden, shops and stalls. Underneath it all was a network of tunnels where slaves treaded the giant wheels that pumped clean water up to bathers. Caracalla's baths were in use until 537, when the Visigoths sacked Rome and severed the city's aqueducts.

Santa Sabina

Piazza Pietro d'Illiria 1 (06 57 941). **Open** 6.30am-12.45pm, 3-6pm daily. **Map** p118 B1 ❷

Santa Sabina was built in the fifth century over an early Christian place of worship; the bit of mosaic floor visible through a grate at the entrance is all that remains. Restored mercilessly in the 1930s, the church is now arguably the closest thing to an unadulterated ancient basilica in Rome. The fifth-century cypress doors are carved with biblical scenes. The nave's Corinthian columns support an arcade decorated with ninth-century marble inlay work; the choir dates from the same period. Selenite has been placed in the windows as it would have been in the ninth century. A window in the entrance porch looks on to the place where St Dominic is said to have planted an orange tree brought from Spain in 1220. The beautiful 13th-century cloister has just been restored.

Testaccio & Ostiense

In the shadow of the exclusive Aventine hill, Testaccio is everything its elegant neighbour isn't: bustling, noisy, workaday and populated by brusquely salt of the earth long-term residents

Testaccio market p126

The slow road to redevelopment

Former abattoir at Testaccio

After years of neglect, Rome's immense former abattoir on the Testaccio riverfront is finally coming back to life – though not assertively enough for most Romans to notice.

The sheer size of the place – more than 46,000 square metres (495,000 square feet) of built space in grounds totalling 90,000 square metres (968,000 square feet) – meant a complete overhaul was out of the question. Instead, the *ex-mattatoio* has been subjected to a jigsaw of partial makeovers, its various splendid pavilions being assigned to lucky users one by one.

Part of the complex is occupied by the architecture department of a Roman university, while the **MACRO** contemporary art gallery's (p98) *Future* branch occupies two enormous refrigeration units, where works are displayed amid the machinery of butchery.

The latest – still largely unsung – addition is a fairtrade/organic food mart (largo Dino Frisullo, open 11am-8pm Tue-Sun), complete with a delightfully wholesome café-snack bar (open same hours) and restaurant (open Tue-Sat dinner and Sun lunch).

The setting is unique, with eccentric **Monte Testaccio** – a hill constructed entirely of Roman potsherds – looming above, and a vast, empty piazza stretching out below towards the cast-iron holding pens of the *campo boario* (cattle market), now occupied by the straggly beasts that pull Rome's horse-drawn buggies. In the centre of the piazza officials used to oversee the goings-on in this source of all the meat in Rome.

The eco-friendly occupants of the newly opened pavilion are doing their best to fill their space, with child-friendly events like juggling and face-painting in the piazza most weekends (ask in the shop for details). But a more concerted effort will be needed to give the abattoir the buzz it deserves.
■ www.cittadellaltraeconomia.org
■ www.macro.roma.museum

ROME BY AREA

Centrale Montemartini p122

who have, however, had to take an influx of young(ish) professionals in their stride.

Locals of all stripes mix happily in the gardens of piazza Santa Maria Liberatrice on warm evenings, linked by an almost universal devotion to the AS Roma football team and an indulgent fondness for the elderly ladies who still traipse to the market in their slippers of a morning.

There are no monuments here, just a few traces of Testaccio's industrious past: an ancient river port, a rubbish tip composed of discarded potsherds (Monte Testaccio) and an abandoned abattoir slowly being made over into an arts centre-cum-alternative marketplace (p121). It's also home to Rome's most happening nightlife.

Further south, via Ostiense slices through once run-down suburbs earmarked for some interesting development: Dutch architectural superstar Rem Koolhaas is turning the former wholesale fruit and vegetable market into a complex of youth-oriented exhibition spaces, sports centres and shopping centres – what the authorities describe as 'Rome's Covent Garden'.

However, the signs of change and renewal have been visible for a while – ever since the **Centrale Montemartini** power station was converted into one of the capital's most striking museums, the **Teatro Palladium** reopened, revamped and with a fascinating programme, and Testaccio's vibrant after-hours activity began seeping south.

Sights & museums

Centrale Montemartini
Via Ostiense 106 (06 574 8042/ www.centralemontemartini.org). **Open** 9am-7pm Tue-Sun. **Admission**

€4.50; €2.50 reductions; extra charge during exhibitions. No credit cards. **Map** p119 B5 ❸
The Centrale Montemartini contains the leftover ancient statuary from the Capitoline Museums – but the dregs are pretty impressive; moreover, the setting itself is worth a visit. Fauns and Minervas, bacchic revellers and Apollos are all starkly white but oddly at home against the gleaming machinery of this former generating station.

Museum of Via Ostiense

Via R Persichetti 3 (06 574 3193).
Open 9.30am-1.30pm, 2.30-4.30pm Tue, Thur; 9.30am-1.30pm Wed, Fri, Sat, 1st & 3rd Sun of mth. **Admission** free. **Map** p118 C3 ❹
This third-century AD gatehouse, called Porta Ostiensis in antiquity and Porta San Paolo today, contains a quaint collection of artefacts and prints describing the history of via Ostiense – the Ostian Way, built in the third century BC to join Rome to its port at Ostia. There's also a large-scale model

of the ancient port. Best of all, you can cross the crenellated walkway for a bird's-eye view of the true finesse of the modern Roman motorist.

Protestant Cemetery

Via Caio Cestio 6 (06 574 1900/ www.protestantcemetery.it). **Open** 9am-5pm Mon-Sat; 9am-1pm Sun. **Admission** free (donation expected). **Map** p118 B3 ❺
This heavenly oasis of calm in the midst of a ruckus of traffic has been the resting place for foreigners who have passed on to a better world since 1784. Officially the 'non-Catholic' cemetery, this charmingly old-world corner of the city accommodates Buddhists, Russian Orthodox Christians and atheists. In the older sector you'll find the grave of John Keats, who coughed his last at the age of 26. Close by is the tomb of Shelley, who died a year after Keats in a boating accident.

San Paolo fuori le Mura

Via Ostiense 184 (06 4543 5574/ www.abbaziasanpaolo.net). **Open** *Basilica* 7am-7pm daily. *Cloister* 9am-1pm, 3-6pm daily. **Map** p119 B6 ❻
Constantine founded this basilica to commemorate the martyrdom of St Paul nearby. The church has been rebuilt several times; most of the present church is only 150 years old. Features to have survived include 11th-century doors; a strange 12th-century Easter candlestick featuring human-, lion- and goat-headed beasts spewing the vine of life from their mouths; and a 13th-century canopy above the altar, by Arnolfo di Cambio. In the nave are mosaic portraits of all the popes from Peter to the present incumbent. There are only seven spaces left; once they are filled, the world, apparently, will end. In the confessio beneath the altar is the tomb of St Paul, topped by a stone slab pierced with holes through which devotees stuff bits of cloth to imbue them with the apostle's holiness. For information on the celebrations marking the 2,000th anniversary of Paul's birth, see p142. Monks chant vespers at 5pm daily.

ROME BY AREA

Eating & drinking

See also Volpetti (p126).

Al Ristoro degli Angeli

Via Luigi Orlando 2 (06 5143 6020/ www.ristorodegliangeli.it). **Meals served** 8-11.30pm Mon-Sat. Closed Aug, 2wks Sept. **€€€**. **Map** p119 C5 ❼

Rather off the beaten track in the charming 1920s workers' suburb of Garbatella, the Ristoro's vibe is old-style French bistro but the excellent food is all Italian. Many organic products go into dishes such as pasta with fresh tuna, capers and wild fennel, or beef millefeuille with radicchio and smoked provola cheese. There are always fish and vegetarian options. The wine list is small but interesting, the home-made desserts are luscious and there are tables outside.

Andreotti

Via Ostiense 54B (06 575 0773). **Open** 7.30am-9.30pm daily. **Map** p119 ❽

The Andreotti family claims to serve up 700 cups of its excellent coffee every day, and that was before a recent overhaul doubled the space and lengthened the counter to allow even more scope for sampling this historic bar's excellent breakfast *cornetti*, cakes, light lunchtime snacks and evening *aperitivi* with nibbles.

Bishoku Kobo

Via Ostiense 110B (06 574 4190). **Meals served** 7.30pm-midnight Mon, Sat; 12.30-3pm, 7.30pm-midnight Tue-Fri. Closed 1wk Aug. **€€**. No credit cards. **Map** p119 B5 ❾

This Japanese restaurant is well placed for visitors to the collection of antique statues in the Centrale Montemartini. The food is classic Japanese, the ambience is pure neighbourhood trattoria.

Checchino dal 1887

Via di Monte Testaccio 30 (06 574 6318/www.checchino-dal-1887.com). **Meals served** 12.30-3pm, 8pm-midnight Tue-Sat. Closed Aug; 1wk Dec. **€€€€**. **Map** p118 A3 ❿

Imagine a pie shop becoming a top-class restaurant, and the odd mix of humble decor, elegant service, hearty food and huge cellar falls into place. Vegetarians should give the Mariani family's restaurant a wide berth: offal is the speciality. Pasta dishes like the *bucatini all'amatriciana* are delicious.

Da Felice

Via Mastro Giorgio 29 (06 574 6800). **Meals served** 12.30-3pm, 8-11.30pm Mon-Sat; 12.30-3pm Sun. Closed 3wks Aug. **€€€**. **Map** p118 B2 ⓫

This former spit-and-sawdust trat has had an industrial-chic makeover but its high-quality traditional fare – including classics such as *tonnarelli cacio e pepe* (p189) and *abbacchio al forno con patate* (baked lamb with potatoes) – remains as good as ever. The wine list is impressive. Be sure to book.

Il Seme e la Foglia

Via Galvani 18 (06 574 3008). **Open** 8am-2am Mon-Sat; 6pm-2am Sun. Closed 3wks Aug. No credit cards. **Map** p118 B3 ⓬

This lively daytime snack bar and evening pre-club stop is always packed with students from the music school opposite. At midday there's generally a pasta dish, plus large salads (€5-€7) and creative filled rolls.

L'Oasi della Birra

Piazza Testaccio 38 (06 574 6122). **Open** 12.30-3pm, 7pm-12.30am Mon-Sat; 7pm-12.30am Sun. Closed 2wks Aug. **Map** p118 B2 ⓭

The 'Oasis of Beer' has more than 500 brews on offer, including beers from award-winning Italian microbreweries. The selection of wines by the bottle is almost as impressive. Food ranges from snacks (*crostini*, *bruschette*, a well-stocked cheese board) to full-scale meals with a Teutonic slant. There are tables outside too.

Piccolo Alpino

Via Orazio Antinori 5 (06 574 1386). **Meals served** 12.30-2.30pm, 6-11pm Tue-Sun. **€**. No credit cards. **Map** p118 A2 ⓮

Protestant cemetery p123

There are no frills in this very cheap, very cheerful eaterie where the pizzas are good and some of the pasta dishes – the *spaghetti con le vongole* stands out – are perfectly acceptable too (though these will push the bill into the €€ bracket).

Remo

Piazza Santa Maria Liberatrice 44 (06 574 6270). **Meals served** 7pm-1am Mon-Sat. Closed 3wks Aug. €. **Map** p118 B2 ⑮

This pizzeria is a Testaccio institution. You can choose to sit at wonky tables on the pavement, or in the deafening interior. The thin-crust Roman pizzas are excellent, as are the *bruschette al pomodoro*.

Satollo

NEW *Via Rubattino 22 (06 5728 9587/ www.satollo.com).* **Meals served** 8-11pm Mon-Sat. €€€. **Map** p118 A2 ⑯

Newcomers to the dining scene Chiara and Davide brought an enthusiastic young team to this venue in Testaccio

in spring 2008. With their home-made bread and pasta, and attentively sourced ingredients – including excellent fish – their creative Italian cuisine and laid-back upmarket-trat ambience seem to have filled a niche successfully from the start.

Tallusa

Via Beniamino Franklin 11 (333 752 3506). **Open** 11am-4pm, 5pm-1.30am daily. €. **Map** p118 A2 ⑰

Always packed, this tiny eat-in or takeaway joint specialises in southern and eastern Mediterranean cuisine – ranging from Sicilian specialities to falafel and a full range of Lebanese-style mezedes. It's very friendly and very cheap but rather erratic in its opening times.

Tuttifrutti

Via Luca della Robbia 3A (06 575 7902). **Meals served** 7.30-11.30pm Mon-Sat. Closed 3wks Aug. €€€. **Map** p118 B2 ⑱

Al Ristoro degli Angeli p124

Behind an anonymous glass door, this trattoria is Testaccio's best-value dining experience, at the lower end of this price bracket. Michele guides you through a changing menu of creative fare. There is usually a veggie option and the wine is excellently priced.

Zampagna

Via Ostiense 179 (06 574 2306).
Meals served 12.30-2.30pm Mon-Sat. Closed Aug. **€€**. No credit cards. **Map** p119 B6 ⑲
This is basic Roman cooking as it once was, with filling dishes for the refined carnivore. Primi include *spaghetti alla carbonara* or *tagliatelle alla gricia* (with bacon and pecorino cheese), while most of the second courses are served swimming in the thick house *sugo* (tomato sauce). Service is brisk.

Shopping

The produce market (Mon-Sat, mornings) in piazza Testaccio is an excellent place to pick up the wherewithal for a picnic. Nearby streets, and the north-western aisle

of the market itself, have been colonised by vendors of shoes of every description, including bargains on last season's models. For men's shoes, stop by the market on Saturday. See also p23.

Volpetti

Via Marmorata 47 (06 574 2352/ www.fooditaly.com). **Open** 8am-2pm, 5-8.15pm Mon-Sat. **Map** p118 B2 ⑳
This is one of the best delis in Rome. It's hard to get away without one of the jolly assistants loading you up with samples – pleasant, but painful on the wallet. Around the corner is Volpetti Più (via A Volta 8-10, 06 574 4306, open 10am-3.30pm, 5.30-9.30pm Mon-Sat), a self-service restaurant where you can taste the deli's delicious cured meats and cheeses, along with pizza, salads and more.

Nightlife

Akab

Via di Monte Testaccio 68-69 (06 5725 0585/www.akabcave.com). **Open** midnight-5am Tue-Sat. Closed Aug.

Admission (incl 1 drink) €10-€20.
Map p118 B3 ㉑
This long-term fixture of the Testaccio scene has an underground cellar and a street-level room, plus a garden for warmer months. Tuesday L-Ektrica sessions feature international DJs. There's retro on Wednesday, R&B on Thursday and house on Friday and Saturday.

Alpheus

Via del Commercio 36 (06 574 7826/ www.alpheus.it). **Open** 10.30pm-4am Fri-Sun; other days vary. Closed July & Aug. **Admission** depends on event. **Map** p119 B4 ㉒
An eclectic club with a varied crowd, the Alpheus has four halls for live gigs, music festivals, theatre and cabaret, all followed by a disco. The music changes nightly and from room to room: rock, chart R&B and Latin alongside world music, retro and happy trash. Watch out for the regular *Gorgeous I Am* gay events.

Caruso-Café de Oriente

Via di Monte Testaccio 36 (06 574 5019/www.carusocafedeoriente.com). **Open** 10pm-4am Tue-Sun. Closed Aug. **Admission** (incl 1 drink) €8-€10; free Sun. No credit cards. **Map** p118 B3 ㉓
A must for lovers of salsa, this club offers Latin American tunes every night apart from Saturday (anything from reggae to hip hop), and live acts almost daily. There's a roof terrace.

Classico Village

Via Libetta 3 (349 596 2398/ www.classicovillage.it). **Open** 9pm-1.30am Mon-Thur; 9pm-4am Fri, Sat. **Admission** €5-€15. **Map** p119 C5 ㉔
This former factory in trendy Ostiense can offer up to three (mainly rock-based) events simultaneously in its large spaces, all of which face on to a courtyard – a heavenly spot to chill on warm evenings. DJ sets usually follow shows.

Goa

Via Libetta 13 (06 574 8277). **Open** midnight-4am Thur-Sat. Closed mid May-mid Sept. **Admission** (incl 1 drink) €10-€25. **Map** p119 C5 ㉕
One of the best of Rome's fashionable clubs, Goa is a techno-ethno fantasy of iron and steel with oriental-style statues and colours. Thursday's Ultrabeat brings Europe's top electronic music DJs. Goa also opens some Sundays (5pm-4am); there's a women-only event on the last Sunday of the month.

L'Alibi

Via di Monte Testaccio 40-44 (06 574 3448/www.lalibi.it). **Open** 11.30pm-5am Thur-Sun. **Admission** (incl 1 drink) €10-€15. **Map** p118 B3 ㉖
Rome's original gay club, the Alibi is still, in theory, a great place to dance away, with a well-oiled sound system. But it's showing its age. And a new straight-friendly approach and Friday hetero night have proved something of a turn-off all round.

La Saponeria

Via degli Argonauti 20 (393 966 1321/ www.saponeriaclub.it). **Open** 11.30pm-5am Fri, Sat. Closed mid May-mid Sept. **Admission** €5-€15. **Map** p119 C5 ㉗
One of the liveliest clubs in Ostiense, this stylish, curvy, white space gets hopelessly packed on weekends. Friday is techno and electronic, Saturday is hip hop and R&B.

Rashomon

Via degli Argonauti 16 (347 340 5710). **Open** 11pm-4am Wed-Sun. Closed July & Aug. **Admission** free-€10. No credit cards. **Map** p119 C5 ㉘
Run by afficionados of alternative clubs in London and Berlin, Rashomon offers electro-rock, indie, electronica and new wave. There are live acts, including emerging locals.

Arts & leisure

Teatro Palladium

Piazza Bartolomeo Romano 8 (06 5733 2768/www.teatro-palladium.it). **Map** p119 C5 ㉙
This beautiful 1920s theatre in Garbatella offers a mix of top-quality electronic music acts, cutting-edge theatre, art performances and, oddly, university seminars on diverse topics.

ROME BY AREA

Statue of Garibaldi p138

Trastevere & the Gianicolo

Trastevere

Located on the Tiber's right bank, picturesque ivy-and-washing draped Trastevere is the Rome of your romantic dreams. It's quaint but buzzing, historical but without the imposing ruins and galleries you feel you have to 'do' on the other side of the river.

Here – across the Tiber: *trans Tiberim* – your main tasks will include rambling through narrow cobbled streets and selecting the likeliest-looking bar for *aperitivi*. And if your fellow ramblers are predominantly tourists (rather than the few genuine *trasteverini* who haven't been priced out of this exclusive enclave), well… that's

not so bad. After all, you can eat well, soak up the rustic charm and generally bask in the laid-back feel of the place.

Trasteverini claim descent from slave stock. Through the Imperial period, much of the *trans Tiberim* area was agricultural, with farms, vineyards, country villas and gardens laid out for the pleasure of the Caesars. Trastevere was a working-class district in papal Rome and remained so until well after Unification.

Viale Trastevere slices the district in two. At the hub of the much-visited western part is piazza **Santa Maria in Trastevere** with its eponymous church. Fewer tourists make it to the warren of cobbled alleys in the eastern half, where craftsmen still ply their trades around the lovely church of **Santa Cecilia in Trastevere**.

Further upriver, Ponte Sisto provides handy pedestrian access back across to the *centro storico*.

Sights & museums

Museo di Roma in Trastevere

Piazza Sant'Egidio 1B (06 581 6563/ www.museodiromaintrastevere.it). **Open** 10am-8pm Tue-Sun. **Admission** €3; €1.50 reductions; extra charge during exhibitions. No credit cards. **Map** p130 C3 ❶

This rather dusty folklore museum, housed in a 17th-century convent, has a series of watercolours of 19th century Rome and some whiskery waxwork tableaux evoking the life of 18th- and 19th-century *trasteverini*.

Orto botanico (Botanical Garden)

Largo Cristina di Svezia 24 (06 4991 7146). **Open** *Nov-Mar* 9am-5.30pm Tue-Sat. *Apr-Oct* 9am-6.30pm Tue-Sat. **Admission** €4; €2 reductions. No credit cards. **Map** p130 B2 ❷

Established in 1883, Rome's Botanical Gardens are a welcome haven from the rigours of a dusty, hot city: plants tumble over steps and into fountains and fish ponds, creating luxuriant hidden corners disturbed only by frolicking children.

Palazzo Corsini – Galleria Nazionale d'Arte Antica

Via della Lungara 10 (06 6880 2323/ www.galleriaborghese.it). **Open** 8.30am-7.30pm Tue-Sun. **Admission** €4; €2 reductions. No credit cards. **Map** p130 C2 ❸

A 17th-century convert to Catholicism, Sweden's Queen Christina established her glittering court here in 1662. The stout monarch smoked a pipe, wore trousers and entertained female and (ordained) male lovers here. Today her home houses part of the national art collection, with scores of Madonnas

and Children (the most memorable is a Madonna by Van Dyck). Other works include a pair of Annunciations by Guercino; two St Sebastians (one by Rubens, one by Annibale Carracci); Caravaggio's *St John the Baptist*; and a triptych by Fra Angelico. There's also a melancholy *Salome* by Guido Reni.

San Francesco a Ripa

Piazza San Francesco d'Assisi 88 (06 581 9020). **Open** 7.30am-noon, 4-7pm Mon-Sat; 7.30am-1pm, 4-7.30pm Sun. **Map** p131 E5 ❹

This church stands on the site of the hospice where St Francis of Assisi stayed when he visited Rome in 1219; a near-contemporary portrait hangs in the cell where the saint stayed. The original 13th-century church was rebuilt in the 1680s. It contains Bernini's sculpture of the Beata Ludovica Albertoni (1674), showing the aristocratic Franciscan nun dying in an agonised, sexually ambiguous Baroque ecstasy.

Santa Cecilia in Trastevere

Piazza Santa Cecilia 22 (06 589 9289). **Open** *Church* 9.30am-1.15pm, 4-8pm daily. *Cavallini frescoes* 10.15am-12.15pm Mon-Sat; 11.30am-12.30pm Sun. *Excavations* 7am-12.30pm, 4-6.30pm daily. **Admission** *Frescoes* €2.50. *Excavations* €2.50. No credit cards. **Map** p131 E4 ❺

This church stands on the site of a fifth-century building that was itself built over an older Roman house, part of which can be visited. According to legend it was the home of the martyr Cecilia: after an attempt to suffocate her in her bath, her persecutors tried to behead her with three strokes of an axe (the maximum permitted). She sang for the several days it took her to die, and so became the patron saint of music. Her tomb was opened in 1599, revealing her undecayed body. It disintegrated, but not before a sketch was made, on which Stefano Maderno based the sculpture below the high altar. Her sarcophagus is in the crypt. In the upstairs gallery is a small fragment of what must have been one of the world's

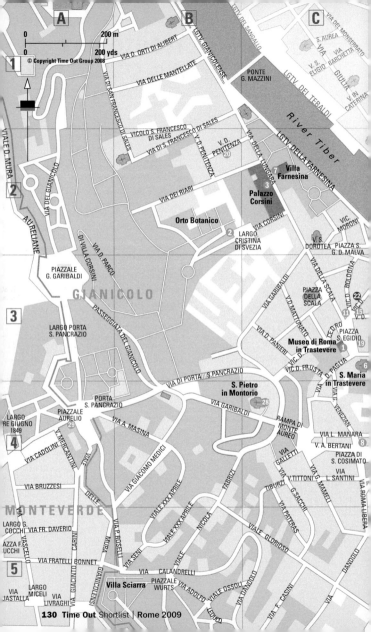

A

200 m
0
200 yds
0
© Copyright Time Out Group 2008

1

VIALE D. MURA

VIA D. ORTI DI ALIBERT

VIA DELLE MANTELLATE

VIA DI SAN FRANCESCO DI SALES

VICOLO S. FRANCESCO DI SALES

VIA DI S. FRANCESCO DI SALES

V. D. PENITENZA

V.D. PENITENZA 20

VIA DEI RIARI

2

VIA DEL GIANICOLO

VIA DEL GIANICOLO

AURELIANE

VIA DI VILLA CORSINI

VIA D. PARCO

PIAZZALE
G. GARIBALDI

Orto Botanico

2 LARGO
CRISTINA
DI SVEZIA

GIANICOLO

PASSEGGIATA DEL GIANICOLO

3

LARGO PORTA
S. PANCRAZIO

VIA DI PORTA S. PANCRAZIO

PORTA
S. PANCRAZIO

**S. Pietro
in Montorio**

28

VIA GARIBALDI

PIAZZALE
AURELIO

LARGO
RE GIUGNO
1849

29

V. MERCANTINI

V. CADOLINI

VIA A. MASINA

VIA GIACOMO MEDICI

4

VIA BRUZZESI

VIALE

DELLE

VIA P. ROSELLI

MURA

MONTEVERDE

LARGO G.
COCCHI VIA FR. DAVERIO

AZZA ROLI
UCCHI

VASCELLO

CARINI

VIA FRATELLI BONNET

VIA
GIACINTO

GIANICOLENSE

VIALE XXX APRILE

VIALE XXX APRILE

VIALE

VIA SENI

VIA G. SACCHI

NICOLAI

FABRIZI

5

VIA
JASTALLA

LARGO
MICELI

VIA
LIVRAGHI

Villa Sciarra

VIA CALANDRELLI

PIAZZALE
WURTS

VIA ADOLFO

VIA F. CASINI

VIALE OSSOLI

VIALE GLORIOSO

B

LGTV. DEL SANGALLO

LGTV. GIANICOLENSE

PONTE
G. MAZZINI

River Tiber

LGTV. DELLA FARNESINA

7 **Villa
Farnesina**

VIA DELLA LUNGARA

**Palazzo
Corsini**

3

VIA CORSINI

VIA GARIBALDI

V.D. MATTONATO

PIAZZA
DELLA
SCALA

VIA D. PANIERI

VIC. D.

PEDRO

VIA D. FRUSTA

VIA DI PORTA S. PANCRAZIO

RAMPA DI
MONTE
AUREO

VIA
GALLETTI

V. TITTONI

TIBURZI

G. SACCHI

VIALE GLORIOSO

VIA PATERAS

VIA DANDOLO

VIA
LEDUC

C

VIA DEL MONSERRATO

S. AUREA

VIA
S. ELIGIO

VIA
BARCHETTA

V. S.

GIULIA

V. IN
CATERINA

LGTV. DEL TEBALDI

PONTE

VIC.
MORONI

V. S.
DOROTEA

PIAZZA S.
G. D. MALVA

VIA DELLA SCALA

VIA DELLA PELLICCIA

VIC. D. BOLOGNA

22

11

15

19

PIAZZA
S. EGIDIO

**Museo di Roma
in Trastevere**

1

VIC. D.

6

**S. Maria
in Trastevere**

VIA F. VENEZIAN

VIA L. MANARA

V. A. BERTANI

8

PIAZZA DI
S. COSIMATO

VIA G. MAMELI

VIA
SANTINI

VIA
ROMA LIBERA

VIA G. MAMELI

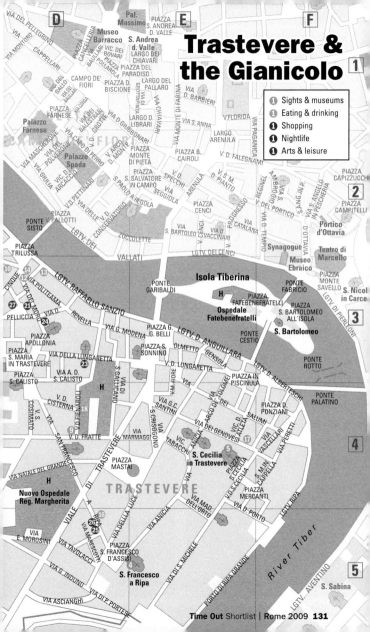

greatest frescoes. In this 13th-century *Last Judgement*, Pietro Cavallini flooded the apostles with a totally new kind of light – the same that was to reappear in Giotto's work.

Santa Maria in Trastevere

Piazza Santa Maria in Trastevere (06 581 4802). **Open** 7.30am-9pm daily. **Map** p130 C3 ⑥

Legend has it that a miraculous well of oil sprang from the ground where Santa Maria now stands the moment that Christ was born, and flowed to the Tiber all day. The first church on this site was begun in the early fourth century; the present building was erected in the 12th, and has wonderful mosaics. Those on the façade – from the 12th and 13th centuries – show Mary breastfeeding Christ, and ten women with crowns and lanterns (they may represent the parable of the wise and foolish virgins). Inside, the apse has a 12th-century mosaic of Jesus and his mother. Lower down, between the windows, there are beautiful 13th-century mosaics showing scenes from the life of the Virgin by Pietro Cavallini. The Madonna and Child with rainbow overhead is also by Cavallini. In the chapel immediately to the left of the high altar is a very rare sixth-century painting on wood of the Madonna.

Villa Farnesina

Via della Lungara 230 (06 6802 7268/ www.lincei.it). **Open** 9am-1pm Mon-Sat. **Admission** €5; €4 reductions. No credit cards. **Map** p130 C2 ⑦

Built in 1508-11 for rich papal banker Agostino Chigi, this palazzo became the property of the powerful Farnese family in 1577. Chigi was one of Raphael's principal patrons. The stunning frescoes in the ground-floor Loggia of Psyche were designed by Raphael but executed by his followers while the master dallied with his mistress. The Grace with her back turned, to the right of the door, is attributed to him. Around the corner, in the Loggia of Galatea, Raphael himself created the victorious goddess in her seashell chariot.

Freni e Frizioni

Eating & drinking

See also Lettere Caffè (p136) and
Cioccolato e vino (p136).

Alberto Ciarla

*Piazza San Cosimato 40 (06 581 8668/
www.albertociarla.com).* **Open**
Bottiglieria noon-midnight Mon-Sat.
Meals served *Restaurant* 8.30pm-
midnight Mon-Sat. Closed 1wk Aug.
€€-€€€€. **Map** p130 C4 ❽

This mirrors-and-glitz time warp of a
restaurant serves some of Rome's best
fish, with the emphasis on raw
seafood. The Ciarla experience is
unfailingly wonderful, but if the
(hefty) bill worries you, go for one of
the taster menus (from €50) or check
out Alberto's stylish wine bar, La
Bottiglieria di Alberto Ciarla, where
traditional Roman dishes are given a
creative twist and offered along with
a daunting selection of excellent wines.
Here you can perch and nibble or go
for a full meal; either way, the price tag
will be considerably lower.

Alle Fratte di Trastevere

*Via delle Fratte di Trastevere 49-50
(06 583 5775/www.allefrattedi
trastevere.com).* **Meals served**
noon-3pm, 6.30-11.30pm Mon, Tue,
Thur-Sat; 6.30-11.30pm Sun. Closed
2wks Aug. **€€**. **Map** p131 D4 ❾

The cheerful Alle Fratte does honest
Roman trattoria fare with Neapolitan
influences. Service is friendly, attentive
and bilingual. First courses, such as
pennette alla sorrentina (pasta with
tomatoes and mozzarella), come in generous portions. *Secondi* include roast
sea bream and veal escalopes in marsala.
Post-prandial *digestivi* flow freely.

Bir & Fud

NEW *Via Benedetta 23 (06 589 4016/
www.birefud.it).* **Meals served** 12.20-
3.30pm, 8pm-midnight daily. Closed 2wks
Aug. **€€**. **Map** p131 D3 ❿

Narrow and buzzing, Bir & Fud
serves exactly what the name
says: interesting beers from lesser-
known breweries, plus pizza,
bruschetta, mixed salads and some

very Roman offal. Food is super-fresh
and additive free. The venue opens at
6.30pm for *aperitivi*.

Dar Poeta

Vicolo del Bologna 45 (06 588 0516).
Meals served 7.30pm-midnight daily.
€€. **Map** p130 C3 ⓫

Dar Poeta does high-quality pizza with
creative toppings, such as the house
pizza (with courgettes, sausage and
spicy pepper) and the *bodrilla* (with
apples and Grand Marnier). The varied *bruschette* are first-rate, and
healthy salads offer a break from all
those carbs. Be prepared to queue, as
it doesn't take bookings.

Enoteca Ferrara

*Piazza Trilussa 41A (06 5833 3920/
www.enotecaferrara.it).* **Open** *Wine
bar & shop* 11am-2am daily.
Map p131 D3 ⓬

This warren of a place may also be a
restaurant (8-11.30pm daily, €€€€),
but we recommend sticking to the comfortable, dimly lit wine bar with its good
choice of wines by the glass, and an
encyclopaedic (though rather expensive) bottle menu. From 6pm to 2am
you can graze through an appetising
selection of bar snacks for €7-€9.

Freni e Frizioni

*Via del Politeama 4-6 (06 5833 4210/
www.frenifrizioni.com).* **Open** 10am-
2am daily. **Map** p131 D3 ⓭

Housed in a former mechanic's workshop, this shabby-chic temple to the
aperitivo cult is now a cool place for
a light lunch (€€) too, especially if
you can bag one of the few tables out
on the square. Of an evening, uncon-
tainable crowds of hipsters hit the
generous (free) snacks table, then spill
out of 'Brakes and Clutches' and
across the square.

Friends Art Café

*Piazza Trilussa 34 (06 581 6111/www.
cafefriends.it).* **Open** 7am-2am Mon-
Sat; 6pm-2am Sun. **Map** p131 D3 ⓭

Habitués meet in this lively bar for
everything from breakfast to after-
dinner cocktails. The chrome detailing

Chocolate box

It has taken a while for Italy's recent love affair with all things chocolatey to hit Rome: perhaps because the city's temperatures swiftly turn chocolate gooey for much of the year... or maybe because Rome has so many other very sensual pleasures.

But finally *cioccolato* has been added to the Eternal City's pantheon of gastronomic delights, and epicurean Romans are spoilt for choice with a slew of the finest, rarest chocolate shops.

Cioccolata e vino (p136) hedges its bets with a double temptation. Half-shop, half-bar, this choc-box-sized Trastevere emporium is full of treats: try a decadent hot chocolate, a delicious espresso with a piece of bitter chocolate in the bottom of your tiny cup, a tasting of naughty handmade chocs or a glass from a small but interesting selection of wine. (For dieting teetotallers there are second-hand books downstairs in the cellars.)

You'll have to cross the river, however, to find most of the capital's grander *cioccolatieri*.

Pop in to the new **Da leccarsi i baffi** (via del Panico 31, 06 9799 7935), and you'll be cajoled into sampling one of its exquisite chocolate cases filled with cherries and liqueur, topped with warm melted chocolate.

Moriondo & Gariglio (p83) is a Rome classic, and has a reassuringly old-fashioned air to prove it. No Roman romance is serious without one of its chocolate offerings on Valentine's Day: take your own gift-trinket and staff will seal it inside a chocolate heart. At Easter, admirers drool over the stunning giant egg window display.

Close by, politicians in need of a chocolate fix dash out of sittings at the Senate and straight into **Chocolat** (via della Dogana Vecchia 12-13, 06 6813 5545).

Named after the Aztec god who took the form of a plumed serpent and gave the cocoa tree to the world, **Quetzalcoatl** (via delle Carrozze 26, 06 6920 2191) is another extraordinary its boutique: try their famed figs in Cointreau, or the chocolate made with honey.

and brightly coloured plastic chairs, plus the constant din of fashion TV, lend the place a retro-'80s funhouse feel. Lunch and dinner menus offer *bruschette*, salads and pastas at reasonable prices. There's an equally lively branch near piazza Navona in via della Scrofa 60.

Glass Hostaria

Vicolo del Cinque 58 (06 5833 5903/ www.glasshostaria.it). **Meals served** 8pm-midnight Tue-Sun. Closed 2wks Jan-Feb. €€€. **Map** p130 C3 ⓰

Ultra-modern Glass kicks against the trad Trastevere dining scene, with unusual creative pan-Italian dishes... most of which work. Service is warm, the wine list is interesting and it's not bad value, given the setting.

Jaipur

Via di San Francesco a Ripa 56 (06 580 3992/www.ristorantejaipur.it). **Meals served** 7pm-midnight Mon; noon-3pm, 7-11.30pm Tue-Sun. €€. **Map** p131 D5 ⓰

Jaipur does some of Rome's best Indian food (not that there's much competition), and it's good value too – which helps make up for the rather garish lighting and colour scheme. The menu ranges from basic starters to an extensive selection of tandoori specials, curries and murghs, plus a range of vegetarian dishes.

Le Mani in Pasta

Via de' Genovesi 37 (06 581 6017/ www.lemaniinpasta.com). **Meals served** 12.30-3pm, 7.30-11.30pm Tue-Sun. Closed 3wks Aug, 1wk Dec. €€€. **Map** p131 E4 ⓱

This relative newcomer offers decent, creative home cooking, huge portions, friendly informal service and great value for money, all of which make it popular, so book ahead. Antipasti such as the chargrilled vegetables or sautéed clams and mussels, and huge mountains of pasta, such as the spaghetti with cuttlefish and artichokes, may mean you never get as far as good main courses like fillet steak with green peppercorns.

Libreria del Cinema

Via dei Fienaroli 31D (06 581 7724/ www.libreriadelcinema.roma.it). **Open** 3-9pm Mon; 10am-9pm Tue-Fri, Sun; 11am-11pm Sat. Closed 2wks Aug. **Map** p131 D4 ⓲

This is heaven for movie buffs, with its vast stock of cinema-related books, its busy events programme and its intimate little bar where aficionados swap cinema tales.

Almost Corner Bookshop p136

Ombre Rosse

Piazza Sant'Egidio 12 (06 588 4155).
Open 7.30am-2am Mon-Sat; 6.30pm-2am Sun. **Map** p130 C3 ⑲

In the heart of Trastevere, this café is a meeting spot day and night: perfect for morning coffee, a late lunch or a light dinner (try the chicken salad or fresh soups). It fills to bursting after dark, when snagging an outside table is a coup. Service is slow but friendly: as the bartender hand-crushes the ice for your next caipiroska, you have plenty of time to watch the world go by.

Rivadestra

NEW *Via della Penitenza 7 (06 683 07053/www.rivadestra.com).* **Open** 8pm-midnight Mon-Sat. **€€€. Map** p130 B2 ⑳

Up a quiet riverside side street, Rivadestra is comfortably stylish with heraldic shields of Roman families on the walls and neo-baroque twists. A menu of Mediterranean cuisine changes every few weeks. The freshest of fish with interesting vegetable combinations feature.

Shopping

Piazza San Cosimato is home to a produce market (early to about 2pm Mon-Sat) that manages to retain a local feel in this heavily touristed area. On Sunday mornings, the Porta Portese flea market engulfs via Portuense and surrounding streets: watch out for pickpockets as you root through bootleg CDs, clothes, bags and fake designer gear.

Almost Corner Bookshop

Via del Moro 45 (06 583 6942). **Open** 10am-1.30pm, 3.30-8pm Mon-Sat; 11am-1.30pm, 3.30-8pm Sun. **Map** p131 D3 ㉑

This English-language bookshop is packed to the rafters with fiction, plus books on history, art, archaeology and more. Charming owner Dermot O'Connell is unfailingly helpful. Check the noticeboard if you're seeking work, lodgings or Italian lessons.

Cioccolata e Vino

Vicolo del Cinque 11A (06 5830 1868/www.cioccolataevino.com). **Open** 2pm-2am daily. **Map** p130 C3 ㉒

See box p134.

Roma – Store

Via della Lungaretta 63 (06 581 8789/www.romastoreprofumi.com). **Open** 10am-8pm daily. **Map** p131 D3 ㉓

This blissful sanctuary of lotions and potions stocks an array of gorgeous scents: old-school Floris, Creed and Penhaligon's rub shoulders with modern classics such as home-grown Acqua di Parma and Lorenzo Villoresi. Staff can be very abrupt, though.

Valzani

Via del Moro 37B (06 580 3792/www.valzani.it). **Open** 2-8pm Mon, Tue; 10am-8pm Wed-Sun. **Map** p131 D3 ㉔

Sachertorte and spicy, nutty *pangiallo* are the specialities in this Trastevere institution, but they are the tip of a sweet-toothed iceberg.

Nightlife

See also Freni e Frizioni (p133), Friends Art Café (p133) and Ombre Rosse (p136).

Big Mama

Vicolo San Francesco a Ripa 18 (06 581 2551/www.bigmama.it). **Open** 9pm-1.30am Tue-Sat. Closed June-mid Sept. **Admission** free with membership (annual €13, monthly €8); extra charge (€8-€22) for big acts. **Map** p131 D5 ㉕

Rome's blues temple, where an array of respected Italian and international artists play regularly, guaranteeing a quality night out for live-music aficionados. There's jazz too. Food is served: book to ensure you get a table.

Lettere Caffè

Via di San Francesco a Ripa 100-101 (06 6456 1919/www.letterecaffe.org). **Open** 2pm-2am daily. Closed Aug. **Map** p131 D5 ㉖

Poetry slams and readings compete with live concerts – from rockabilly to jazz beginning at 10.30pm – and DJ sets

Take your blanket and run

It's a common sight, around Castel Sant'Angelo, or on the Ponte Sisto: at some invisible signal, the dozens of mainly Senegalese traders hawking fake Vuitton bags and counterfeit CDs grab the corners of the blankets on which their wares are spread, and scarper. The police have been spotted approaching, and this trade is strictly illegal.

Some estimates put the number of unlicensed traders in Rome as high as 10,000. These, coupled with the 2,200 licensed vendors – 5,000, if you count the ones with permits to trade in food markets – are a formidable army. And the hard sell can be overwhelming.

It's a problem that Rome's city council has sought to deal with recently. In the first seven months of 2007 the *Guardia di Finanza* (finance police) confiscated 4.6 million counterfeit items and charged over 1,000 people for illegal street trading.

In Trastevere's Porta Portese market, a crackdown in 2007-8 saw the number of stalls fall from 2,000 to 1,050 after the unlicensed stalls were evicted.

But it's not only the illegal hawkers who have come in for a clean-up. Much to their annoyance, the legal sellers of nylon football shirts and plaster replicas of St Peter's are also being forced to adopt new standards and venues.

The Tridente area of the *centro storico* was the first to feel the pinch, with only booksellers allowed to continue plying their wares there. Other districts were ordered to designate total-ban, partial-ban and free-for-all zones. And the vendors were told that their trading could only be done from standard *bancarelle* (stalls), colour-coded for different types of merchandise – and costing anything from €6,000 to €18,000 – pricey for a humble street trader.

Hardest hit, however, are not Rome's traders, but the Vatican's. In a surprise move in late 2007, the 112 *urtisti* (from *urtare*, 'bump into') selling plaster Padre Pios on St Peter's square were thrown out of the temple, a move they were still fighting as this guide went to press. Almost exclusively Jewish, *urtisti* were first given permission to trade in the 16th century by Paul IV, the same pope who enclosed the ghetto. Their permits – passed down through families – have been renewed ever since, with their rights enshrined in a papal bull in the 19th century. Unable to operate in Rome proper, the *urtisti* are deprived of their traditional living by the Vatican's ruling, and are understandably furious.

in this bookish bar where well-priced wines and spirits and yummy home-made cakes complete the picture.

Arts & leisure

L'Albero e la Mano

Via della Pelliccia 3 (06 581 2871/ www.lalberoelamano.it). Closed Sat, Sun & mid July-mid Sept. **Rates** €12-€15 per class. No credit cards. **Map** p131 D3 ㉗

This incense-scented studio offers Shiatsu, Ayurvedic and Thai massages. There are also classes in Astanga and Hatha yoga, stretching and Pilates.

Gianicolo & Monteverde

The leafy slopes of the Gianicolo hill seem the epitome of calm; only the equestrian statue of Unification hero Giuseppe Garibaldi – in the hilltop gardens with their spectacular view over the city – is a reminder of the bloody battle fought here between Unification forces and the French in 1849. A cannon is fired each day at noon from below the panoramic terrace in the gardens.

To the south, tortuous via Garibaldi passes by the Baroque Fontana Paola, a fountain made in 1612 to celebrate the reopening of an ancient Roman aqueduct; the columns come from the original St Peter's. Between the fountain and the church of **San Pietro in Montorio** – with the exquisite **Tempietto** in its courtyard – stands the unlikely Fascist-era Ossario Garibaldo (open 9am-1pm Tue-Sun) containing the remains of heroes of the Risorgimento, Italy's struggle for Unification.

West of here stretches the leafy well-heeled suburb of Monteverde, home to vast, green expanses of the Villa Pamphili park. Rome's largest public green space, it's a wonderful place to stroll of a summer evening.

Nearby is the smaller but equally lovely Villa Sciarra garden, with rose arbours, a children's play area and a miniature big dipper.

Sights & museums

Tempietto di Bramante & San Pietro in Montorio

Piazza San Pietro in Montorio 2 (06 581 3940). **Open** *Tempietto* Oct-Mar 9.30am-12.30pm, 2-4pm Tue-Sun; Apr-Sept 9.30am-12.30pm, 4-6pm Tue-Sun. *Church* 8.30am-noon, 4-6pm daily. **Map** p130 C4 ㉘

High up on the Gianicolo, on one of the spots where St Peter was said to have been crucified (St Peter's is another), San Pietro in Montorio conceals an architectural gem in its courtyard: the Tempietto, designed by Bramante in 1508. This round construction, with its Doric columns, was the first modern building to follow exactly the proportions of one of the classical orders. In 1628, Bernini added the staircase down to the crypt. The 15th-century church has a chapel by Bernini (the second on the left). Paintings include a Sebastiano del Piombo and a Guido Reni.

Eating & drinking

Antico Arco

Piazzale Aurelio 7 (06 581 5274/ www.anticoarco.it). **Meals served** 7.30-11.30pm Mon-Sat. Closed 1wk Aug, 1wk Christmas. €€€€. **Map** p130 A4 ㉙

A 2007 refit gave the Antico Arco a minimalist-but-warm new interior, served up with some interesting innovations – including a delicious *tonnarelli* pasta with mullet roe, artichokes and coriander – in the kitchen. But the old favourites are still there too, from the amazing onion flan with grana cheese sauce, to *primi* like risotto with castelmagno cheese. There is a range of delicious *secondi*, and the desserts are fantastic. Sommelier Maurizio will steer you through an extensive, well-priced wine list. Book at least a couple of days in advance. The winebar opens at 6pm.

St Peter's

The Vatican & Prati

The Vatican & Borgo

The area now occupied by the Vatican state has a connection with Christianity stretching back well before the establishment of the first basilica here.

In AD 54, Emperor Nero built a circus in the *campus vaticanus*, a marshy area across the river from the city centre. Ten years later, when fire destroyed two-thirds of Rome, Nero blamed the Christians, and the persecution of this new cult began, with much of the Christian-bating taking place in Nero's circus.

Top apostle Peter is believed to have been crucified here and buried on the spot where, in 326, Emperor Constantine built the first church of St Peter.

Not all of the following popes resided in the Vatican but,

throughout the Christian era, pilgrims have flocked to the tomb of the founder of the Roman Church. Around it, the Borgo district grew up to service the burgeoning Dark Age tourist industry. Pope Leo IV (847-55) enclosed Borgo with the 12-metre-high (40-foot) Leonine Wall. Pope Nicholas III (1277-80) extended the walls and provided a papal escape route, linking the Vatican to the huge, impregnable Castel Sant'Angelo by way of a long *passetto* or covered walkway.

After the Sack of Rome in 1527, Pope Paul III got Michelangelo to build bigger, better walls but the popes moved to the Lateran, then the Quirinal, palaces. Only in 1870, with the Unification of Italy, were they forced back across the Tiber once more. Until 1929, the pope

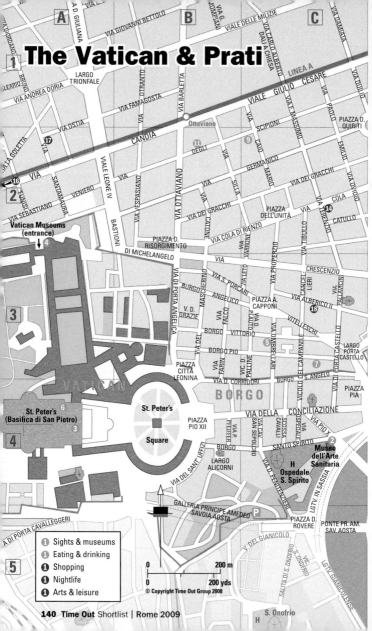

The Vatican & Prati

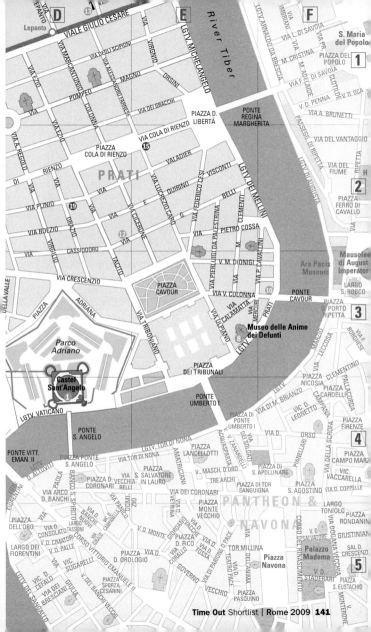

Year of Paul

San Paolo fuori le Mura

The jury is still out over when St Paul was born: in AD 7, 8, 9 or 10. Benedict XVI decided to hedge his bets and celebrate the 2,000th anniversary of the apostle's birth with celebrations beginning on 28 June 2008. The Pauline year ends 12 months later on June 29, the day on which both Saints Peter and Paul are believed to have died – though in different years – and which is Rome's annual holiday.

Pauline activities started with a papal inauguration and Handel's *Messiah*, performed by Lorin Maazel, conducted in the basilica of **San Paolo fuori le Mura** (p123).

Built over what is said to be Paul's tomb, the basilica has been an important pilgrimage site since the first Holy Year in 1300. A fire in 1823 destroyed most of the old church; but, in 2002-6, Vatican archaeologists excavated beneath a tombstone inscribed *Paulo Apostolo Mart* and found a fourth-century sarcophagus that, they believe, may hold the martyred apostle's remains (or part of them

– the heads of Peter and Paul are in **San Giovanni Laterano**, p109).

San Paolo fuori le Mura is the fulcrum of Pauline celebrations. But Rome abounds with sites connected with the apostle.

Christian-hating Saul was blinded by a flash of light on the road to Damascus and converted, taking the name Paul. The dramatic scene is portrayed in Caravaggio's **Santa Maria del Popolo** (p85).

Paul spent the rest of his life organising, preaching and firing off epistles to the communities of what became the Christian Church. Imperial authorities saw him as a threat: he was jailed (in the **Mamertine prison**, p59), tried and executed during the reign of Nero.

The site of his execution – now the **Abbazia delle Tre Fontane** (p155) – has been venerated since earliest Christian times. A church was built on this spot in the fifth century, though the current structure dates from the 16th.

■ www.annopaolino.org
■ www.vatican.va

pronounced the Italian state to be sacrilegious. But on 11 February 1929, Pius XII and Mussolini signed the Lateran Pacts, awarding the Church a huge cash payment, tax-free status and a constitutional role that led to an important and continuing moral influence over legislation on social issues.

The Vatican City occupies an area of less than half a square kilometre, making it the world's smallest state. Despite having fewer than 800 residents, it has its own diplomatic service, postal service, army (the Swiss Guard), heliport, station, supermarket, and radio and TV stations. It has observer status at the UN, and issues its own stamps and currency. Outside in Borgo, locals mingle with off-duty Swiss Guards and priests from the Vatican Curia (administration).

Vatican tips

■ **Dress code**: the Vatican enforces its dress code strictly, both in St Peter's and in the Vatican Museums. Anyone wearing shorts or a short skirt, or with bare shoulders or midriff, will be turned away.

■ **Timing**: the queues to visit both St Peter's and the Vatican Museums (ten minutes' brisk walk between the two) are usually huge. Factor in an hour or more of waiting time for each.

■ **Papal audiences**: when in Rome, the pope addresses crowds in St Peter's square at noon on Sunday. On Wednesday mornings he holds a general audience in St Peter's square, if the weather is fine, otherwise in the modern Sala Nervi audience hall. If you wish to attend, make your request well in advance to the Prefettura della Casa Pontificia (06 6988 4857, fax 06 6988 5863, open 9am-1.30pm Mon-Sat).

■ **Vatican Gardens**: the Vatican walls surround splendid formal gardens, which can be visited on Tuesday, Thursday and Saturday – weather permitting – on guided tours (€18, €14 reductions). Send a fax to book at least one week in advance to 06 6988 4019.

Sights & museums

Castel Sant'Angelo

Lungotevere Castello 50 (06 681 9111). **Open** 9am-7.30pm Tue-Sun. **Admission** €5; €2.50 reductions. Extra charge during exhibitions. No credit cards. **Map** p141 D4 ❶

Begun by Emperor Hadrian in AD 135 as his own mausoleum, Castel Sant'Angelo has been a fortress, prison and papal residence. It now plays host to temporary art shows, although the real pleasure of a visit lies in wandering from Hadrian's original spiralling ramp entrance to the upper terraces, with their superb views over the city. Between, there is much to see: lavish Renaissance salons, decorated with spectacular frescoes and trompe l'oeils; the glorious chapel in the *Cortile d'Onore* designed by Michelangelo; and, halfway up an easily missed staircase, Clement VII's tiny bathroom, painted by Giulio Romano.

Museo Storico Nazionale dell'Arte Sanitaria

Lungotevere in Sassia 3 (06 689 3051). **Open** 10am-noon Mon, Wed, Fri. Closed Aug. **Admission** €4. No credit cards. **Map** p140 C4 ❷

A hostel and church was established here in around 726 by King Ine of Wessex to cater for weary pilgrims from the north. Known as the *burgus saxonum* or 'in Sassia', this became the nucleus of the world's first purpose-built hospital. British funds for the hostel were cut off with the Norman invasion of England in 1066, after which it passed into papal hands and thence to the Templar knight Guy de Montpellier, who founded the Order of the Holy Spirit. A few rooms of the modern hospital here house a gruesome collection of medical artefacts. Two massive 15th-century frescoed wards were emptied not all that long ago of their beds to provide space for itinerant exhibitions.

St Peter's (Basilica di San Pietro)

Piazza San Pietro (06 6988 1662/ 06 6988 5518/www.vatican.va). No credit cards. **Map** p140 A4 ❸
Basilica Open *Oct-Mar* 7am-6pm daily. *Apr-Sept* 7am-7pm daily. **Admission** free.
Dome Open *Oct-Mar* 8am-5pm daily. *Apr-Sept* 8am-6pm daily. **Admission** €5; €7 with lift.
Grottoes Open *Oct-Mar* 7am-5pm daily. *Apr-Sept* 7am-6pm daily. **Admission** free.
Necropolis Apply at the Excavations Office (fax 06 6987 3017/scavi@fsp.va). **Open** *Guided tours* 9am-5pm Mon-Sat. **Admission** €10.
Treasury Museum Open *Oct-Mar* 9am-5.15pm daily. *Apr-Sept* 9am-6.15pm daily. **Admission** €6; €4 reductions.

The current St Peter's was consecrated on 18 November 1626 by Urban VIII, exactly 1,300 years after the consecration of the first basilica on the site. By the mid 15th century, the south wall of the original basilica was collapsing. Pope Nicholas V had 2,500 wagonloads of masonry from the Colosseum carted here, just for running repairs. It took the arrogance of Pope Julius II and his pet architect Donato Bramante to knock the millennia-old basilica down, in 1506.

Following Bramante's death in 1514, Raphael took over the work. In 1547, he was replaced by Michelangelo; he died in 1564, aged 87, after coming up with a plan for a massive dome. Completed in 1590, this was the largest brick dome ever constructed, and is still the tallest building in Rome. In 1607, Carlo Maderno designed a new façade, crowned by enormous statues of Christ and the apostles.

After Maderno's death Bernini took over and became the hero of the hour with his sumptuous baldachin and elliptical piazza. This latter was built between 1656 and 1667; the oval measures 340 by 240m (1,115 by 787ft), and is punctuated by the central Egyptian obelisk and two symmetrical fountains by Maderno and Bernini. The 284-column, 88-pillar colonnade is topped by 140 statues of saints.

In the portico (1612), opposite the main portal, is a mosaic by Giotto (c1298), from the original basilica. Five doors lead into the basilica: the central ones come from the earlier church, while the others are all 20th century. The last door on the right is opened only in Holy Years by the pope himself. Inside, a series of brass lines in the floor show the lengths of other churches around the world that are not as big. Bernini's vast *baldacchino* (1633), cast from bronze purloined from the Pantheon, hovering over the high altar, is the real focal point. Below the altar, two flights of stairs lead to the *confessio*, where a niche contains a ninth-century mosaic of Christ, the only thing from old St Peter's that stayed in the same place. Far below lies the site of what is believed to be St Peter's tomb, discovered during excavations in 1951.

Pilgrims head straight for the last pilaster on the right before the main altar, to kiss the big toe of Arnolfo da Cambio's statue of St Peter (c1296), or to say a prayer by the crystal casket containing the mummified remains of Pope John XXIII, who was beatified in 2002. Tourists make a beeline for the first chapel on the right, where Michelangelo's *Pietà* (1499) is found. Following an anti-clockwise direction, the third chapel has a tabernacle and two angels by Bernini, plus St Peter's only remaining painting: a *Trinity* by Pietro da Cortona (the others have been replaced by mosaic copies).

Bernini's Throne of St Peter (1665) stands at the far end of the nave. Encased in it is a wood and ivory chair, probably dating from the ninth century but for many years believed to have belonged to Peter himself. To the right of the throne is Bernini's 1644 monument to his patron Urban VIII.

On the pillars supporting the main dome are venerated relics, including a chip off the True Cross. In the left aisle,

The *passetto* at Castel Sant'Angelo p143

beyond the pilaster with St Veronica holding the cloth with which she wiped Christ's face, Bernini's tomb for Pope Alexander VII shows the pope shrouded with a cloth of reddish marble, from beneath which struggles a skeleton clutching an hourglass. Near the portico end of the left aisle is a group of monuments to the Old Pretender James Edward Stuart and family.

Beneath the basilica are the Vatican grottoes – Renaissance crypts containing papal tombs. The Necropolis, where St Peter is said to be buried, lies under the grottoes. The small treasury museum off the left nave of the basilica contains stunning liturgical relics. The dome, reached via hundreds of stairs (there's a cramped lift as far as the basilica roof, then 320 steps to climb to get to the very top), offers fabulous views.

Vatican Museums

Viale del Vaticano (06 6988 3333/www.vatican.va). **Open** 8.30am-6pm Mon-Sat (ticket office closes 2hrs before). *Year-round* last Sun of mth 9am-1.45pm. Closed Catholic holidays. **Admission** €14; €8 reductions; free last Sun of mth. No credit cards. **Map** p140 A2 ④

Begun by Pope Julius II in 1503, this immense collection represents the accumulated fancies and obsessions of a long line of strong, often contradictory personalities. The signposted routes cater for anything from a dash to the Sistine Chapel to a five-hour plod. There are also itineraries for wheelchair users. Wheelchairs can be borrowed at the museum: you can book them on 06 6988 5433.

Borgia Rooms

This six-room suite was adapted for the Borgia Pope Alexander VI (1492-1503) and decorated by Pinturicchio with a series of frescoes on biblical and classical themes.

Galleria Chiaramonte

Founded by Pius VII in the early 19th century, this is an eclectic collection of Roman statues, reliefs and busts.

Gallerie dei Candelabri & degli Arazzi

The long gallery, which is studded with candelabra, contains Roman statues, while the next gallery has ten huge tapestries (*arazzi*), woven by Flemish master Pieter van Aelst from cartoons by Raphael.

Galleria delle Carte Geografiche

A 120m-long (394ft) gallery, with the Tower of the Winds observation point at the north end. Ignazio Danti drew the extraordinarily precise maps of Italian regions and cities.

Egyptian Museum

Founded in 1839, this selection of ancient Egyptian art from 3000 BC to 600 BC includes statues of a baboon god, painted mummy cases, real mummies and a marble statue of Antinous, Emperor Hadrian's lover.

Etruscan Museum

This collection contains Greek and Roman art as well as Etruscan masterpieces, including the contents of the Regolini-Galassi Tomb (c650 BC).

Museo Paolino

Highlights of this collection of Roman and neo-Attic sculpture include a beautifully draped statue of Greek tragedian Sophocles and a trompe l'oeil mosaic of an unswept floor.

Museo Pio-Clementino

The world's largest collection of classical statues fills 16 rooms. Don't miss the first-century BC *Belvedere Torso* by Apollonius of Athens, the Roman copy of the bronze *Lizard Killer* by Praxiteles and, in the octagonal Belvedere Courtyard, the exquisite *Belvedere Apollo* and *Laocoön*.

Pinacoteca

The Pinacoteca (picture gallery) holds many of the pictures that the Vatican managed to recover from France after Napoleon whipped them in the early 19th century. The collection ranges from Byzantine school works and Italian primitives to 18th-century Dutch and French old masters, and includes Giotto's *Stefaneschi Triptych*; a *Pietà* by Lucas Cranach the Elder; several delicate Madonnas by Fra Filippo Lippi, Fra Angelico, Raphael and Titian; Raphael's last work, *The Transfiguration*; Caravaggio's *Entombment*; and a chiaroscuro *St Jerome* by Leonardo da Vinci.

Sistine Chapel

The world's most famous frescoes cover the ceiling and one immense wall of the Cappella Sistina, built by Sixtus IV in 1473-84. For centuries it has been used for popes' private prayers and papal elections. In the 1980s and '90s, the 930sq m (10,000sq ft) of *Creation* (on the ceiling) and the *Last Judgement* (on the wall behind the altar) were subjected to a controversial restoration.

In 1508, Michelangelo was commissioned to paint some undemanding decoration on the ceiling of the chapel. He offered to do far more than that, and embarked upon his massive venture alone, spending the next four and a half years standing (only Charlton Heston lay down) on 18m-high (60ft) scaffolding. A sequence of biblical scenes, from the Creation to the Flood, begins at the *Last Judgement* end; they are framed by monumental figures of Old Testament prophets and classical sibyls.

In 1535, aged 60, Michelangelo returned. Between the completion of the ceiling and the beginning of the wall, Rome had suffered. From 1517, the Protestant Reformation threatened the power of the popes, and the sack of the city in 1527 by Imperial troops was seen by Michelangelo as the wrath of God. The *Last Judgement* dramatically reflects this gloomy atmosphere. In among the larger-than-life figures, Michelangelo painted his own miserable face on the human skin held by St Bartholomew, below and to the right of the powerful figure of Christ.

Before Michelangelo set foot in the chapel, the stars of the 1480s – Perugino, Cosimo Roselli, Botticelli, Ghirlandaio – had created the paintings along the walls.

Raphael Rooms

Pope Julius II gave 26-year-old Raphael carte blanche to redesign four rooms of the Papal Suite. The Study (Stanza della

Vatican tours

Vatican Museums

There *are* ways to admire the Sistine Chapel in peace. You could, say, become a head of state and ask the pope to show you round. Or you could try an exclusive agency (such as Bellini Travel, www.bellini travel.com) and pay over €3,000 to enjoy the Vatican Museums (almost) to yourself one evening.

Otherwise, you may have to join the other four million annual visitors in the notorious queue. And you'll have to squeeze in with them for a quick squint at the world's most famous ceiling.

Alternatively, you *can* queue-jump, and maybe find yourself inside with slightly smaller crowds, by joining a pre-arranged tour.

Plenty of private tour companies offer 'exclusive' guided Vatican visits. Be sure to read the small print, though. If your tour costs less than €130 a head, then it's likely that you'll get a guide, but will still have to wait in line. Pay more, and you'll be able to bypass the line – a lucrative business for the Holy See, which levies a hefty charge for this privilege. The earlier your private tour is, the smaller the crowds will be: the Vatican Museums and Sistine Chapel officially open at 8.30am. In fact, only pre-booked private tour groups can get in before 10am.

Far cheaper than this – and offering the same queue-jumping opportunities – are the Vatican's own tours. At €23.50 (€18.50 reductions; includes ticket) for a two-hour sprint, these are good value. They are also a Holy Grail. You must book well in advance by fax (06 6988 5100), then wait for a faxed response confirming your booking. If the fax doesn't arrive, you're not in – and more often than not, it doesn't.

At which point the best solution is to visit when the faithful are busy in St Peter's square for the pope's Wednesday morning general audience; or to try at lunchtime when hungry pilgrims are seeking bodily rather than cultural sustenance.

■ www.vatican.va

ROME BY AREA

Segnatura, 1508-11) covers philosophical and spiritual themes. The star-packed *School of Athens* fresco has contemporary artists as classical figures: Plato is Leonardo; the glum thinker on the steps at the front – Heraclitus – is Michelangelo; Euclid is Bramante; and Raphael himself is on the far right-hand side behind a man in white. Raphael next turned to the Stanza di Eliodoro (1512-14), where the portrayal of God saving the temple in Jerusalem from the thieving Heliodorus was intended to highlight the divine protection enjoyed by Pope Julius. The Dining Room (Stanza dell'Incendio; 1514-17) is dedicated to Pope Leo X (the most obese of the popes, he died from gout aged 38). The room is named for the *Fire in the Borgo*, which Leo IV apparently stopped with the sign of the

cross. The Reception Room (Sala di Constantino, 1517-24) was completed by Giulio Romano after Raphael's death in 1520, and tells the legend of Emperor Constantine's miraculous conversion. The Loggia di Raffaello (usually closed) has a beautiful view over Rome; started by Bramante in 1513, and finished by Raphael, it has 52 small paintings on biblical themes, and leads into the Sala dei Chiaroscuri. The adjacent Chapel of Nicholas V has scenes from the lives of saints Lawrence and Stephen by Fra Angelico (1448-50).

Eating & drinking

Enoteca Nuvolari

Via degli Ombrellari 10 (06 6880 3018). **Open** 6.30pm-2am Mon-Sat. Closed Aug. No credit cards. **Map** p140 C3 **⑤**

The younger denizens of Borgo hang out in this welcoming *enoteca*. The lively *aperitivo* hour (6.30-8.30pm) is accompanied by a free buffet; more filling soups and patés are on offer next door (8pm-1am) in the candlelit dining room.

Il Ristoro

Basilica di San Pietro (06 6988 1662). **Open** *Oct-Mar* 8.30am-5pm Mon-Sat. *Apr-Sept* 8.30am-6pm Mon-Sat. No credit cards. **Map** p140 A4 **⑥**

Take the St Peter's dome lift for Rome's most unlikely 'cappuccino with a view' – on the roof of the basilica. There's nothing but water, coffee and soft drinks on the menu, but the wonder of being up here between those giant marble saints will make you feel light-headed anyway.

Paninoteca da Guido

Borgo Pio 13 (06 687 5491). **Open** 8am-4pm Mon-Sat. Closed 3wks Aug. No credit cards. **Map** p140 C3 **⑦**

This hole-in-the-wall joint in Borgo Pio is one of the best places to grab a snack in the Vatican area. Guido does filled rolls, made up while you wait from the ingredients behind the counter: ham, mozzarella, rocket, olive paste, etc. There are also a couple of pasta dishes. You'll have to fight for one of the few outside tables, though.

Settembrini p150

Prati

The Prati district was a provocation. Built over meadows (*prati*) soon after Rome became capital of the newly unified Italian state in 1871, its grand *palazzi* housed the staff of the ministries and parliament. But its broad avenues were named after historic figures who had fought against the power of the Papal States, and the largest of its *piazze* – nestling beneath the Vatican walls – was named after the Risorgimento, the movement that had destroyed the papacy's hold on Italy.

A solidly bourgeois district, Prati has a main drag – via Cola di Rienzo – that provides ample opportunities for retail therapy. Imposing military barracks line viale delle Milizie, and the bombastic Palazzo di Giustizia (popularly known as *il palazzaccio*, 'the big ugly building') sits between piazza Cavour and the Tiber. On the riverbank is one of Catholic Rome's truly weird experiences: the Museo delle Anime dei Defunti.

Sights & museums

Museo delle Anime dei Defunti
Lungotevere Prati 12 (06 6880 6517). **Open** 7.30-11am, 4.30-7pm daily. **Map** p141 E3 ❽
This macabre collection, attached to the church of Sacro Cuore di Gesù in Prati, contains hand- and fingerprints left on the prayer books and clothes of the living by dead loved ones, to request masses to release their souls from purgatory. Shuts earlier in summer.

Eating & drinking

Del Frate
Via degli Scipioni 118 (06 323 6437). **Meals served** 1-3pm, 6.30pm-12.30am Mon-Fri; 6.30pm-1.30am Sat. Closed 2wks Aug. €€€. **Map** p140 C2 ❾
This venerable Prati bottle shop expanded into a wine bar annexe a few years back. Of an evening, tables spill over into the *enoteca* itself, amid tall shelves crammed with bottles. The oven-baked ravioli with salmon and courgette sauce is a good demonstration of the modern approach; seconds might include a scallop of sea bass with pan-fried cicoria. The only off-note is the steep mark-up on wines.

Gran Caffè Esperia
Lungotevere dei Mellini 1 (06 3211 0016). **Open** *Oct-Apr* 7am-9.30pm daily. *May-Sept* 7am-midnight daily. **Map** p140 F3 ❿
The pavement tables at this newly restored café are hotly contested when the sun shines on them in the morning. Work on your tan while eating toasted *cornetti* with ham and cheese, or smoked salmon sandwiches. The coffee's great… or go straight for a prosecco.

Franchi p150

Isola della Pizza

Via degli Scipioni 43, 45, 47 (06 3973 3483/www.isoladellapizza.com). **Open** 12.30-3pm, 7.30pm-12.30am Mon, Tue, Thur.-Sun. Closed 2wks Aug. €-€€€ **Map** p140 B2 ⓫

This huge Island of Pizza is a throbbing eating factory, with noisy, hungry hordes digging into immense pizzas (served at lunch too, a rarity in Rome), a range of good pasta dishes or great hunks of meat slung on an open fire.

L'Arcangelo

Via GG Belli 59-61 (06 321 0992/ www.ristorantidiroma.com/arcangelo). **Meals served** 12.30-2.30pm, 8-11.30pm Mon-Fri; 8-11pm Sat. Closed Aug. €€€. **Map** p141 D2 ⓬

The sombre L'Arcangelo has dark wood panelling below tobacco-sponged walls, linen tablecloths and a jazz soundtrack. The seasonal dishes are impressive: a tartlet of octopus and potato with olive oil is simple but delicious, and potato gnocchi with lamb and artichokes is a worthy follow-up. *Secondi*, like tripe with mint and pecorino, are clever variations on the Roman tradition.

Settembrini

Via Luigi Settembrini 25 (06 323 2617/ www.settembriniroma.it). **Meals served** 12.30-4pm, 8-11.30pm Mon-Sat. €€€. Closed 2wks Aug. **Map** off p141 D1 ⓭

Settembrini mixes design and tradition both in its warmly minimalist decor and in its menu. In chef Luigi Nastri's Italo fusion approach, the flavours of southern Italy are prominent and ingredients are sourced with an obsessive regard for quality. The place is open all day, from 11am on, with *aperitivi* served from 6pm to 8pm.

Shopping

Franchi

Via Cola di Rienzo 200 (06 687 4651/ www.franchi.it). **Open** 8am-9pm Mon-Sat. **Map** p140 C2 ⓮

This dream of a deli has just about anything you could ever want to eat: cheeses from everywhere, cured meat and fresh, ready-to-eat seafood dishes.

Iron G

Via Cola di Rienzo 50 (06 321 6798). **Open** 10.30am-7.30pm Mon-Sat. Closed 2wks Aug. **Map** p141 E2 ⓯

This boutique supplies clubwear to the fashion victims of this well-heeled neighbourhood. Hip labels mix with ethnic and local accessories.

Studio Massoni

Via della Meloria 90 (06 3975 4840). **Open** 9am-1pm, 3-7pm Mon-Sat. No credit cards. **Map** off p140 A2 ⓰

There's a selection of classical busts in plaster, while copies of just about any statue you want can be made to order.

Nightlife

Alexanderplatz

Via Ostia 9 (06 3974 2171/ www.alexanderplatz.it). **Open** 8pm-1.30am daily. Closed June-Sept. **Admission** free with monthly (€10) membership. **Map** p140 A2 ⓱

Rome's pioneer jazz club offers nightly concerts with famous names from Italy and beyond. In summer, Alexanderplatz shifts to Villa Celimontana for the Jazz & Image festival (p41).

The Place

Via Alberico II 27-29 (06 6830 7137/ www.theplace.it). **Open** 8.30pm-2.30am Tue-Sun. Closed mid June-mid Sept. **Admission** €5-€15. **Map** p140 C3 ⓲

A vibrant jazz club with a stage for live acts, The Place draws a 30- to 40-something crowd for mostly Italian jazz bands, plus DJs after the weekend acts. The restaurant serves from 7.30pm, during the 'Sound Check' rehearsal session.

Arts & leisure

El Spa

Via Plinio 15C/D (06 6819 2869/ www.elspa.it). **Open** 10am-9pm Mon-Thur, Sun; 10am-10pm Fri, Sat. Closed Aug. **Map** p141 D2 ⓳

Decorated in warm, Middle Eastern style, the spa specialises in holistic treatments. Try the *mandi lulur*, an ancient Indonesian treatment that leaves you with silky-soft skin.

The Appian Way

Out of Town

The Appian Way

So impressive was the via
Appia Antica, Rome's first great
military road, that it was known
as the *Regina viarum* – the
'queen of roads'.

Built in the fourth century BC
by statesman and censor Appius
Claudius Caecus, the Appia went
first to the strategic southern city
of Capua, and was later extended
to link *Caput mundi* with the
Adriatic at Brindisi in 121 BC.

By the time it reached Brindisi,
the Appia was the Romans' main
route to their eastern Empire, a
perfect thoroughfare for speeding
troops and supplies to where they
were most needed. In 71 BC,
6,600 followers of rebellious
gladiator-slave Spartacus were
crucified along the Appia as a
warning to other underlings with
ideas above their station. But well-
to-do Romans chose to end their
days here too, building their family
mausoleums alongside the road,
which was soon lined with tombs,
vaults and sarcophagi.

Today only a fraction of this
magnificent funerary decoration
remains, but it suffices to make
this the most fascinating, and
the most picturesque, of the
ancient roads.

Christians, too, began burying
their dead here (burial was always
performed outside a sacred city
boundary known as the *pomerium*),
initially in necropoli and later
underground, creating the

300-kilometre (200-mile) network of tunnels known as the **catacombs**. This system wasn't used for secret worship, as was once thought: authorities were perfectly aware of their existence. A Jewish catacomb still exists at via Appia Antica 119.

Via Appia Antica suffered at the hands of marauding Goths and Normans; successive popes did as much damage, grabbing any good pieces of statuary or marble that remained and reducing the ancient monuments to unrecognisable stumps. But this is still a wonderful place to spend a day, preferably a Sunday or holiday when all but local traffic is banned. The www.parcoappiaantica.org website provides exhaustive information.

You can explore more extensively by renting a bike at the **Punto Informativo** (via Appia Antica 58-60, 06 512 6314, €10 per day) or at the **Catacombs of San Sebastiano** (p153, €9 per day, closed Sun).

Another ancient route lies nearby: the great Roman aqueduct that brought fresh water from the hills near Tivoli dominates the **Parco degli Acquedotti**, accessible from viale Appio Claudio.

Museo delle Mura

Porta San Sebastiano

Centro Visite Parco dell'Appia Antica

Via Latina

Catacombe di San Callisto

Domine Quo Vadis?

Fortified Farmhouse

Fosse Ardeatine

Catacombe Ebraiche

Catacombe di Domitilla

Mausoleo di Romolo

Basilica e Catacombe di S. Sebastiano

Circo di Massenzio

Sacro Bosco

Tomba di Cecilia Metella

Via Ardeatina

Appia Pignatelli

Via Appia Antica

Via Appia Nuova

0   300 m
0   300 yds
© Copyright Time Out Group 2008

Villa dei Quintili

Getting there

You can take the hop-on, hop-off **Archeobus** (tickets €13, €8 reductions), which leaves from Termini railway station about every 20 minutes between 9am and 4pm, and stops by most major sights. Alternatively, the following regular bus services ply part of the way:
118 from viale Aventino (Circo Massimo metro) to the catacombs of San Callisto and San Sebastiano.
218 from piazza San Giovanni to Porta San Sebastiano, down the Appia to the Domine Quo Vadis? church, then along via Ardeatina.
660 from Colli Albani metro to the Circus of Maxentius and Tomb of Cecilia Metella.

Sights & museums

Catacombs of San Callisto
Via Appia Antica 110 (06 5130 1580/www.catacombe.roma.it).
Open 8.30am-noon, 2.30-5pm Mon, Tue, Thur-Sun. **Admission** €5; €3 reductions.
This is Rome's largest underground burial site. Buried in the 29km (12.5 miles) of tunnels were nine popes,

The Appian Way

take you into the crypt of St Sebastian, the martyr always depicted nastily pierced by a hail of arrows (though these were just one of several unpleasant tortures), who was buried here in the late third century. Above, the fourth-century basilica of San Sebastiano was originally called Basilica Apostolorum, because the remains of Saints Peter and Paul were hidden here. On display is the marble slab in which Christ left his footprints during his miraculous apparition at the spot on the via Appia where the Domine Quo Vadis? church (open for mass only) now stands.

Circus of Maxentius

Via Appia Antica 153 (06 780 1324).
Open 9am-1pm Tue-Sun. **Admission**
€3; €1.50 reductions. No credit cards.
This area of lovely green countryside contains one of the best-preserved Roman circuses. It was built by Emperor Maxentius for his private use, before his defeat and death at the hands of co-ruler Constantine in AD 312. Remains of the Imperial palace are perched above the track, at its northern end. Also found on this part of the site is the mausoleum Maxentius built for his beloved son Romulus.

Museo delle Mura

*Via di Porta San Sebastiano 18
(06 7047 5284/www.museodellemura
roma.it).* **Open** 9am-2pm Tue-Sun.
Admission €3; €1.50 reductions.
No credit cards.
Housed inside the mighty San Sebastiano gate, at the head of the Appian Way, this delightful museum not only charts the history of Rome's walls, but allows visitors to hike along the top of them for 350m (1,150 ft).

Tomb of Cecilia Metella

*Via Appia Antica 161 (06 780
0093).* **Open** 9am-4.30pm Tue-Sun.
Admission €6 (includes Baths of Caracalla & Villa dei Quintili);
€3 reductions. No credit cards.
Note opening hours are erratic.
This colossal cylinder of travertine is the final resting place of a woman who

dozens of martyrs and thousands of Christians. They are stacked down, with the oldest on the top. Named after third-century Pope Callixtus, the area became the first official cemetery of the Church of Rome. The crypt of St Cecilia is the spot where this patron saint of music is believed to have been buried, before she was transferred to her eponymous church in Trastevere.

Catacombs of San Sebastiano

*Via Appia Antica 136 (06 785 0350/
www.catacombe.org).* **Open** 8.30am-
noon, 2.30-5pm Mon-Sat. Closed
mid Nov-mid Dec. **Admission**
€5; €3 reductions.
The name 'catacomb' originated here, where a complex of underground burial sites situated near a tufa quarry was described as being *kata kymbas* – 'near the quarry'. The guided tour will

married into the wealthy Metella family in the first century BC. During the 14th century, the powerful Caetani family incorporated the tomb into a fortress, adding the crenellations to the top of the structure. The spot where Cecilia was buried is a fine example of brick dome-making. Downstairs, pieces of the volcanic rock used in the construction of via Appia Antica can be seen.

Villa dei Quintili

Via Appia Nuova 1092 (06 712 9121).
Open 9am-4.30pm Tue-Sun.
Admission €6 (includes Baths of Caracalla & Tomb of Cecilia Metella); €3 reductions. No credit cards.
Magnificently situated between the ancient and the modern vie Appia (but accessible only from the latter), this sumptuous second-century AD villa was owned by the influential Quintili brothers, who were murdered by the Emperor Commodus. The villa closes one hour before sunset through the summer months.

EUR

Italian Fascism was at once monstrous and absurd, but out of it came some of 20th-century Europe's most fascinating architecture and urban planning.

In the early 1930s, Rome's governor Giuseppe Bottai – the leading arbiter of taste among the Fascists – had the idea of expanding landbound Rome along via Ostiense towards the sea, some 20 kilometres (12.5 miles) away. Using as an excuse the universal exhibition pencilled in for 1942, he intended to combine cultural and exhibition spaces with a monument to the regime.

Architect Marcello Piacentini was charged with co-ordinating the ambitious project, but the planning committee became so bogged down in argument that very little had been achieved by

the outbreak of World War II. After the war, work resumed in an entirely different spirit. Still known as EUR (*Esposizione universale romana*), it's now a business district, where unrelieved planes of icy travertine and reinterpretations of classical monuments let you know you're not in Kansas any more.

A number of didactic museums – the Museo dell'Alto Medioevo, **Museo della Civiltà Romana** (now containing a new and very active astronomy museum and planetarium), the Museo Preistorico ed Etnografico – allow visitors a glimpse inside these grandiose monuments to the hubris of Italian Fascism.

Getting there

Take metro B to EUR Fermi or EUR Palasport, or buses 30Exp, 170, 714.

Abbazia delle Tre Fontane

Via Acque Salvie 1 (06 540 1655/ www.abbaziatrefontane.com).
Open *Santi Vincenzo e Anastasio* 6am-12.30pm, 3-8pm daily. *Other churches* 8am-1pm, 3-6pm daily. *Shop* 9am-1pm, 3.30-7pm daily.
North-east of EUR centre (and reachable by bus 767) lies a haven of ancient, eucalyptus-scented green, with three churches commemorating the points where St Paul's head supposedly bounced after it was severed in AD 67. (Being a Roman citizen, Paul was eligible for the relatively quick head-chop, as opposed to the long, drawn-out crucifixion.) These are the grounds of the Trappist monastery of Tre Fontane, where water has gurgled and birds have sung since the fifth century. The church of San Paolo delle Tre Fontane is said to be built on the spot where the apostle was executed; apart from a column to which Paul is supposed to have been tied, all traces of the fifth-century church were destroyed in 1599 by architect Giacomo della Porta, who was also responsible for the two other churches. Monks planted the eucalyptus trees in the 1860s, believing they would drive away the malarial mosquitoes; a liqueur is now brewed from the trees and sold in a little shop along with chocolate and remedies for all ills.

Museo dell'Alto Medioevo

Viale Lincoln 3 (06 5422 8199). **Open** 9am-2pm Tue-Sun. **Admission** €2; €1 reductions. No credit cards.
Focusing on the decorative arts from the period between the fall of the Roman Empire and the Renaissance, this museum has gold- and silver-decorated swords, buckles and horse tackle, plus more mundane objects: ceramic bead jewellery and the metal frames of what may be Europe's earliest folding chairs.

Museo della Civiltà Romana

Piazza G Agnelli 10 (06 5422 0919/ www.museociviltaromana.it). **Open** *Museum* 9am-2pm Tue-Sat; 9am-1pm Sun. *Planetarium* 9am-2pm Tue-Fri;

Airline flights are one of the biggest producers of the global warming gas CO_2. But with **The CarbonNeutral Company** you can make your travel a little greener.

Go to **www.carbonneutral.com** to calculate your flight emissions then 'neutralise' them through international projects which save exactly the same amount of carbon dioxide.

Contact us at **shop@carbonneutral.com** or call into the office on **0870 199 99 88** for more details.

CarbonNeutral®flights

9am-7pm Sat, Sun. **Admission**
Museum €6.50; €4.50 reductions.
Planetarium (booking obligatory
06 0608) €6.50; €4.50 reductions.
No credit cards.
With its blank white walls and lofty,
echoing corridors, this building, from
1937, is Fascist-classical at its most
grandiloquent. There's a fascinating
cutaway model of the Colosseum's maze
of tunnels and lifts, as well as casts of
the intricate reliefs on Trajan's column.
The centrepiece is a giant model of
Rome in the fourth century AD, which
puts the city's scattered fragments and
artefacts into context. The palazzo also
contains the Museo dell'Astrologia and
a planetarium (www.planetarioroma.it).

Museo Preistorico ed Etnografico L Pigorini

*Piazza G Marconi 14 (06 549 521/
www.pignorini.art.beniculturali.it).*
Open 10am-6pm Tue-Sun. **Admission**
€4; €2 reductions. No credit cards.
This museum displays prehistoric
Italian artefacts together with material from a range of world cultures. The
lobby contains a reconstruction of the
prehistoric Guattari cave near Monte
Circeo, south of Rome, with a genuine
Neanderthal skull. On the first floor is
the ethnological collection; the second
floor has archaeological finds from
digs all over Italy.

Ostia Antica

If you're contemplating the
punishing day trip from Rome to
Pompeii, do yourself a favour and
come here instead. The excavated
ruins (*scavi*) of Ostia Antica convey
the everyday life of a working
Roman town every bit as well
as Pompeii does.

Five minutes' walk from the
entrance to the excavations, the
medieval village of Ostia Antica
has a castle (built in 1483-86 for
the bishop of Ostia, the future Pope
Julius II) and picturesque cottages,
which were inhabited by the people
who worked in the nearby salt pans.

EUR p154

Ostia Antica

Getting there

Ostia Antica is a 20-minute train ride from Roma-Lido station, next to Piramide metro.

Sights & museums

Scavi di Ostia Antica

Viale dei Romagnoli 717, Ostia Antica (06 5635 8099/www.itnw.roma.it/ostia/scavi). **Open** *Nov-Feb* 8.30am-4pm Tue-Sun. *Mar* 8.30am-5pm Tue-Sun. *Apr-Oct* 8.30am-6pm Tue-Sun. **Admission** €6.50; €3.25 reductions. No credit cards.

Legend says that Ostia was founded by Ancus Martius, the fourth king of Rome, in the seventh century BC, although the oldest remains date 'only' from c330 BC. Ostia was Rome's main port for more than 600 years.

Abandoned after sackings by barbarians in the fifth century, the town was gradually buried by river mud. Over the centuries, the coastline has receded, leaving Ostia landlocked and obsolete. Visit on a sunny weekday and bring a picnic (not actually allowed but keep a low profile and you probably won't be ejected).

The *decumanus maximus* (high street) runs from the Porta Romana for almost a kilometre (half a mile), past the theatre and forum, before forking left to what used to be the seashore. The right fork, via della Foce, leads to the Tiber. Either side of these main arteries lies a network of intersecting lanes where the best discoveries can be made.

Behind the theatre is one of Ostia's most interesting features: the Forum of the Corporations. Here the trade guilds had their offices, and mosaics on the floor of shops that ring the open square refer to the products each guild dealt in – shipowners had ships on the floor, ivory dealers had elephants. Further along on the right is the old mill, where the furrows ploughed by the blindfolded donkeys that turned them are still visible. In the tangle of

streets between the decumanus and the museum, don't miss the *thermopolium* – an ancient Roman bar. Located off the forum to the south-east are the forum baths and nearby is the *forica*, or ancient public latrine. Off via della Foce, the House of Cupid and Psyche is an elegant fourth-century construction; the House of the Dioscuri has beautiful mosaics; the Insula of the Charioteers still has many of its frescoes.

A dusty old museum (same hours) contains bits of statuary etc from the digs, plus there's a shiny new café and bookshop... though mangy dogs may bar your path as you approach.

Tivoli

Just 20 kilometres (12.5 miles) from Rome, Tivoli (ancient Tibur) is home to two UNESCO World Heritage Sites – **Villa d'Este**, in Tivoli itself, and **Hadrian's Villa**, five kilometres (three miles)

down the hill – which make it an ideal destination for a day trip.

Getting there

Take the COTRAL bus from Ponte Mammolo metro station; note that the bus marked *autostrada* is a quicker service. If you're travelling by bus, visit Tivoli town first (the regular service is marked 'via Tiburtina' and takes about 45mins to Tivoli) and get off at the main square (piazza Garibaldi) for Villa d'Este. From the bus stop in front of the tourist office in piazza Garibaldi, frequent orange (local) buses serve Villa Adriana (10mins) down the hill. From Villa Adriana, both local and COTRAL buses travel to Rome.

Local trains go to Tivoli from Tiburtina station; bus 4 goes from Tivoli station to the centre of town for the Villa d'Este.

Sights & museums

Hadrian's Villa (Villa Adriana)

Via di Villa Adriana, Villa Adriana (0774 382 733). **Open** *Nov-Jan* 9am-5pm daily. *Feb* 9am-6pm daily. *Mar, Oct* 9am-6.30pm daily. *Apr, Sept* 9am-7pm daily. *May-Aug* 9am-7.30pm daily. **Admission** €6.50; €3.25 reductions; extra charge during exhibitions. No credit cards.

Villa Adriana, the retreat of Emperor Hadrian, is strewn across a gentle slope. Built from AD 118 to 134, it has some fascinating architectural spaces and water features.

Hadrian was an amateur architect and it is believed that he designed many of the elements in his magnificent villa himself. In the centuries following the fall of the Roman Empire the villa became a luxury quarry for treasure-hunters. At least 500 pieces of statuary in collections around the world have been identified as coming from this site.

The restored remains lie amid olive groves and cypresses and are still impressive. The model in the pavilion just up the hill from the entrance gives an idea of the villa's original size.

Where the original entrance to the villa lay is still uncertain; today the first space you'll encounter after climbing the road from the ticket office is the *pecile* (or *poikile*), a large pool that was once surrounded by a portico with high walls, of which only one remains. Directly east of the *poikile*, the *Teatro marittimo* (Maritime Theatre) is one of the most delightful inventions in the whole villa. A circular brick wall, 45m (150ft) in diameter, encloses a moat, at the centre of which is an island of columns and brickwork; today a cement bridge crosses the moat, but originally there would have been wooden bridges, which could be removed.

Beneath the building called the winter palace, visitors can walk along the perfectly preserved *cryptoporticus* (covered corridor).

ROME BY AREA

In the valley below is the lovely *canopus*: a long, narrow pool, framed on three sides by columns and statues, including a marble crocodile. At the far (southern) end of the pool is a structure called the *serapeum*, used for lavish entertaining. Summer guests enjoyed an innovative form of air-conditioning – a sheet of water poured from the roof over the open face of the building, enclosing diners.

Villa d'Este

Piazza Trento 1, Tivoli (0774 332 920/ www.villadestetivoli.info). **Open** 8.30am-1hr before sunset Tue-Sun. **Admission** €6.50; €3.25 reductions. No credit cards.

Dominating the town of Tivoli is the Villa d'Este, a lavish pleasure palace built in 1550 for Cardinal Ippolito d'Este, son of Lucrezia Borgia, to a design by architect Pirro Ligorio. Inside the villa there are frescoes and paintings by Correggio, Da Volterra and Perin Del Vaga (including views of the villa shortly after its construction).

But the gardens are the main attraction. Ligorio developed a complex 'hydraulic machine' that channelled water from the River Aniene (still the source today) through a series of canals under the garden. Using know-how borrowed from the Romans, he created 51 fountains spread around the terraced gardens. The sibyls (pagan high-priestesses) are a recurring theme – it was at Tivoli that the Tiburtine sibyl foretold the birth of Christ – and the grottoes of the sibyls behind the vast fountain of Neptune echo with thundering artificial waterfalls.

Technological gimmickry was another big feature; the Owl Fountain (operates every two hours from 10am) imitated an owl's song using a hydraulic mechanism, while the *Fontana dell'organo idraulico* (restored and now in operation every two hours from 10.30am) used water pressure to compress air and play tunes.

Electric carts are provided free for disabled visitors to tour the gardens; booking is essential (0774 335 850/332 920).

Long an anchor
of the restaurant scene
along the upscale
Via Veneto, the delicate
Mediterranean flavors
of Restaurant Doney
are reflected in the pale
marble floors, stone walls
and light wood finishes
in the recently remodeled
dining room.

Via Vittorio Veneto, 141 Roma
Orario apertura 12.30/15.30 -19.30/22.30
Domenica brunch dalle ore 12.30
Per informazioni e prenotazioni
telefono 06.47.08.27.83
email Restaurant.Doney@westin.com
web westin.com/doney

RISTORANTE
doney

Essentials

Hotels **164**

Getting Around **180**

Resources A-Z **184**

Vocabulary **188**

Menu Glossary **189**

Index **190**

The Beehive

Hotels

Until recently, Rome offered exorbitantly expensive four- and five-star options. And cheap *pensioni* of dubious cleanliness. In the middle was a depressing void. Nowadays, the extremes still exist but the middle ground has, to some extent, been filled with mid-priced boutiques, a raft of B&Bs and cleaner, smarter two- and three-stars. The city's ever-increasing popularity means, however, that it remains a seller's market: this is a more expensive place to stay than many other European capitals.

The luxury hotel market has exploded recently, due partly to a council scheme to revamp old *palazzi* in down-at-heel areas like the Esquilino, and partly to upscale districts such as via Veneto experiencing a resurgence. The recent Italian trend for hotels

created by fashion designers had seen haute couturiers sidelining Rome in favour of trendier Florence and Milan for their temples to style; a much-needed injection of glamour came in May 2006 with the opening of fashion designer Ferragamo's swanky **Portrait Suites** (p175).

The mid-range market is also flourishing, and fierce competition from the boutique hotels popping up all over the *centro storico* means that older-style hotels and *pensioni* are being forced to upgrade both amenities and decor if they want to stay in business.

It's only at the lower end that Rome lags behind: in all but a few notable cases – for example, the **Beehive** (p176) – the gulf in standards between rock bottom and the lower edge of moderate is immense: in Rome, it's worth

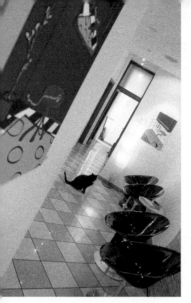

SHORTLIST

Newcomers
- Okapi Rooms (p175)
- Portrait Suites (p175)
- St George Roma (p171)

Utter luxury
- De Russie (p173)
- Exedra (p176)
- Hassler Villa Medici (p175)
- St Regis Grand (p178)
- Westin Excelsior (p176)

Stunning views
- Abruzzi (p170)
- Eden (p173)
- Sole al Pantheon (p171)
- View at the Spanish Steps (p175)

Cool pools
- Exedra (p176)
- Radisson SAS es. Hotel (p176)

Best B&Bs
- Arco del Lauro (p178)
- Buonanotte Garibaldi (p178)

Chic & cheap
- The Beehive (p175)
- Daphne Inn (p173)
- Relais Palazzo Taverna (p171)

Old-style *pensioni*
- Pensione Barrett (p170)
- Pensione Panda (p175)

Bargain hotels & hostels
- Colors Hotel & Hostel (p179)
- Foresteria Orsa Maggiore (p178)
- Pensione Paradise (p179)

Stunning suites
- Garden Suite at the Inn at the Roman Forum (p176)
- Grand Suite at the Exedra (p176)
- La Cupola at the Westin Excelsior (p176)
- Royal Suite at the St Regis Grand (p178)

paying just that little bit more. Either that, or go out on a limb, for example with a very un-Roman camping experience (see box p177).

Location

There are now three five-star hotels within a stone's throw of Termini station, but the vast majority of hotels in this area – the **Esquilino** – are cheap *pensioni* swarming with budget backpackers. It's not Rome's most picturesque corner, and almost certainly not what you dreamt of for your Roman holiday. It's definitely worth considering looking further afield. Termini is only a few minutes' bus ride from the centre, but you're likely to end up wishing you were more in the thick of things.

A room in the *centro storico* offers many advantages, not least of which are a shower between sightseeing and dinner, and a pleasant stroll (rather than a bus) back to the hotel afterwards. The

ESSENTIALS

FORTY47 SEVEN
ALBERGO IN ROMA

Fortysevenhotel
Via Petroselli 47, 00186 – Rome
Tel +39.06.6787816; Fax +39.06.69190726
contact@fortysevenhotel.com
www.fortysevenhotel.com - www.circusbar.it

area around **campo de' Fiori** offers mid-priced hotels with lots of character, and a central piazza that is a lively market by day and a hip Roman hangout by night (though don't stay too late, as it gets very seedy as the evening wears on); the area around the **Pantheon** and **piazza Navona** is generally a bit pricier. Moving distinctly up the price range, Rome's top-end hotels have traditionally clustered around **via Veneto**; it's nothing like as lively as it was in its *dolce vita* heyday, and there's a strong whiff of expense accounts in the air. But brave efforts are underway to relaunch this famous street, and it definitely has a certain grandeur. The **Tridente** area near the Spanish Steps, hub of designer shopping, is full of elegant hotels at the upper end of the price scale.

If you're looking for some peace, the **Celio**, just beyond the Colosseum, offers a break from the frantic activity of the *centro storico*, as does another of Rome's seven hills: the **Aventine**, an exclusive residential outpost no distance at all from the *centro*.

Heading across the river, the characterful **Trastevere** district is a pleasant place to stay, with good bus and tram connections to the major sights; in recent years it has blossomed from hotel-desert to hotel-bonanza, offering an array of price options. Just north of here, the medieval alleys around the **Vatican** give on to the busy retail thoroughfares of **Prati**: it's lively during the day but hushed at night.

Booking a room

Always reserve a room well in advance, especially at peak times, which now means most of the year, with lulls during winter (January to March) and in the dog days of

Aleph p171

ESSENTIALS

August. If you're coming at the same time as a major Christian holiday (Christmas or Easter) it's recommended to book weeks, or even months, ahead.

Increasingly, booking is via hotel websites, but you may also be asked to fax confirmation of a booking, with a credit card number as deposit. In high season, smaller hotels may ask for a money order to secure rooms. The www.venere.com booking service offers many hotels in all price ranges. If you arrive with nowhere to stay, try the **APT** tourist office (p187), which provides a list of hotels; you have to do the booking yourself. The **Hotel Reservation** (www.hotelreservation.it/06 699 1000) service, which has desks at Fiumicino airport, Ciampino airport and at Termini station, offers a free booking service.

Avoid the touts that hang around Termini: you're likely to end up paying more than you should for a very grotty hotel.

Standards & prices

Italian hotels are classified on a star system, from one to five. One star usually indicates *pensioni*, which are cheap but have very few facilities; you may have to share a bathroom. The more stars, the more facilities a hotel will have, but bear in mind that a higher rating offers no guarantee of friendliness, cleanliness or decent service.

Prices generally rise by a relentless ten per cent a year in Rome, but it's worth keeping an eye out for low-season deals on hotel websites. If you're staying in a group or for a longish period, ask about discounts.

If you're visiting with children, most hotels will be happy to squeeze a cot or camp bed into a room, but they will probably charge 30 to 50 per cent extra for the privilege.

Alternative accommodation

If you're travelling with children and/or staying for a while, you might prefer to opt for an apartment rental. Websites like www.myhomeyourhome.it, www.romanreference.com and www.flatinrome.com have many on their books; London-based www.aplaceinrome.com has a delightful few. For B&B accommodation, check out www.bbitalia.it, www.b-b.rm.it or www.bedandbreakfastroma.com.

Our choice

The hotels listed in this guide have been chosen for their location, because they offer value for money, or simply because they have true Roman character. Unless stated, rates are for rooms with bathrooms, and include breakfast.

In the deluxe category (€€€€) the emphasis is on luxury; a standard double in high season is likely to set you back €400 plus. Those in mid- to upper-price ranges (€€-€€€) are smaller, many in old *palazzi*, with pretty, though often small, bedrooms. Expect to pay €150 to €300 for a moderately priced hotel, and anywhere from €300 to €400 for an expensive room. *Pensioni* (€-€€) are fairly basic, but those listed here are friendly and usually family-run; you'll be very hard pressed to find anything half-decent for less than €100 per night.

Few Roman hotels – with the exception of the grander ones – have access for the disabled. Though staff are generally very willing to help guests who have mobility difficulties, the real problem is that most places have so many stairs that there's not much they can do. As hotels renovate, they do tend to add a room for the disabled if they can.

ESSENTIALS

Il Palazzetto p175

A no-smoking law introduced in 2005 applies to hotels' public areas but most are still fairly laissez-faire when it comes to guests lighting up in the rooms so long as they open a window. Hotels that are strictly non-smoking, or that have designated non-smoking rooms, have been indicated in the text.

Il Centro

Abruzzi
Piazza della Rotonda 69 (06 9784 1369/www.hotelabruzzi.it). €€.
The location is this hotel's main selling point. Recent renovations have upgraded what used to be a dingy establishment. Many rooms have great views of the Pantheon; some are very small.

Campo de' Fiori
Piazza del Biscione 6 (06 6880 6865/ www.hotelcampodefiori.com). €€.
Just off busy campo de' Fiori, this hotel underwent a complete renovation in 2006, with impressive results: though not spacious, the rooms are finely fitted out in rich colours. The small but elegant bathrooms have bronze-effect tiles with antique mirrors. The pretty roof terrace has great views.

Due Torri
Vicolo del Leonetto 23-25 (06 6880 6956/www.hotelduetorriroma.com). €€.
In a labyrinth of cobbled streets, the Due Torri has a welcoming feel. The 26 rooms are cosy rather than spacious, and kitted out with dark wooden furniture. If you're persistent, you might get one of the rooms with a private terrace overlooking the rooftops.

Pensione Barrett
Largo Argentina 47 (06 686 8481/ www.pensionebarrett.com). €.
A bewildering number of antiques and curios decorate the hotel, giving it a vaguely eccentric feel. Rooms are a mishmash of faux-classical columns and mouldings, dark wood furniture,

original wood-beamed ceilings and pastel walls; some have great views over largo Argentina. Breakfast (which costs extra) is served in the rooms. Poet Elizabeth Barrett Browning stayed here in 1848.

Relais Palazzo Taverna & Locanda degli Antiquari

Via dei Gabrielli 92 (06 2039 8064/ www.relaispalazzotaverna.com). €€.
In a 15th-century building, these twin *residenze* have sleek, modern decor. Spacious bedrooms have white-painted wood ceilings, wallpaper with bold graphics and bedlinen in spicy tones. Breakfast is served in the rooms.

Residenza in Farnese

Via del Mascherone 59 (06 6821 0980/ www.residenzafarneseroma.it). €€€.
This converted convent in a narrow ivy-lined alley has been refurbished without losing its charm. A chandelier in the lobby lends a sense of opulence; details like home-made baked goods and jams for breakfast reflect the homely charm of the place. Rooms run the gamut from basic updated cells with small marble bathrooms to more comfortable pastel-hued rooms with hand-painted furnishings.

Sole al Pantheon

Piazza della Rotonda 63 (06 678 0441/ www.hotelsolealpantheon.com). €€€.
Dating back to the 15th century, the Sole al Pantheon is one of Europe's oldest hotels. Rooms have a fresh feel, though, with tiles and pretty frescoes. Bathrooms are not luxurious but they do have whirlpool baths. Rooms at the front have great views of the Pantheon.

St George Roma

NEW *Via Giulia 62 (06 686 611/ www.stgeorgehotel.it).* €€€€.
This new five-star on gorgeous via Giulia is a study in coolly elegant designer neutrals and dark wood, with lashings of travertine in public spaces and bathrooms, and the odd deco-inspired detail. There's a spa – with small indoor pool – in the basement, a cigar lounge and a rooftop terrace.

Teatro di Pompeo

Largo del Pallaro 8 (06 6830 0170/ www.hotelteatrodipompeo.it). €€.
This small, friendly hotel occupies a palazzo that was built on the site of the ancient Teatro di Pompeo; its *pièce de résistance* is its cave-like breakfast room, tucked away inside the ancient ruins. The guest rooms are simply decorated in neutral tones, with terracotta floors and high, wood-beamed ceilings. Opt for one of the rooms in the main hotel building rather than those in the more basic annexe a few streets away.

Teatro Pace 33

Via del Teatro Pace 33 (06 687 9075/ www.hotelteatropace.com). €€.
Hidden away on a cobbled alley near busy piazza Navona, this 17th-century former cardinal's residence has a Baroque spiral staircase that winds up four floors (there's no lift, but chairs are provided every couple of floors for the out-of-breath). Rooms are spacious and elegantly decorated with wood floors, heavy drapes and marble bathrooms; all have their original beamed ceilings. Breakfast is served in the rooms. Excellent low-season deals on the hotel website.

Tridente & Borghese

Aleph

Via di San Basilio 15 (06 422 901/ www.boscolohotels.com). €€€€.
This Adam Tihany-designed hotel with a theme – heaven and hell – with common areas in various intensities of devil-red, and bright, 'heavenly' bedrooms. It's a world away from the luxe-but-dull decor of many of via Veneto's megahotels, making it a favourite of the fashion set. A top-floor terrace bar and restaurant operate in warmer months; there's a subterranean spa in white and icy blue. Rooms are modern and luxurious.

Casa Howard

Via Capo le Case 18 (06 6992 4555/ www.casahoward.com). €€.
All rooms in this beautiful *residenza* near piazza di Spagna have been

designed with an emphasis on quality.
Some rooms have (private) bathrooms
along the hall. There's a Turkish bath
too. The five new (and slightly more
expensive) rooms added around the
corner at via Sistina 149 have ensuite
bathrooms. Massages can be arranged
at both properties.

Daphne Inn

*Via degli Avignonesi 20; via di San
Basilio 55 (06 8745 0087/06 4782
3529/www.daphne-rome.com).* €€.
The Daphne Inn has two locations: one
near the Trevi Fountain, the other off
via Veneto. Each has seven rooms –
some with ensuite baths and some that
share – all of which are fitted out in
organic-modern style with terracotta
floors, neutral tones and simple framed
leaf prints on the walls. Excellent value
and a warm welcome.

De Russie

*Via del Babuino 9 (06 328 881/
www.hotelderussie.it).* €€€€.
The De Russie's modern elegance is a
million miles away from the luxury-
schmaltz of many hotels on via Veneto.
Fabulous gardens and a state-of-the-art
health centre make it a star-magnet.
Some rooms are smaller and less opulent than you might expect.

Eden

*Via Ludovisi 49 (06 478 121/
www.lemeridien.com/eden).* €€€€.
Elegantly understated, the Eden offers
the attentiveness and attention to detail
of a top-notch hotel without the stuffi-
ness. Handsome reception rooms, tastefully decorated bedrooms, and a roof
terrace with restaurant, piano bar –
and truly spectacular views.

Fontanella Borghese

*Largo Fontanella Borghese 84
(06 6880 9504/www.
fontanellaborghese.com).* €€.
This hotel is elegantly done out in
relaxing cream and muted colours.
Shopping meccas via del Corso and
via Condotti are just around the corner: it's an ideal bolthole when the
credit cards start to melt.

Hotel Art p175

Hassler Villa Medici

Piazza Trinità dei Monti 6 (06 699 340/
www.hotelhasslerroma.com). €€€€.
This is one of Rome's classic hotels,
with all the trimmings you might
expect: chandeliers everywhere, pol-
ished wood and marble, plush fabrics
and grand oil paintings, and a garden
out back. The attentiveness of the staff
distinguishes the Hassler from the
impersonal service at Rome's top chain
hotels. A few steps away, and with
a royal box view over the Spanish
Steps, is Il Palazzetto (www.ilpalazzet-
toroma.com), an annexe under the
same ownership.

Hotel Art

Via Margutta 56 (06 328 711/
www.hotelart.it). €€€€.
Opened in 2002 on a street famed for
its art studios, this hotel's lobby has
white pods serving as check-in and
concierge desks. Hallways are in reti-
na-burning shades, but bedrooms have
creamy bedlinens and dark wood furniture. There's a small gym.

Inn at the Spanish Steps

Via Condotti 85 (06 6992 5657/
www.atspanishsteps.com). €€€€.
The Inn at the Spanish Steps offers luxury boutique-hotel accommodation
right on one of the world's most
famous shopping streets. Rooms are an
extravagant mix of plush fabrics and
antiques; some of the deluxe rooms
have 17th-century frescoes. Just down
the road, its sister establishment –
View at the Spanish Steps – has more
restrained decor, with sober grey and
blue fabrics, darkwood floors and
black-and-white tiled bathrooms. The
junior suite boasts a dead-ahead view
of the Spanish Steps.

Okapi Rooms

NEW *Via della Penna 57 (06 3260*
9815/www.okapirooms.it). €.
Sticking with the exotic beast theme,
owners of the Pensione Panda (see
below) have opened this fresh, bright
outpost a stone's throw from piazza del
Popolo. Though pretty basic and

reportedly noisy at times, Okapi Rooms
offers air-con and internet access, and
one room has a little terrace.

Pensione Panda

Via della Croce 35 (06 678 0179/
www.hotelpanda.it). €.
Panda's location, near the piazza di
Spagna, is its main selling point. Its
rooms are clean but very basic; newly
renovated rooms have high, wood-
beamed ceilings and terracotta floors.
There's no lift and no breakfast, but
centro storico bargains are hard to
come by, and Panda is usually booked
solid in high season.

Portrait Suites

Via Bocca di Leone 23 (06 6938 0742/
reservations 055 2726 4000/
www.lungarnohotels.com). €€€€.
Opened in spring 2006, the stylish
Portrait Suites is owned by fashion
designer Salvatore Ferragamo.
Memorabilia from the designer's
archives decorate the hallways;
in the bedrooms, a black-and-slate
colour scheme is offset with touches
of pink and lime. There are spacious
marble bathrooms, walk-in wardrobes
and a glamorous kitchenette.
Breakfast is served in the rooms or on
the spectacular terrace.

Residenza A

Via Veneto 183 (06 486 700/
www.hotelviaveneto.com). €€€.
On the first floor of an imposing palazzo, Residenza A is a boutique hotel
with splashy modern art enlivening
its grey and black colour scheme. The
rooms have been luxuriously finished,
with great extras such as flat-screen
computers and free internet, roomy
showers and Bulgari bath products.

Residenza Cellini

Via Modena 5 (06 4782 5204/
www.residenzacellini.it). €€.
This luminous and spacious *residenza* has huge guest rooms decorated
with faux-antique wooden furniture.
The bathrooms have jacuzzis or showers with hydro-massage. On the floor
that opened in January 2007, three

rooms have balconies and all are decorated in the same classic style; there's a terrace too. Non-smoking.

Westin Excelsior
Via V Veneto 125 (06 47 081/ www.starwood.com). €€€€.
After its wildly expensive makeover in 2002, the Excelsior's entrance is lavish and its rooms – with marble bathrooms – are a Hollywood-style fantasy. The Villa La Cupola suite is the priciest bed in Rome, rumoured to cost over €20,000 a night.

Esquilino & Celio

The Beehive
Via Marghera 8 (06 4470 4553/ www.the-beehive.com). €.
American owners Steve and Linda Brenner mix their penchant for design-icon furnishings with reasonable rates and basic amenities to create a 'youth hostel meets boutique hotel' vibe. There's a sunny garden, an all-organic restaurant and a yoga studio, plus free internet access. Breakfast not included.

Capo d'Africa
Via Capo d'Africa 54 (06 772 801/ www.hotelcapodafrica.com). €€€€.
The Capo d'Africa's lobby may be somewhat hotel-design-by-numbers but its location, on a quiet street near the Colosseum, is great. The rooms are spacious and comfortable, if bland; the rooftop breakfast room has knock-out views of the Colosseum.

Domus Sessoriana
Piazza Santa Croce in Gerusalemme 10 (06 706 151/www.domussessoriana.it). €€.
Reminders of this hotel's past – it's set in the monastery attached to the church of Santa Croce in Gerusalemme – are everywhere, from huge religious canvases to the narrow ex-refectory where breakfast is served. Tastefully decorated rooms are divided into two wings; the rooms in the 'Conventual' wing overlook the monastery's gorgeous vegetable garden, are more pleasant.

Exedra
Piazza della Repubblica 47 (06 489 381/ www.boscolohotels.com). €€€€.
From its splendid porticoed exterior to its opulent lobby, the Exedra is very glamorous. The rooms run from plush and utterly comfortable to outrageous. From May to September, the rooftop bar/restaurant and pool offer spectacular views. There's a spa too. The only drawback is the location: it's a little too close to Termini station for comfort.

Inn at the Roman Forum
Via degli Ibernesi 30 (06 6919 0970/ www.theinnattheromanforum.com). €€€€.
Opened in 2006, this boutique hotel's location, on a quiet, picturesque street near the Forum, gives it an exclusive feel. The rooms are a sumptuous mix of rich fabrics and antiques; the spacious deluxe rooms have canopied beds and marble bathrooms. Breakfast is served on the roof terrace, or in a cosy room with open fire. The two executive suites can be booked together as the Master Garden Suite, an exclusive apartment with a walled garden.

Lancelot
Via Capo d'Africa 47 (06 7045 0615/ www.lancelothotel.com). €€.
This beautifully kept and attractive family-run hotel has elegant mixes of linen, wood and tiles in the bedrooms, some of which have terraces facing the Palatine and the Colosseum. The reception has been given a personal touch with tiled floors and antique furniture, along with some unusual *objets*.

Nerva
Via Tor de' Conti 3 (06 678 1835/ www.hotelnerva.com). €€.
The family-run Nerva is handy for the Forum, and the rather old-fashioned rooms have all been refurbished. The staff are a friendly bunch.

Radisson SAS es. Hotel
Via F Turati 171 (06 444 841/ www.rome.radissonsas.com). €€€.
Built on the site of an ancient cemetery (digs are on show by the entrance), this

Happy campers

Flaminio Village

'Rome' and 'cheap' are words that sit badly together, at least where accommodation is concerned. And lower-end options look set to diminish still further, with the threatened closure of Rome's only official youth hostel, a 330-bed facility in a striking Brutalist building (miles from the centre...) near the Olimpico football stadium. Mind you, as a random selection of user comments found on various travel sites described the hostel as 'crap', 'completely sucks', 'toilets were disgusting' and 'dirty, loud and out of the way', this may not be a huge loss.

There are a host of private hostels, of varying salubriousness, thoughout the city. The best of these, we believe, are listed here: places like the **Beehive** (p175), **Colors** (p179) and the women-only **Foresteria Orsa Maggiore** (p178).

If you don't mind cell-like rooms and curfews, then seek out those religious establishments that take guests (see websites below), though beware: those in the *centro* tend to charge market rates for their generally sparse rooms.

Or, for something completely different – and very un-Roman – bring a tent. None of Rome's (very few) campsites are anywhere near the city centre: space problems alone prevent that. But what they lack in historic atmosphere, they make up for in amenities.

Besides allowing you to pitch your tent (€32 for two adults, a tent and a car) in a shady grove on the edge of the Veio nature reserve, the **Flaminio Village** (via Flaminia Nuova, 06 333 2604/ 1429/06 3322 0505, website below) campsite has bungalows (prices from €70 for two to €185 for five people), a huge swimming pool, a fine restaurant and squeaky-clean bathrooms with piped muzak. It will take you 15 minutes on a grotty commuter train to get into the centre, and transport dries up completely in the evening, but if you're on a budget and/or touring by car, this might just be the answer.

■ www.monasterystays.com
■ www.santasusanna.org
■ www.hospites.it
■ www.villageflaminio.it

'concept' hotel caters for business clients – who don't baulk at the location, by the train station – and diehard design fans. The large rooftop has a bar and pool. In the all-white rooms, the bed is on a low platform, divided from the bathroom by a glass screen; the only splash of colour is the turf-effect rugs. All very mod... but doesn't feel like Rome.

St Regis Grand
Via VE Orlando 3 (06 47 091/ www.starwood.com. €€€€.
The hotel's original chandeliers dazzle in massive marbled reception rooms, decorated in opulent gold, beige and red. Rooms have been individually designed using rich fabrics, and are filled with silk-covered Empire and Regency-style furnishings. There's a gym and a sauna.

Aventine & Testaccio

Sant'Anselmo, Villa Pio & Aventino
Piazza di Sant'Anselmo 2/via di Santa Melania 19 (06 570 057/ www.aventinohotels.com). €€€.
The three hotels in this group are within a stone's throw of one another in an exclusive, leafy residential area. The more ornate Sant'Anselmo has recently reopened after refurbishment. The Villa San Pio consists of three separate buildings that share the same pretty gardens and an airy breakfast room; it has a light feel, making it a pleasant place to stay. The Aventino is less manicured. Some rooms have jacuzzis.

Trastevere & the Gianicolo

Arco del Lauro
Via dell'Arco de' Tolomei 27 (06 9784 0350/www.arcodellauro.it). €.
On a picturesque backstreet, Arco del Lauro has six tasteful rooms decorated in modern, fresh neutrals. Budget *residenze* are few and far between in chichi Trastevere: this one is airy and spotlessly clean. Breakfast is taken in a bar in a nearby piazza.

Buonanotte Garibaldi
Via Garibaldi 83 (06 5833 0733/ www.buonanottegaribaldi.com). €€.
Artist Luisa Longo's three rooms around a courtyard garden act as a showcase for her distinctive creations: wall panels, bedcovers and curtains in hand-painted silk, organza and velvet. Guests are greeted after a day's sightseeing with a restorative glass of wine.

Casa di Santa Francesca Romana
Via dei Vascellari 61 (06 5812 1252/ www.sfromana.it). €.
This ex-convent is now a hotel with a noticeably churchy feel. It's popular with businessmen on a budget and with families (for the spacious quad rooms). The tree-lined central courtyard makes a pleasant spot for breakfast.

Foresteria Orsa Maggiore
Via San Francesco di Sales 1A (06 689 3753/www.foresteriaorsa. altervista.org). €.
Inside a 16th-century convent that for years has been home to a hopping

Colors Hotel & Hostel

feminist cultural centre, this women-only hostel offers B&B accommodation in bright, clean, recently redecorated single, double and dorm rooms at rock-bottom prices. The right-on complex also has eateries, exhibition spaces, a bookshop and a fairtrade store.

Hotel San Francesco
Via Jacopa de' Settesoli 7 (06 5830 0051/www.hotelsanfrancesco.net). €€.
On the quieter eastern side of viale Trastevere, the San Francesco has an attractive marble-floored entrance hall and a lovely roof terrace where breakfast is served when the weather's warm. Rooms are well equipped and reasonably big, though they have a slightly corporate feel. At the lower end of this price range.

Hotel Santa Maria
Vicolo del Piede 2 (06 589 4626/5474/ www.hotelsantamaria.info). €€.
On the site of a 16th-century convent, the Santa Maria has rooms with cool tiled floors, slightly anonymous floral print decor and spacious bathrooms. They all open on to a sunny central courtyard planted with orange trees.

Residenza Arco de' Tolomei
Via dell'Arco de' Tolomei 27 (06 5832 0819/www.inrome.info). €€.
This bijou *residenza* projects a cosy, welcoming feel. There's beautiful wood flooring, plentiful antiques and a sunny breakfast room. All of the bedrooms are individually designed in a whimsical, English country-house style; the three on the upper floor have terraces, the two below are slightly larger.

Vatican & Prati

Bramante
Vicolo delle Palline 24 (06 6880 6426/ www.hotelbramante.com). €€.
Once home to 16th-century architect Domenico Fontana, this became an inn in 1873. It has a large, pleasant reception and a little patio for the summer. The 16 rooms of varying sizes are simple yet elegant; most have high-beamed ceilings, some have wrought-iron beds.

Colors Hotel & Hostel
Via Boezio 31 (06 687 4030/ www.colorshotel.com). €.
A short walk from St Peter's, Colors has bright, clean dorm and hotel accommodation, plus self-catering kitchen and laundry facilities, and a terrace. A new floor opened in 2005; its superior rooms have breakfast included. All rooms have air-con. Credit cards are accepted for the superior rooms only.

Pensione Paradise
Viale Giulio Cesare 47 (06 3600 4331/ www.pensioneparadise.com). €.
Rooms in this budget hotel are on the poky side, but friendly staff and a decent location not far from the Vatican ensure that backpackers keep on coming. There's no breakfast and no air-con, but if you're willing to rough it a little, you could do far worse.

ESSENTIALS

Getting Around

Airports

Aeroporto Leonardo da Vinci, Fiumicino

Via dell'Aeroporto di Fiumicino (06 65 951/www.adr.it). **Open** 24hrs daily.

There's an express **rail** service between Fiumicino airport and Termini railway station, which takes 31mins and runs every 30mins from 6.36am until 11.36pm daily (5.52am-10.52pm to Fiumicino). A one-way ticket costs €11.

The regular service from Fiumicino takes 25-40mins, and stops at Trastevere, Ostiense, Tuscolana and Tiburtina stations. Trains leave about every 15mins (less often on Sun) between 5.57am and 11.27pm (5.05am-10.33pm to Fiumicino). Tickets cost €5.50.

Tickets for either service can be bought with cash or credit card from ticket booths or self-ticketing machines. Stamp your ticket in the machines at the head of the platform before boarding, or you risk a fine.

Terravision (06 6595 8646, www.terravision.it) runs a coach service from Fiumicino to Termini, which also makes stops in the northern suburbs (along via Aurelia) and at Lepanto (journey time to Termini: 70mins). Departures are about every 2hrs between 8.30am and 8.30pm daily. Coaches from Termini to Fiumicino leave from via Marsala 7 (opposite the multi-storey car park) from 6.30am to 6.30pm. Tickets cost €7 one way, €12 return (€3.50/€6 reductions), and can either be booked in advance online (all major credit cards are accepted), or paid for in cash at the Terravision desk or on the bus.

During the night, a Cotral **bus** service runs between Fiumicino (outside Terminal C) and Termini and Tiburtina railway stations in Rome; tickets cost €4.50. Buses leave Tiburtina at 12.30am, 1.15am, 2.30am and 3.45am, stopping at Termini railway station 10mins later. Departures from Fiumicino are at 1.15am, 2.15am, 3.30am and 5am. Neither Termini nor Tiburtina are attractive places at night, so it's advisable to get a taxi on from there to your final destination. Buses are infrequent; metro line B at Termini and Tiburtina closes at 11.30pm (1.30am Fri & Sat); for the time being, metro line A closes at 10pm daily, with shuttle buses replacing the service at night.

Aeroporto GB Pastine, Ciampino

Via Appia Nuova 1651 (06 65 951/www.adr.it). **Open** 24hrs daily.

Though bus services claim to run into the early morning, often they don't. Booking tickets online before you leave home may signal to bus drivers not to pack up early. Taxi drivers who hang out at this airport are known for praying on tourists.

On paper at least, the most hassle-free way to get into town from Ciampino is to take a coach. **Terravision** (06 7949 4572/4621, www.terravision.it) runs services to Termini station (journey time: 40mins). Buses leave from outside the arrivals hall after each arrival. Buses from Termini to Ciampino leave from via Marsala. This is a dedicated service for low-cost airlines, so you'll need to show your ticket or boarding pass to buy a ticket (€8 single, €14 return; €4/€7 reductions), which can be booked online, or bought (cash only)

ESSENTIALS

in the arrivals hall at Ciampino, at the Terravision office in the Termini forecourt or on the bus.

SIT Bus Shuttle (06 591 6826, www.sitbusshuttle.it) runs a frequent service from Termini (via Marsala) to Ciampino (€6, 4.30am-9.15pm), and Ciampino to Termini (€6, 8.30am-00.30am). Tickets can be bought on the bus or online.

Schiaffini buses (800 700 805, www.schiaffini.it) runs a service between Ciampino and Anagnina metro station every 30-40mins (6am-10.40pm daily), and to Ciampino station (where frequent trains depart for Rome Termini) 5.45am-23.25pm daily; both cost €1. It also runs a direct service (€5) from the airport to Termini station at 11.50am and 00.15am; from Termini to Ciampino at 4.45am. Buy tickets on board.

By bus

There is no central long-distance bus station in Rome. Most coach services terminate outside the following metro stations: Cornelia, Ponte Mammolo and Tiburtina (routes north); Anagnina and EUR Fermi (routes south).

By train

Most long-distance trains arrive at Termini station, also the hub of Rome's transport network. Beware of pickpockets. Night trains may arrive at Tiburtina or Ostiense.

For bookings and information on mainline rail services across Italy, call **Trenitalia** (24hrs daily) on 892 021 (06 6847 5475 from abroad) or go to www.trenitalia.it. Tickets can be bought at stations (credit cards accepted over the counter and by ticket machines) or online. Under-12s pay half fare; under-4s travel free.

Slow trains (*diretti, espressi, regionali* and *interregionali*) are cheap; fast services – InterCity (IC),

EuroCity (EC), Eurostar Italia (ES) – are closer to the European norm.

You must stamp your ticket in the yellow machines at the head of the platform before boarding. You risk being fined if you don't.

Rome's main stations are **Ostiense** (piazzale dei Partigiani), **Termini** (piazza dei Cinquecento), **Tiburtina** (circonvallazione Nomentana) and **Trastevere** (piazzale Biondo).

Public transport

Rome's transport system is co-ordinated by **ATAC** (06 57 003, toll-free 800 431 784, www.atac.roma.it). You can download maps of the transport network from the website (click on *percorsi e mappe*), which also has a useful journey planner.

City-centre and inner-suburb routes are served by the buses and trams of the **Trambus** transport authority. The system is relatively easy to use and as efficient as the traffic-choked streets allow.

Pickpocketing is a problem on buses and metros, particularly on major tourist routes, notoriously the 64 and 40 Express between Termini station and the Vatican.

Tickets

The same tickets are valid on all city bus, tram and metro lines, whoever the operator is. They are not valid on services to Fiumicino airport. Though the latest generation of buses has ticket dispensers on board, in most cases you'll have to buy before you board, from ATAC automatic ticket machines, information centres, some bars and newsstands and all *tabacchi*. Before purchasing a three-day ticket, consider whether the three-day **Roma Pass** (p11) might not be better value.

BIT valid for 75mins, during which you can take an unlimited number

of city buses, plus one metro trip; €1.
BIG valid for one day, until midnight;
covers the whole urban network; €4.
BTI three-day pass, covering all bus
and metro routes, and local mainline
trains to Ostia; €11.
CIS valid for seven days; it covers
all bus routes and the metro system,
including the lines to Ostia; €16.
You must stamp tickets on board.

Under-10s travel free; older kids
and pensioners must pay the adult
fare. If you are caught without a
stamped ticket, you'll be fined €51
on the spot, or €104.40 if you opt
topay later at a post office.

Buses

Bus is the best way to get around
Rome. Once you get the hang of it,
the system is easy to use; a sign at
each bus stop tells you the routes
each line stopping there takes.

Most services run 5.30am-
midnight daily, every 10-45mins.
The doors for boarding (usually
front and rear) and alighting
(usually centre) are clearly marked.
Note that 'Express' buses make
few stops along their route: check
before boarding so you don't get
whisked past your destination.

Trams

Tram routes mainly serve suburban
areas. An express tram service
– No.8 – links largo Argentina to
Trastevere and the western suburbs.
Tram 3 had been replaced by a bus
as this guide went to press.

Metro

MetRo runs Rome's two metro
lines, which cross beneath Termini
train station. Line A runs from
south-east to north-west; line B
from EUR to the north-east. Line B
is open 5.30am-11.30pm (to 1.30am
Fri & Sat). Line A opens 5.30am but
closes at 10pm daily for work on
the long-awaited line C (due in
2011). Shuttle bus services replace
metro line A from 10pm to 11.30pm
(until 12.30am Sat & Sun).

Taxis

Licensed taxis are white and have a
meter. Touts are rife at major tourist
magnets; ignore them if you don't
want to risk an extortionate fare.

Recent changes in taxi tariffs
have made them super-complicated.
When you pick up a taxi at a rank
or hail one in the street, the meter
should read zero. The minimum fare
is currently €2.80 (€4 on Sundays
and public holidays), or €5.80 if you
board 10pm-7am. Each kilometre
after that is €0.92. The first piece
of luggage put in the boot is free,
then it's €1 per piece. Tariffs outside
the GRA, Rome's major ring road,
are much higher. There's a 10%
discount for trips to hospitals, and
for women travelling alone 9pm-
1am, and a €2 surcharge for any trip
starting at Termini station.

Fixed airport tariffs from
anywhere inside the Aurelian walls
(ie most of the *centro storico*) are
€40 to/from Fiumicino; €30 to/from
Ciampino. This is for up to four
people and includes luggage: don't
let taxi drivers tell you otherwise.

Most of Rome's taxi drivers are
honest; if you do think you're being
fleeced, take down the driver's details
from the metal plaque inside the
car's rear door. The more obviously
you do this, the more likely you
are to find the fare returning to
its proper level. Report complaints
to the drivers' co-operative (phone
number on the outside of each car)
or, in serious cases, the police.

When you phone for a taxi, you'll
be given the taxi code-name (always
a location followed by a number)
and a time, as in *Bahama 69, in tre
minuti* ('Bahamas 69, in three
minutes'). Besides the minimum
fare, you'll be charged the following
'call' rates depending on how long

your taxi takes to arrive: €2 (up to five mins), €4 (five-ten mins) or €6 (more than ten minutes). If the meter shows more than this when the taxi arrives, the difference must be deducted at the end of the trip.

Cooperativa Samarcanda 06 5551/ *www.samarcanda.it.*
Cosmos Radio Taxi 06 88 177/ 06 8822.
Società Cooperativa Autoradio Taxi Roma 06 3570/*www.3570.it.*
Società la Capitale Radio Taxi 06 49 94.

Driving

Much of central Rome is off-limits during the day for anyone without a permit. Police and cameras guard these ZTL areas; any car without a pass will be fined €70 if it enters at restricted times. A strict no-car policy applies in the centre on some Sundays too; check www.comune. roma.it or www.atac.roma.it for info.

Most motoring associations have break-down service agreements with either **Automobile Club d'Italia** (24hr info and emergency 06 49 981, toll-free 800 116, www.aci.it) or **Touring Club Italiano** (06 3600 5281, www.touringclub.it).

Remember:

■ You are required to wear a seatbelt at all times, in front and back seats, and to carry a warning triangle and reflective jacket in your car.

■ You must keep your driving licence, vehicle registration and ID documents on you at all times.

■ Traffic lights flashing amber mean stop and give way to the right.

Parking

Residents park for free and visitors pay to park in many areas. It's well policed, so look for the telltale blue lines. Buy parking tickets (€1/hr) at pay-and-display ticket dispensers or from *tabacchi*. In some areas you can park for free at certain times,

so check the instructions on the machine first. €1 parking cards (*scheda per il parcheggio*), available from *tabacchi*, save you the bother of scrabbling for small change.

In zones with no blue lines, anything resembling a parking place is up for grabs, with some exceptions: watch out for signs saying *Passo carrabile* ('access at all times') or *Sosta vietata* ('no parking'), and disabled parking spaces (marked by yellow stripes). The sign *Zona rimozione* ('tow-away area') means no parking, and is valid for the length of the street or until the sign is repeated with a red line through it. If a street or square has no cars parked in it, assume it's a strictly enforced no-parking zone.

In some areas, self-appointed *parcheggiatori* will 'look after' your car for a small fee; it may be illegal and an absurd imposition, but it's probably worth paying up to ensure your tyres remain intact.

Cars are safe in most central areas, but you may prefer to use a car park to keep your car off the street. The following are central:
ParkSì Villa Borghese *viale del Galoppatoio 33 (06 322 5934/7972/ www.sabait.it)*. **Rates** €1.60/hr for up to 12hrs, €1/hr thereafter.
Valentino *via Sistina 75E (06 678 2597)*. **Rates** €3/hr for up to six hours.

Vehicle removal

If your car is not where you left it, it may have been towed. Phone the municipal police (*Vigili urbani*) on 06 67 691 and quote your number plate to find out which pound it's in.

Vehicle hire

Avis 06 481 4373/199 100 133/ *www.avisautonoleggio.it.*
Europcar 199 307 030/ *www.europcar.it.*
Hertz 06 488 0049/199 112 211/*www.hertz.it.*
Maggiore 06 2245 6060/199 151 120/*www.maggiore.it.*

ESSENTIALS

Resources A-Z

Accident & emergency

To call an **ambulance**, dial 118; for the **fire brigade**, dial 115; for **police**, see p185. The hospitals listed below offer 24hr casualty services. If your child needs emergency treatment, head for the Ospedale Bambino Gesù.

Ospedale Fatebenefratelli
Isola Tiberina (06 68 371).
Ospedale Pediatrico Bambino Gesù *Piazza Sant'Onofrio 4 (06 68 591/www.opbg.net).*
Ospedale San Camillo-Forlanini *Via Portuense 332 (06 55 551/06 58 701/www.scamilloforlanini.rm.it).*
Ospedale San Giacomo *Via Canova 29 (06 36 261/ www.aslromaa.it/ospedali/osg.htm).*
Ospedale San Giovanni *Via Amba Aradam 8 (06 7705 3444/ www.hsangiovanni.roma.it).*
Policlinico Umberto I *Viale Policlinico 155 (06 49 971/ www.policlinicoumberto1.it).*

Pharmacies

Normal pharmacy opening hours are 8.30am-1pm, 4-8pm Mon-Sat. Outside these hours, a duty rota system operates. A list by the door of any pharmacy (and in local papers) indicates the nearest ones.
Farmacia della Stazione *Piazza dei Cinquecento 49-51 (06 488 0019).* **Open** 24hrs daily.
Piram *Via Nazionale 228 (06 488 0754).* **Open** 24hrs daily.

Credit card loss

The following are open 24hrs.
American Express *06 7228 0371/ US cardholders 800 874 333*
Diners Club *800 864 064*
MasterCard *800 870 866*
Visa *800 877 232*

Customs

Travellers arriving from EU countries are not required to declare goods imported into or exported from Italy if they are for personal use, up to the following limits:
■ 800 cigarettes or 400 cigarillos or 200 cigars or 1kg of tobacco
■ ten litres of spirits (over 22% alcohol) or 20 litres of fortified wine (under 22% alcohol).

For people arriving from non-EU countries the following limits apply:
■ 200 cigarettes or 100 cigarillos or 50 cigars or 250g of tobacco
■ one litre of spirits or two litres of wine; one bottle of perfume (50g)
■ 250ml of eau de toilette or various merchandise not exceeding €175.

Anything above will be subject to taxation at the port of entry. There are no restrictions on the importation of cameras, watches or electrical goods. Call Italian customs (*dogana*) on 041 251 0250 or check its website (www.agenziadogane.it).

Dental emergency

For serious dental emergencies, use hospital casualty departments (see above). Children should be taken to the Ospedale Bambino Gesù.

Disabled

With cobbled streets, narrow pavements and old buildings, Rome is difficult for disabled people. That said, many city-centre buses are now wheelchair accessible and most museums and larger hotels have facilities.

The non-profit **CO.IN** (www.coinsociale.it) gives information on disabled facilities at museums, restaurants, shops, theatres, stations and hotels. The group also organises transport for disabled people (up to 8 places), which must be booked several days in advance. It runs a phone service in Italian and English (toll-free 800 271 027, from within Italy only). Guided tours with transport can be booked.

Roma per Tutti (06 5717 7094, www.romapertutti.it) is an info line run by CO.IN and the city council. English-speaking staff answer questions on accessibility in hotels, buildings and monuments.

Information for disabled people is also available from the APT tourist office (p187).

Electricity

Italy uses 220V – compatible with British-bought appliances (with a plug adaptor); US 110V equipment requires a current transformer.

Embassies & consulates

For a full list of embassies, see *Ambasciate* in the phone book.
Australia *Via Antonio Bosio 5 (06 852 721/www.italy.embassy.gov.au).*
Britain *Via XX Settembre 80A (06 4220 0001/www.britain.it).*
Canada *Via Zara 30 (06 854 441/ 06 8544 43937/www.canada.it).*
Ireland *Piazza Campitelli (06 697 9121/www.ambasciata-irlanda.it).*
New Zealand *Via Clitunno 44 (06 853 7501/www.nzembassy.com).*
South Africa *Via Tanaro 14 (06 852 541/www.sudafrica.it).*
US *Via Vittorio Veneto 119 (06 46 741/www.usembassy.it).*

Internet

Much of central Rome, plus major parks (*ville* Borghese, Pamphili, Ada, Torlonia), EUR and the Auditorium – Parco della Musica zone, is covered by the ever-growing city-sponsored free wireless network. When you open your browser in one of the 100+ hotspots, you'll be asked to log on. Initially, you'll need to register, giving a mobile phone number. For information, including a map of hotspots, see www.romawireless.com.

Opening hours

For shopping hours, see p23; for pharmacies, see p184.

Most banks open 8.30am-1.30pm, 2.45-4.30pm Mon-Fri. Some central branches also open until 6pm Thur and 8.30am-12.30pm Sat. All banks work reduced hours the day before a holiday (many close by 11am).

Police

For emergencies, call one of the following helplines:
Carabinieri *(English-speaking helpline) 112*
Polizia di stato *113*
The principal *Polizia di Stato* station, the Questura Centrale, is at via San Vitale 15 (06 46 861, www.poliziadistato.it). Others, and the Carabinieri's *Commissariati*, are listed in the phone directory under *Polizia* and *Carabinieri*. Incidents can be reported to either.

Post

The once-notorious Italian postal service is now generally efficient (try the Vatican Post Office, run in association with the Swiss postal service, if in doubt). For postal information, call 803 160 (8am-8pm Mon-Sat) or visit www.poste.it.

There are local post offices (*ufficio postale*) in each district; opening hours are generally 8.30am-6pm Mon-Fri (8.30am-2pm

ESSENTIALS

Aug), 8.30am-1.30pm Sat and any day preceding a public holiday. They close two hours earlier than normal on the last day of each month. Main post offices in the centre have longer opening hours. Some services are available via the website (www.poste.it); check it first to avoid the queues.

Posta Centrale *Piazza San Silvestro 19 (info 803 160).*

Vatican Post Office *Piazza San Pietro (06 6988 3406).* **Open** 8.30am-6pm Mon-Fri; 8.30am-5pm Sat.

Smoking

A law introduced in January 2005 prohibits smoking in all public places in Italy except for those that provide a distinct, ventilated smokers' room. Possible fines of between €27.50 and €275 (or up to €550 if you smoke in the presence of children or pregnant women) are the reason why you'll find small groups puffing away *outside* most restaurants, pubs and clubs.

Tabacchi

Tabacchi, identified by signs with a white T on a black background, are the only places where you can buy tobacco products. They also sell stamps, phone cards, tickets for public transport and lottery tickets.

Telephones

Dialling & codes

■ Land-lines have the area code 06, which must be used whether calling from within or outside the city. When phoning Rome from abroad, do *not* omit the initial 0.
■ Numbers beginning 800 are toll-free. Numbers beginning 840 and 848 are charged at low set rates but can only be called within Italy.
■ Mobile numbers begin with a 3.

GSM phones can be used on both 900 and 1800 bands; British, Australian and New Zealand mobiles work fine, but US phones (unless they're tri-band) don't work.
■ For international calls, dial 00, followed by the country code, area code (omitting the initial zero, if applicable) and number. Codes include: Australia 61; Canada 1; Irish Republic 353; New Zealand 64; United Kingdom 44; United States 1.

Directory enquiries

This is a jungle, and charges for information given over the phone are steep. The major services are 1254 (Italian and international numbers, in Italian) and 892 412 (international numbers, in Italian and English, from mobile phones). Italian directory information can be accessed for free at www.1254 .it and www.paginebianche.it.

Operator services

To reverse the charges (make a collect call), dial 170 for the international operator. If you are reversing the charges from a phone box, insert a 10¢ coin (refunded after your call).

Public phones

Rome has no shortage of public phone boxes, and many bars have payphones, which are rarely busy as locals are addicted to mobiles. Most only accept phone cards (*schede telefoniche*); a few also accept major credit cards. Phone cards cost €5, €15 and €30 and are available from *tabacchi*, some newsstands and some bars.

Tickets

For pre-booking tickets for sights, galleries and exhibitions, see p11, and Tourist Infomation below.

Expect to pay *diritti di prevendita* (booking fees) on tickets bought anywhere except at the venue on the night. **Feltrinelli Libri e Musica** (Galleria Alberto Sordi, piazza Colonna, 06 679 4957) sells tickets for classical concerts and for rock, jazz and other events.

Hello Ticket (800 907 080, www.helloticket.it) takes bookings over the phone and online for most concerts, plays and sporting events.

Time

Italy is on Central European Time, making it an hour ahead of GMT and six hours ahead of Eastern Standard Time. In all EU countries clocks move forward an hour in early spring, and then back again in late autumn.

Tipping

Foreigners are generally expected to tip more than Italians, but the ten or more per cent usual in many countries is seen as generous even for the richest-looking tourist. Anything between €1 and €5 is normal; some smarter places now include a 10-15% service charge. For drinks, leave 10¢-20¢ when ordering at the counter. Taxi drivers will be happy if you round the fare up to the nearest euro.

Tourist information

The offices of Rome's tourist board, **APT**, have English-speaking staff. The city council has well-stocked, green tourist information kiosks (**PIT**), 9.30am-7/7.30pm daily; the most central are in piazza Pia (by Castel Sant'Angelo), piazza delle Cinque Lune (by piazza Navona) and piazza Sonnino (in Trastevere).

The fastest one-stop shop for tourist information, however, is a new phone service, 060608,

sponsored by the city council. Information on sights, opening times, shows and much else is dispensed in English and Italian; phone operators will put callers through to the appropriate booking agency if they want to reserve tickets or seats. The www.060608.it website is an excellent source of information.

APT (Azienda per il Turismo di Roma) *Via Parigi 5 (infoline 060608/ www.romaturismo.com).* **Open** 9.30am-1pm, 2.30-4.30pm Mon, Thur.

Ufficio Pellegrini e Turisti (Vatican Tourist Office) *Piazza San Pietro (06 6988 1662/www.vaticano.va).* **Open** 8.30am-6.30pm Mon-Sat.

Visas

EU nationals and citizens of the US, Canada, Australia and New Zealand do not need visas for stays of up to three months. For EU citizens a passport or national ID card valid for travel abroad is sufficient; non-EU citizens must have full passports. In theory, all visitors must declare their presence to the local police within eight days of arrival. If you're staying in a hotel, this will be done for you.

What's on

Listings mags *Roma C'è* (www. romace.it, out Wed) and *Trovaroma* (free with *La Repubblica* on Thur) are the best sources of information about shows, concerts and nightlife. The latter has an English section.

Major events are listed on the city of Rome's website (www.roma turismo.it). For an alternative look at Rome's nightlife, check out www.romastyle.info and www. musicaroma.it. For information on Rome's gay scene, contact **Arcigay Roma** (06 6450 1102, www.arcigay roma.it) or **Arci-Lesbica Roma** (www.arcilesbica.it/roma). For other gay organisations, see p28.

ESSENTIALS

Vocabulary

Pronunciation

a – like a in ask
e – like a in age or e in sell
i – like ea in east
o – like o in hotel or hot
u – like oo in boot
c – as in cat before a, o and u;
otherwise like ch in cheat
g – as in good before a, o and u;
otherwise like g in giraffe; **gl** – like
lli in million; **gn** – like ny in canyon
h – after any consonant makes it
hard (ch – cat; gh – good)
sc – like sh in shame; **sch** – like
sc in scout

Useful phrases

hello/goodbye (informal) *ciao, salve*;
good morning *buon giorno*; **good
evening** *buona sera*; **good night**
buona notte
please *per favore, per piacere*; **thank
you** *grazie*; **you're welcome** *prego*;
excuse me, sorry *pardon*, (formal)
mi scusi, (informal) *scusa*
I don't speak Italian (very well)
non parlo (molto bene) l'italiano
do you speak English?
parla inglese?
can I use/where's the toilet?
posso usare/dov'è il bagno?
open *aperto*; **closed** *chiuso*;
entrance *entrata*; **exit** *uscita*

Transport

bus *autobus, auto*; **car** *macchina*;
coach *pullman*; **plane** *aereo*; **taxi**
tassi, taxi; **train** *treno*; **tram** *tram*;
bus stop *fermata (dell'autobus)*;
platform *binario*; **station** *stazione*;
ticket *biglietto*; **one-way** *solo andata*;
return *andata e ritorno*

Directions

where is? *dov'è?*; **(turn) left** *(giri a)
sinistra*; **(it's on the) right** *(è a/sulla)
destra*; **straight on** *sempre dritto*;
is it near/far? *è vicino/lontano?*

Communications

attacco per il computer *dataport*;
broadband *ADSL (adiesselle)*;
cellphone *telefonino*; **courier**
corriere, pony; **fax** *fax*; **letter** *lettera*;
phone *telefono*; **postcard** *cartolina*;
stamp *francobollo*; **a stamp for
England/the US** *un francobollo
per l'Inghilterra/gli Stati Uniti*

Days

Monday *lunedì*; **Tuesday** *martedì*;
Wednesday *mercoledì*; **Thursday**
giovedì; **Friday** *venerdì*; **Saturday**
sabato; **Sunday** *domenica*;
yesterday *ieri*; **today** *oggi*;
tomorrow *domani*; **weekend**
fine settimana, weekend

Numbers, weights & sizes

0 *zero*; **1** *uno*; **2** *due*; **3** *tre*; **4** *quattro*;
5 *cinque*; **6** *sei*; **7** *sette*; **8** *otto*; **9** *nove*;
10 *dieci*; **11** *undici*; **12** *dodici*;
13 *tredici*; **14** *quattordici*; **15** *quindici*;
16 *seidici*; **17** *diciasette*; **18** *diciotto*;
19 *dicianove*; **20** *venti*; **30** *trenta*;
40 *quaranta*; **50** *cinquanta*;
60 *sessanta*; **70** *settanta*; **80** *ottanta*;
90 *novanta*; **100** *cento*; **200** *duecento*;
1,000 *mille*; **2,000** *duemila*
I take (shoe/dress) size *porto il
numero/la taglia…*; **100 grams of…**
un'etto di…; **300 grams of…**
tre etti di…; **a kilo of…** *un kilo di…*;
five kilos of… *cinque chili di…*

Booking & paying

booking, reservation *prenotazione*
I'd like to book… *vorrei prenotare…*
…a table for four at eight *un tavolo
per quattro alle otto*
…a single/twin/double room *una
camera singola/doppia/matrimoniale*
how much is it? *quanto costa?*
do you take credit cards?
si accettano le carte di credito?

Menu Glossary

Sauces & toppings

aglio, olio e peperoncino *garlic, oil and chilli*; **alle vongole** *clams*; **al pomodoro fresco** *fresh/raw tomatoes*; **al ragù** *'bolognese' (a term that doesn't exist in Italian)*; **al sugo** *puréed cooked tomatoes*; **all'amatriciana** *tomato, chilli, sausage and onion*; **alla gricia** *as above without tomato*; **all'arrabbiata** *tomato and chilli*; **alla carbonara** *egg, bacon and parmesan*; **alla puttanesca** *olives, capers and garlic*; **cacio e pepe** *cheese and black pepper*; **in bianco** *with oil or butter and parmesan*; **(ravioli) ricotta e spinaci** *filled with curd cheese and spinach*.

Meat & meat dishes

abbacchio, agnello *lamb*; **animelle** *fried pancreas and thymus glands*; **bresaola** *thinly sliced cured beef*; **coda alla vaccinara** *oxtail in celery broth*; **coniglio** *rabbit*; **lardo** *fatty bacon*; **lingua** *tongue*; **maiale** *pork*; **manzo** *beef*; **ossobuco** *beef shins with marrow jelly inside*; **pajata** *veal/lamb intestines*; **pancetta** *bacon*; **pollo** *chicken*; **porchetta** *roast suckling pig*; **prosciutto cotto** *ham*; **prosciutto crudo** *Parma ham*; **straccetti** *thin strips of pan-tossed beef*; **trippa** *tripe*; **vitello** *veal*.

Fish & seafood

alici, acciughe *anchovies*; **aragosta, astice** *lobster*; **arzilla, razza** *skate*; **baccalà** *salt cod*; **branzino, spigola** *sea bass*; **calamari** *squid*; **cernia** *grouper*; **dentice, fragolino, marmora, orata, sarago** *forms of bream*; **cozze** *mussels*; **gamberi** *prawns*; **granchio** *crab*; **mazzancolle** *king prawns*; **merluzzo** *cod*; **moscardini** *baby octopus*; **ostriche** *oysters*; **pesce sanpietro** *john dory*; **pesce spada** *swordfish*; **polpo, polipo** *octopus*; **rombo** *turbot*; **salmone** *salmon*; **seppie** *cuttlefish*; **sogliola** *sole*; **tonno** *tuna*; **trota** *trout*; **vongole** *clams*.

Vegetables

asparagi *asparagus*; **broccoli siciliani** *broccoli*; **broccolo** *green cauliflower*; **broccoletti** *turnip tops*; **carciofo** *artichoke*; **cavolfiore** *cauliflower*; **cicoria** *green leaf vegetable, like dandelion*; **cipolla** *onion*; **fagioli** *beans*; **fagiolini** *green beans*; **fave** *broad beans*; **funghi** *mushrooms*; **insalata verde/mista** *green/mixed salad*; **melanzana** *aubergine, eggplant*; **patate** *potatoes*; **patatine fritte** *french fries*; **piselli** *peas*; **puntarelle** *bitter salad vegetable usually served with anchovy sauce*; **rughetta** *rocket*; **sedano** *celery*; **spinaci** *spinach*; **zucchine** *courgettes*.

Fruit

ananas *pineapple*; **anguria, cocomero** *watermelon*; **arance** *oranges*; **ciliegi** *cherries*; **fichi** *figs*; **fragole** *strawberries*; **mele** *apples*; **nespole** *loquats*; **pere** *pears*; **pesche** *peaches*; **uva** *grapes*.

Desserts

gelato *ice-cream*; **pannacotta** *'cooked cream', a thick blancmange-like cream*; **sorbetto** *water ice*; **tiramisù** *mascarpone and coffee sponge*; **torta della nonna** *flan of pâtisserie cream and pinenuts*; **millefoglie** *flaky pastry cake*.

Miscellaneous

antipasto *hors d'oeuvre*; **primo** *first course*; **secondo** *main course*; **contorno** *side dish, vegetable*; **dessert, dolce** *dessert*; **fritto** *fried*; **arrosto** *roast*; **alla griglia** *grilled*; **all'agro** *with oil and lemon*; **ripassato in padella** *(of vegetables) cooked then tossed in a pan with oil, garlic and chilli*; **formaggio** *cheese*; **parmigiano** *parmesan*; **pane** *bread*; **sale** *salt*; **pepe** *pepper*; **aceto** *vinegar*; **olio** *oil*.

ESSENTIALS

Index

Sights & Areas

a
Abbazia delle Tre Fontane p155
Appian Way, The p151
Ara Pacis Museum p85
Aventine p117

b
Baths of Caracalla p117
Baths of Diocletian p101
Bioparco-Zoo p92
Borgo p139

c
Campo de' Fiori p65
Capitoline Museums p56
Caracalla p117
Castel Sant'Angelo p143
Catacombs of San Callisto p152
Catacombs of San Sebastiano p153
Celio p108
Centrale Montemartini p122
Centro, Il p54
Chiesa Nuova/Santa Maria in Vallicella p78
Circus Maximus p57
Circus of Maxentius p153
Colosseum p57
Crypta Balbi p69

d
Domus Aurea p101
Doria Pamphili Gallery p78

e
Esquilino p100
Explora – Museo dei Bambini di Roma p92
EUR p154

g
Galleria Borghese p92
Galleria Colonna p95
Galleria Nazionale d'Arte Moderna e Contemporanea p92
Galleria Spada p69
Gesù, Il p69
Ghetto, The p65
Gianicolo p138

h
Hadrian's Villa (Villa Adriana) p160

i
Imperial Fora Museum p57

j
Jewish Museum p69

k
Keats-Shelley Memorial House p85

m
MACRO p98
Mamertine Prison p59
MAXXI p98
Monteverde p138
Monti p100
Museo Barracco p70
Museo Carlo Bilotti p94
Museo della Civiltà Romana p155
Museo dell'Alto Medioevo p155
Museo delle Anime dei Defunti p149
Museo delle Mura p153
Museo di Roma p78
Museo di Roma in Trastevere p129
Museo Nazionale d'Arte Orientale p101
Museo Nazionale delle Paste Alimentari p95
Museo Nazionale di Villa Giulia p94
Museo Preistorico ed Etnografico L Pigorini p157
Museo Storico Nazionale dell'Arte Sanitaria p143
Museum of Via Ostiense p123

o
Orto botanico (Botanical Garden) p129
Ostia Antica p157
Ostiense p120

p
Palazzo Altemps p78
Palazzo Barberini – Galleria Nazionale d'Arte Antica p95
Palazzo Corsini – Galleria Nazionale d'Arte Antica p129
Palazzo delle Esposizioni p101
Palazzo del Quirinale p96

Palazzo Massimo alle Terme p104
Palazzo Ruspoli-Fondazione Memmo p85
Palazzo Venezia Museum p60
Pantheon, The p76, p78
Piazza Navona, p76, p79
Portico D'Ottavia p70
Prati p149
Protestant Cemetery p123

q
Quirinale p95

r
Roman Forum & Palatine p60

s
San Carlino alle Quattro Fontane p96
San Clemente p109
San Francesco a Ripa p129
San Giorgio in Velabro p61
San Giovanni p108
San Giovanni in Laterano p109
San Gregorio Magno p111
San Lorenzo p114
San Lorenzo fuori le Mura p114
San Lorenzo in Lucina p85
San Luigi dei Francesi p79
San Marco p63
San Nicola in Carcere p63
San Paolo fuori le Mura p123
San Pietro in Vincoli p104
Santa Cecilia in Trastevere p129
Santa Croce in Gerusalemme p111
Sant'Agnese in Agone p79
Sant'Agostino p79
Santa Maria della Concezione p94
Santa Maria della Pace p79
Santa Maria della Vittoria p96
Santa Maria del Popolo p85
Santa Maria in Aracoeli p63
Santa Maria in Cosmedin & the Mouth of Truth p64
Santa Maria in Domnica p111
Santa Maria in Trastevere p132
Santa Maria Maggiore p105
Santa Maria sopra Minerva p79

Index

Sant'Andrea al Quirinale p97
Sant'Andrea della Valle p70
Santa Prassede p105
Santa Pudenziana p106
Santa Sabina p120
Santi Giovanni e Paolo p111
Sant'Ignazio di Loyola p80
Santi Quattro Coronati p112
Sant'Ivo alla Sapienza p80
Santo Stefano Rotondo p112
Scala Santa & Sancta
  Sanctorum p112
Scavi di Ostia Antica p158
Scuderie Papali al Quirinale
  p97
Spanish Steps & Piazza
  di Spagna p88
St Peter's (Basilica di
  San Pietro) p144

t
Tempietto di Bramante &
  San Pietro in Montorio
  p138
Testaccio p120
Theatre of Marcellus p70
Tiber Island & Ponte Rotto
  p72
Tivoli p159
Tomb of Cecilia Metella
  p153
Trastevere p128
Tridente, The p84
Trevi Fountain p95, p97

v
Vatican, The p139
Vatican Museums p145
Via Veneto p91
Villa Borghese p91
Villa dei Quintili p154
Villa d'Este p161
Villa Farnesina p132
Villa Torlonia p99
Vittoriano p64

Eating & Drinking

a
Agata e Romeo p106
Alberto Ciarla p133
Alberto Pica p72
Alle Fratte di Trastevere
  p133
Al Presidente p98
Al Ristoro degli Angeli
  p124
Altro Mastai, L' p107
Al Vino al Vino p106
Andreotti p124
Antica Birreria Peroni p98
Antico Arco p138
Arancia Blu p114
Arcangelo, L' p150
Ar Galletto p72
Armando al Pantheon p81

b
Bar à Book p114
Bar della Pace p81
Bar Sant'Eustachio p81
Bartaruga p72
Bernasconi p72
Bir & Fud p133
Bishoku Kobo p124
Bocconcino, Il p113
Bruschetteria degli Angeli
  p72
B-Said p116
Buccone p88

c
Café Café p113
Caffè Bernini p81
Caffè Canova-Tadolini p88
Caffè Fandango p81
Caffettiera, La p82
Cantina Castani p94
Casa Bleve p81
Checchino dal 1887 p124
Ciampini al Café du Jardin
  p88
Cinecaffè – Casina
  delle Rose p94
Cribbio! P116
Crudo p72

d
Da Felice p124
Da Francesco p81
Da Giggetto p73
Da Gino p88
Dagnino p107
Da Michele p98
Dar Poeta p133
Da Vezio p81
Del Frate p149
Ditirambo p73
Doozo p107

e
Enoteca Corsi p82
Enoteca Ferrara p133
Enoteca Nuvolari p148
Etabli p82

f
Forno Campo de' Fiori p73
Freni e Frizioni p133
Friends Art Café p133

g
Gelato di San Crispino, Il p98
GiNa p88
Glass Hostaria p135
Gloss p73
Goccetto, Il p73
Gran Caffè Esperia p149
'Gusto p88

h
Hang Zhou p107

i
Indian Fast Food p107
Isola della Pizza p150

j
Jaipur p135

l
Libreria del Cinema p135
Lo Zozzone p82
Luzzi p113

m
Mani in Pasta, Le p135
Marcello p116
Matricianella p89
Moma p94

o
Oasi della Birra, L' p124
Ombre Rosse p136
Osteria dell'Arco p99

p
Pagliaccio, Il p73
Palatium p89
Paninoteca da Guido p148
Piccolo Alpino p124
Piramidi, Le p75
Pizza Ciro p89

r
Remo p125
Ristoro, Il p148
Rivadestra p136
Rosati p89

s
Salotto 42 p82
San Teodoro p65
Satollo p125
Seme e la Foglia, Il p124
Settembrini p150
Société Lutèce p82
Sora Margherita p75
Stardust p82
Stravinskij Bar p89

t
Tallusa p125
Trattoria p89
Trattoria Monti p107
Tuttifrutti p125

u
Uno e Bino p116

v
Vic's p91
Vineria, La p75

z
Zampagna p126

ESSENTIALS

ROME

VIA VITTORIO VENETO 62 A/B
METRO STOP: PIAZZA BARBERINI
+39-06-4203051 • HARDROCK.COM
FOR INFO:
ROME_SALES@HARDROCK.COM

VIP Entrance- First available table

RESTAURANT • COCKTAIL BAR • ROCK SHOP

FREE COLLECTIBLE SOUVENIR
WITH MINIMUM PURCHASE
OF 25 EUROS